PREACHING
THE
NEW COMMON LECTIONARY

YEAR A

After Pentecost

Commentary by:

Fred B. Craddock
John H. Hayes
Carl R. Holladay
Gene M. Tucker

ABINGDON PRESS
Nashville

Preaching the New Common Lectionary
Year A After Pentecost
Copyright © 1987 by Abingdon Press
Second Printing 1990

This book is printed on acid-free paper.

Library of Congress Cataloging in Publication Data

Main entry under title:
  Preaching the new common lectionary. Year A,
  After Pentecost
  Includes index.
  1. Bible—Homiletical use. 2. Bible—Liturgical
  lessons, English. I. Craddock, Fred B.
  BS534.5.P7273   1986   251   786-26524

(pbk.: alk. paper)
ISBN 0-687-33853-0

MANUFACTURED IN THE UNITED STATES OF AMERICA

PREACHING
THE
NEW COMMON LECTIONARY

Contents

---

* Propers 1, 2, and 3 are part of Epiphany

Christ the King

Special Days

Introduction

It might be helpful to the reader if we make a few remarks about our understanding of our task and what we have sought to accomplish in this volume. The following comments will touch on four topics.

The Scripture in Preaching

There is no substitute for direct exposure to the biblical text, both for the preacher in preparation and for the listener in worship. The Scriptures are therefore not only studied privately but read aloud as an act of worship in and of itself and not solely as prelude to a sermon. The sermon is an interpretation of Scripture in the sense that the preacher seeks to bring the text forward into the present in order to effect a new hearing of the Word. In this sense the text has its future and its fulfillment in preaching. In fact, the Bible itself is the record of the continual rehearing and reinterpreting of its own traditions in new settings and for new generations of believers. New settings and new circumstances are properly as well as inescapably integral to a hearing of God's Word in and through the text. Whatever else may be said to characterize God's Word, it is always appropriate to the hearers. But the desire to be immediately relevant should not abbreviate study of the text or divorce the sermon from the biblical tradition. Such sermons are orphaned, released without memory into the world. It is the task of the preacher and teacher to see that the principle of fidelity to Scripture is not abandoned in the life and worship of the church. The endeavor to understand a text in its historical, literary, and theological contexts does create, to be sure, a sense of distance between the Bible and the congregation. The preacher may grow impatient during this period of feeling a long way from a sermon. But this time of study can be most fruitful. By holding text and parishioners apart for a while, the preacher can hear each more clearly and exegete each more honestly. Then, when the two intersect in the sermon, neither the text nor the congregaton is consumed by the other. Because the Bible is an ancient book, it invites the preacher back into its world in order to understand; because the Bible is the church's Scripture, it moves forward into our world and addresses us here and now.

The Lectionary and Preaching

Ever increasing numbers of preachers are using a lectionary as a guide for preaching and worship. The intent of lectionaries is to provide for the church over a given period of time (usually three years) large units of Scripture arranged according to the seasons of the Christian Year and selected because they carry the central message of the Bible. Lectionaries are not designed to limit one's message or restrict the freedom of the pulpit. On the contrary, churches that use a lectionary usually hear more Scripture in worship than those that do not. And ministers who preach from the lectionary find themselves stretched into areas of the canon into which they would not have gone had they kept to the path of personal preference. Other values of the lectionary are well known: the readings provide a common ground for discussions in ministerial peer groups; family worship can more easily join public worship through shared readings; ministers and worship committees can work with common biblical texts to prepare services that have movement and integrity; and the lectionary encourages more disciplined study and advance preparation. All these and other values are increased if the different churches share a common lectionary. A common lectionary could conceivably generate a community-wide Christian conversation.

INTRODUCTION

This Book and Preaching

This volume is not designed as a substitute for work with the biblical text; on the contrary, its intent is to encourage such work. Neither is it our desire to relieve the preacher of regular visits to concordances, lexicons, and commentaries; rather it is our hope that the comments on the texts here will be sufficiently germinal to give direction and purpose to those visits to major reference works. Our commentaries are efforts to be faithful to the text and to begin moving the text toward the pulpit. There are no sermons as such here, nor could there be. No one can preach long distance. Only the one who preaches can do an exegesis of the listeners and mix into sermon preparation enough local soil so as to effect an indigenous hearing of the Word. But we hope we have contributed to that end. The reader will also notice that, while each of us has been aware of the other readings for each service, there has been no attempt to offer a collaborated commentary on all texts or a homogenized interpretation as though there were not four texts but one. We have tried to respect the integrity of each biblical passage and remain within the limits of our own areas of knowledge. It is assumed that the season of the year, the needs of the listeners, the preacher's own abilities, as well as the overall unity of the message of the Scriptures will prompt the preacher to find among the four readings the word for the day. Sometimes the four texts will join arm in arm, sometimes they will debate with one another, sometimes one will lead while the others follow, albeit at times reluctantly. Such is the wealth of the biblical witness.

A final word about our comments. The lections from the Psalter have been treated in the same manner as the other readings even though some Protestant churches often omit the reading of the psalm or replace it with a hymn. We have chosen to regard the psalm as an equal among the texts, primarily for three reasons. First, there is growing interest in the use of Psalms in public worship, and comments about them may help make that use more informed. Second, the Psalms were a major source for worship and preaching in the early church and they continue to inspire and inform

Christian witness today. And third, comments on the Psalms may make this volume helpful to Roman Catholic preachers who have maintained the long tradition of using the Psalms in Christian services.

This Season and Preaching

The liturgical year begins with Advent, the coming of the Christ into the world, and concludes with Pentecost, the coming of the Holy Spirit to the church.

The Season After Pentecost begins with Trinity Sunday, important for two reasons. First, it reminds the church to set the emphasis on the Holy Spirit at Pentecost within the inclusive doctrine of the Trinity. Second, the proclamation of the Trinity announces the tradition of faith within which the texts of this season will be explicated and heard. This season concludes with the celebration of Christ the King on the Sunday preceding the beginning of Advent.

In some traditions these Sundays between Pentecost and Advent are called "ordinary time." During this period there is no concerted movement toward a day of high significance or the clustering of texts with a governing focus as is the case in the seasons from Advent to Pentecost. What this means for the preacher is the opportunity to work with texts that do not possess the thematic unity that characterizes the lections for the remainder of the year. Although the readings for each Sunday are not unhappily joined, an effort has been made to provide continuity of readings from books of both Old and New Testaments. The benefits of this opportunity to develop sustained themes and to deepen one's understanding and appreciation of texts that continue for several weeks are not inconsiderable, both for the preacher and the hearer.

Fred B. Craddock (Gospels)
John H. Hayes (Psalms)
Carl R. Holladay (Epistles)
Gene M. Tucker (Old Testament)

Trinity Sunday

Deuteronomy 4:32-40; Psalm 33:1-12; II Corinthians 13:5-14; Matthew 28:16-20

Trinity Sunday was introduced into the liturgical cycle of the church as the celebration of a doctrine. The texts for the day enable the church at worship to reflect upon that doctrine but, more than that, they direct attention to the reality that called forth the doctrine in the first place. In the biblical tradition, the one God is experienced as transcendent creator, as incarnate, and as present in and among the lives of believers. The Old Testament reading alludes to God as creator and marvels at the Lord who acted in history to save Israel and continues to be present with the people. Psalm 33:1-12 praises the faithful God by whose word the heavens were made and whose counsel endures forever. Both the Gospel and epistolary lections, the concluding sections of their respective books, contain pronouncements in the name of the triune God.

Deuteronomy 4:32-40

Virtually every paragraph in the book of Deuteronomy properly begins with quotation marks. That is so because the contents of the book, with the exception of the introduction (1:1-5), the conclusion (34:1-12), and a few other bits of narrative, are presented as a speech of Moses. The assumed situation is on the plains of Moab at the conclusion of Israel's wandering in the wilderness, before the settlement of the land promised to the ancestors. The narrative framework of the introduction and conclusion makes the final form of the book a report of the last words and deeds of Moses. This situation lends urgency and authority to the speeches. Because of its title (Deuteronomy, "second law") and some of its contents, the book frequently is identified as a law book, but the individual units of discourse are better characterized as instructions, admonitions, and even sermons, many of which interpret the old laws and apply them to the new circumstances of the people (e.g., Deut. 15:1-11).

Because of the similarity of the book's specific contents and the report of the reform of King Josiah in 621 B.C. (II Kings 22–23), at least the core of Deuteronomy has long been associated with that date. However, it is clear from evidence both within and beyond the book that it is the result of a long history of growth and composition, emerging from ancient oral traditions and not reaching its final form until ca. 560 B.C., during the Babylonian Exile. Chapter 4:1-40 must stem from that latest stage, when the book of Deuteronomy was made part of the long history of Israel that runs from Deuteronomy through Second Kings (excluding the Book of Ruth). In Deuteronomy 4:27-28 the writer almost loses the perspective in the time of Moses, presuming the situation of the Exile. Thus the passage before us was written by and for people at the end of a long history in which their ancestors included not only those who had heard the promise of the land but others who had experienced its fulfillment. They themselves, however, had lost the inheritance, and many had to wonder if the ancient covenant was ended. At one level, this passage is part of the answer to such questions.

Our text concludes a longer speech (4:1-40) that stresses the importance of Israel's obedience to the one God who had brought them thus far on their journey. It is especially concerned with the prohibition against worshiping images. The speech presumes the Decalogue (Exod. 20:1-17; Deut. 5:6-21) and aims at persuading the hearers to obey the first and second commandments in particular. Moses is heard to argue the case for Israel's devotion to her Lord, to contrast graven images with the God of history, to threaten punishment if the people are disobedient, and promise blessing if they are faithful. In view of the actual situation in the Babylonian Exile, experienced as punishment for the sins of the past, it is important that the speaker holds open every possibility that the Lord is still available and willing to take back a repentant people and renew his covenant (4:28-31).

The goal of that larger speech is reached in the concluding verse of our assigned reading: "Therefore you shall keep his statutes and his commandments . . . that it may go well with you, and with your children after you." The deuteronomistic preachers insisted at every turn that faithfulness to God and to the divine law led to life and peace in a land they could call their own.

Leading up to that goal is a theological argument, demonstrating why the Lord is the only one worthy of Israel's devotion. In today's reading, that argument is developed in two movements, verses 32-34 and 35-39. The first part, characterized by rhetorical questions, begins by inviting the hearers to ask if anything at all—from the beginning to the present and from one end of heaven to the other—compares with what Israel has experienced (verse 32). The initial rhetorical question (verse 33) focuses on Israel's experience of the voice of God, alluding to the revelation on Mount Sinai (Exod. 19:16-18). The other rhetorical question (verse 34) directs attention to Yahweh's mighty acts in rescuing a people from Egypt, in the full view of everyone. In the second movement of the argument the speaker further elaborates on God's acts in history, explaining their purpose and reasons. Israel was witness to these mighty deeds "that you might know that the Lord is God; there is no other besides him" (verse 35). God revealed his will to the people so that he might discipline them (verse 36). Why did the Lord save this people? Not because they deserved it, or even because he loved them, but because he loved their ancestors (verse 37).

This passage is appropriate for reading and reflection on Trinity Sunday because of its understanding of God. The emphasis is on the uniqueness and the unity of the God of Israel. Although the language is uncompromising—"The Lord is God in heaven above and on the earth beneath; there is no other" (verse 39)—the main issue is not monotheism, the explicit doctrine that there is but one God. Elsewhere the writer suggests that while Israel is by no means to worship the sun, the moon, the stars, and all the hosts of heaven, the Lord has allotted them to all other peoples (4:19). Whether other gods are said to exist or not, or whether they actually do, Israel's devotion to her Lord is to be steady and strong, and not diluted by even the recognition of other deities.

While no trinitarian structure can be discerned here, the one God is characterized in various ways. The incomparability of the Lord stresses a transcendent God. This passage contains the sole allusion in Deuteronomy to the Lord as creator (verse 32) and that in reference to the creation of human beings. Above all, God is active in and through events in history. He is known through such actions and is known to be the one who saves a people and establishes a covenant with them. All these actions are through his very "presence" (verse 37). Thus, the one who is not to be identified with anything in the created order is present in and with creation through acts of salvation on behalf of his chosen creatures.

Psalm 33:1-12

This portion of Psalm 33 is appropriate for Trinity Sunday, first of all because of its emphasis on the word of Yahweh (verses 4 and 6). In describing Jesus, the Christ, as the second person of the Trinity, the church has frequently drawn upon the imagery of the word of God. Already in the New Testament, the prologue to the Gospel of John employs this imagery in such a way as to bind together the word made flesh in Jesus with the word present with God at the creation of the world.

A second factor contributing to the appropriateness of this text for the day is its concern with the nations of the world, its universalistic emphasis (verses 8 and 13-15). Thus, the text joins rank with the emphases of the Great Commission of Matthew 28:16-20.

Finally, the thought of the text, in spite of its universal interests, does not dissolve into a nebulous, pious sentimentalism that gushes over the human propensity to be religious. It does not expound or glory in some lowest common denominator religiosity. Verse 12 preserves a rock bottom particularism that sets the boundaries within which the rest of the psalm can be viewed. On Trinity Sunday the church gives testimony to the theological doctrine that gives

Christianity its particularistic status in the world of religion and marks off Christians from all other practitioners of religious life.

The following is an outline of the entire psalm: communal calls to praise (verses 1-3), hymnic praise of the Deity (verses 4-19), communal response expressing confidence in God (verses 20-21), and a communal appeal addressed to the Deity (verse 22).

The psalm opens with calls to the community to join in celebration. Five imperative verbs are employed: "rejoice" (a better translation is "shout out"), "praise," "make melody," "sing," and "play skillfully." All are terms denoting making music or singing loudly.

Israelite worship differed drastically from that of most modern church services. Nothing comparable to our sitting and listening to a sermon expounding scripture actually existed or if so it was the unusual rather than the normal. (The structure of worship centering on scripture reading and preaching was borrowed by Christians from the later synagogue.) Cultic celebrations in the Jerusalem temple were characterized by throngs of pilgrims, processions, chanting, singing, dancing, and so forth. Even acrobatic and simulated games were performed. (See the activities noted in II Sam. 6:12-19.) Theological affirmations were carried by the rituals and the singing.

In such worship, the congregation that assembled for worship often joined in the singing/chanting of hymns. These hymns performed two functions for the participants. On the one hand, they allowed the congregation to give expression to their feelings. On the other hand, they served to indoctrinate the community in proper theology. (The hymns, probably like all the Psalms, were written by religious professionals associated with or members of the temple staff.)

Hymns generally offer reasons stating why God should be praised or give the motivations for praise. These warrants for praise generally speak about the qualities or acts of Yahweh which evoke doxology and commendation. Two groups of these reasons are found in today's lection.

The first following the introductory "for" (*ki* in Hebrew)

17

occurs in verses 4-7. Verses 4-5 comprise what reads like a small confession of faith (for similar texts see Exod. 34:6-7; Ps.145:8-9). The five imperatives in verses 1-3 are matched by five terms describing Yahweh or his characteristics: "upright," "faithfulness," "righteousness," "justice," and "steadfast love" (or "mercy"). Two parallels are drawn between the worshipers in verse 1 and the statements about the divine in verse 4. Both are upright and righteous.

The description of the divine and the world in verses 4-5 assumes a well-ordered universe, stability and consistence in the world, and an optimistic attitude toward the status quo.

If verses 4-5 depict present realities, then verses 6-7 look back to creation, to the past. The word that manifests itself in the present is the word through whom God created the heavens and their host (the angelic beings). Just as the identification of Christ with the word incarnate and with the creative word at the beginning so here the identification emphasizes the unity and consistency of divine purpose and action.

Verse 7 stresses both the greatness of Yahweh and the dependency of the world (see Isa. 40:12-17). God collects the waters of the oceans like a water-fetcher filling a bottle. Even the deeps (= Tehoms; the name of the divine chaos monster in Mesopotamian mythology) God keeps in storage.

Verse 8 may be taken as a second call to "praise" although it does not open with an imperative verb form. As verses 1-3 called on the Israelites to manifest certain attitudes of celebrative praise, so verse 8 calls on all the earth and its inhabitants to fear Yahweh and be in awe of him. Perhaps fear of Yahweh is here seen as a universal attitude before the Deity rather than just an attitude demanded of non-Yahwistic worshipers.

The call to "fear" in verse 8 is followed by a description of the reasons in verses 9-11. Again creation by word and command is noted (verse 9). Such an emphasis on creation by the word stresses two factors: (1) God is distinct from the world of creation and yet Lord over creation; and (2) just as spoken word makes sense and communicates so also the world makes sense and its structures and orders communicate the divine will.

In verses 10-11, contrast is drawn between the plans and counsels of the nations and the counsel and thoughts of God. God can frustrate the plans of nations and empires whether they be ancient like Assyria and Babylon or modern like the world powers of today.

The particularism of the psalm shines through in verse 12 with its emphasis on Israel as the one nation that worships Yahweh and as the one nation out of all others that he has chosen.

II Corinthians 13:5-14

What makes this epistolary lesson especially appropriate as a text for Trinity Sunday is the final verse, "the most explicitly Trinitarian formula in the entire Pauline corpus" (Spicq). It reflects Paul's triadic understanding of Deity (cf. I Cor. 12:4-6), which he shared with other early Christian traditions (cf. Matt. 28:18-20). It is remarkable because it is formulaic, occurring as the prayer of benediction concluding this letter.

The unusual order is worth noting: "Grace of the Lord Jesus Christ . . . the love of God . . . the fellowship of the Holy Spirit." This in itself sets it apart from later Trinitarian formulations in which God occupies the prominent first position (cf. Matt. 28:19). God is not further defined as Father nor is Christ identified as Son. There seems to be less emphasis on identifying personal, or relational aspects between each of the members of the Godhead. Rather, the emphasis falls on certain attributes, or active aspects, typical of them, or to state it more dynamically, acts done by them on our behalf, "grace . . . love . . . fellowship."

One exegetical question is whether each phrase is to be understood as an objective genitive or a subjective genitive. The former would be rendered, "grace whose object or goal is Christ . . . our love toward or for God . . . fellowship that exists, or reaches fruition, in the Holy Spirit." The latter would be rendered, "grace displayed by, or bestowed in, Christ . . . God's love for us . . . fellowship created, enabled, sustained by the Holy Spirit." The question is left unresolved in RSV, JB, NIV, and only partially resolved in NEB, which

renders the third phrase as "fellowship in the Holy Spirit."
We may comment briefly about each of the three.

First, *the grace of the Lord Jesus Christ*. This is a form of
benediction typically, and frequently, used by Paul (cf. Rom.
16:20; I Cor. 16:23; Gal. 6:18; Phil. 4:23; I Thess. 5:28; Philem.
25). Because the death of Christ is to be understood as an act
of uncalculated generosity by Christ in which he exchanged
wealth for poverty (II Cor. 8:9), this most certainly is to be
understood as grace displayed by the Lord Jesus Christ (in
our behalf). It is thus understood as a "free gift in the grace"
(Rom. 5:15-16).

Second, *love of God*. This should be understood in light of
the most unusual reference earlier to "the God of love" (verse
11), which occurs only here in the New Testament, and never
in the Greek or Hebrew Old Testament. By contrast, "God of
peace" is more frequent in the New Testament (Rom. 15:33;
16:20; Phil. 4:9; I Thess. 5:23; cf. I Cor. 14:33), although
infrequent in Jewish writings. The assurance in verse 11 is
that a loving and peaceful God will be with us. Paul's stress
here on the "love of God" is best understood in close
connection with the grace of Christ. Christ's life and death
become the supreme demonstration of God's love for us (cf.
Rom. 5:5, 8; cf. John 3:16). Indeed, God's love has its focus in
Christ (Rom. 8:39). Through the work of Christ and in the
person of Christ, God's love reaches its most intensely
brilliant radiance as a dazzling shaft of light. The direct result
of God's love is our election (I Thess. 1:4).

Third, *fellowship of the Holy Spirit*. "Fellowship" translates
koinonia, which may be rendered more dynamically as
"sharing" or "participation" (Furnish). It suggests an active
relationship in which there is dynamic, mutual interplay
among the participants. Those who participate both give and
receive, and as a result it is a relationship of sharing. The idea
of partnership is central (cf. II Cor. 1:7; 6:14; 8:4, 23; 9:13). For
this reason, Paul aptly uses *koinonia* to designate financial
contributions made as free-will offerings (II Cor. 8:4). In
urging the Philippians to be one, Paul speaks of the
possibility of "participation in the Spirit" (Phil. 2:1). The
Spirit they share as a common possession serves as the basis
for their solidarity. Most likely, then, this third phrase is to be

taken as an objective genitive: the fellowship, or participation, which we have in the Holy Spirit. This not only suggests that the Spirit is that which we possess in common, but also the common sphere in which our life together is sustained. The Spirit is, after all, living proof that God's love has been bestowed on us (Rom. 5:5).

Scholars have noted the eucharistic overtones of today's passage. The exhortation toward self-examination in the opening section (verse 5) recalls Paul's earlier instructions about appropriate behavior at the Eucharist (I Cor. 1:23-32). The charge to greet one another (verse 12; Rom. 16:3-16; I Cor. 16:20; Phil. 4:21; I Thess. 5:16) fits well within a eucharistic setting. In later Christian worship following the prayer, the saints greeted one another with a holy kiss before presenting the elements for consecration (Justin, *Apology* 1.65; cf. I Cor. 16:20; also Rom. 16:16; I Thess. 5:26; I Pet. 5:14).

As for homiletical possibilities, the preacher should note that the Trinitarian benediction occurs at the end of a series of moral exhortations. Paul commends a life of self-examination and mutual edification within the church (verses 5-10). The readers are charged with responsibility for developing a form of life together that is coherent, harmonious, peaceful, and upbuilding (verses 11-13). They are responsible for repairing broken relationships within their midst and for adjusting their course. It is a reminder that Christian conduct should be self-correcting, responding to the demands of life as well as to the demands of the gospel. Trinity may be a doctrine, but in this text it relates to praxis.

Second, one may wish to explore the relationship between the three Persons in verse 14. To what extent, in Christian experience, does Christ become the primary Way or One through whom we are led to, and experience, God, and in whom we experience participation in God's Spirit?

Matthew 28:16-20

It is understandable that the Sunday following Pentecost suffers by comparison. However, to say that is not to accept a place of lesser importance for this day designated Trinity Sunday. In fact, it is vital for the experience and the theology of the church that the historic faith in one God, creator, redeemer, and sustainer, be reaffirmed. This is especially important after a season of centering our attention on Jesus and a day of focusing on the Holy Spirit. It is, after all, God who sent Jesus Christ and God who sends the Holy Spirit. Today's Gospel statement of the Trinity is Matthew 28:16-20. These verses conclude not only the resurrection narrative of Matthew but also the entire Gospel. We may assume, therefore, that this lection will gather up central themes both of the resurrection story and of the Gospel as a whole.

Matthew 28:16-20 falls naturally in two parts: verses 16-17 which describe the disciples and verses 18-20 which present the appearance and words of the risen and exalted Christ. Verse 16 assumes that Jesus had appointed (commanded) a specific mountain as the place of rendezvous with his disciples. The reader is not told of that instruction nor is the place specified, if, indeed, a mountain in the geographical sense is intended. Mountains are frequently referred to in the Bible as the scenes of theophanies and Christophanies. What we do know is that the passage affirms Matthew's and Mark's designation of Galilee as the center of post-Easter experiences with Christ, a noticeable difference from Luke's insistence that Jesus would have his disciples stay in Jerusalem (24:47-53). The meeting in Galilee between the risen Christ and his disciples was, according to Matthew, in keeping with the word of the pre-Easter Jesus (26:32), the angel at the tomb (28:7), and the risen Christ (28:10; see Mark 14:28; 16:7).

According to verse 17, seeing the risen Christ produced both worship and doubt. Since none other than the Eleven are mentioned, we must assume they are the worshipers and the doubters. Worshiping Christ is a response found elsewhere in Matthew (2:11; 8:2; 14:33), and the doubt is in keeping not only with reason but also with the accounts of the other Evangelists (Mark 16:8; Luke 24:11, 36-41; John 20:4-10; 24-29).

The second part of the reading, verses 18-20, begins rather unusually. Why would the writer, after saying that the disciples saw and worshiped Jesus, say, "And Jesus came and said to them"? Was he not already there? It could be that verses 18-20 were not a part of the original text, and the fact that verse 18 has its own narrative beginning testifies to its being a separate unit added by Matthew or a later edition. Or it could be that the expression "Jesus came" simply refers to his drawing nearer, approaching the disciples who thus far had only seen, worshiped, and doubted. It may be important that in only two stories in Matthew does Jesus draw near or come to anyone; in all others it is the people who come to Jesus. Those two are in the text before us (verse 18) and in the account of the Transfiguration (17:7), both of which are stories of the appearance of the glorified Christ.

But even if the reference to Jesus coming to his disciples does not persuade the reader that Matthew is here presenting the exalted and enthroned Christ who has come and will come, the claim of Jesus does: "All authority in heaven and on earth has been given to me" (verse 18). Although stated differently, Matthew has here offered the readers (the church) the enthroned Christ and Lord no less than in the more familiar enthronement passages (Phil. 2:9-11; I Tim. 3:16) which draw more directly on Psalm 110:1 and Daniel 7:14. This text expresses one of the earliest, if not the earliest meaning of Easter: the exaltation of Jesus as Lord. And to that universal lordship is tied the natural corollary: the universal mission of the church (verse 19) to which Matthew had referred earlier in anticipation of Jesus' exaltation (8:11; 12:21; 25:31-32).

The accents in Jesus' commission are clearly Matthean, touching upon central themes of the Gospel: "make disciples" and "observe all that I have commanded you." Going, baptizing, and teaching are participles in the service of the command to make disciples. The Trinitarian formula is attached to baptism which, however obscure its origins, was the common practice of the early churches. Except at this point, baptism is in the New Testament associated with the name of Jesus (Acts 2:38; 8:16; 10:48; Rom. 6:3; I Cor. 1:13, 15; 6:11). Perhaps by the time of Matthew the church felt the need to set baptism and, in fact, Jesus and the Holy Spirit into the larger context of its understanding of the one God who creates, redeems, and sustains.

The expression "to the close of the age" (verse 20) very

likely involves the triumphal return of Christ, but the accent of the passage is not there in the sense of Christ rescuing his disciples who have been very much alone in the world. The close of the age is rather a finale, a consummation of Christ's work through the church which has labored all the while in the assurance that the enthroned Christ is also present in and with his church.

Proper 4

Sunday Between May 29 and June 4 Inclusive
(If after Trinity Sunday)

Genesis 12:1-9; Psalm 33:12-22; Romans 3:21-28; Matthew
7:21-29

It is a season for the serious and continuous study of
Scripture. The Old Testament lessons provide a series of
twenty readings from the Pentateuch, from the call of
Abraham to the death of Moses, and conclude the season
with texts from the Book of Ruth and the Minor Prophets. All
of the epistolary lections are from three Pauline letters,
sixteen from Romans and the remainder from Philippians
and First Thessalonians. Matthew is the Gospel for continuous study this year. The advantage of such selections is that
the church can hear and reflect upon single books or other
units of the Bible in some depth. The disadvantage, of
course, is that often on given Sundays the themes of the texts
do not converge.

However, the texts for today focus on the common theme
of the human response to God's initiative. The readings from
the Pentateuch begin with the report of the call of Abraham
and his response, initiating the history of salvation that will
find its center in the Exodus from Egypt. The responsorial
psalm celebrates and expresses trust in the might and mercy
of the God of salvation. From the epistolary reading we hear
Paul's classical statement concerning righteousness, grace,
and redemption. The sequence of readings from Matthew
begins with sayings of Jesus concerning those who profess to
follow him.

Genesis 12:1-9

These verses that introduce the story of Abraham may also
be said to introduce the patriarchal narrative as a whole.
Moreover, the events recounted here are, according to the

Yahwist who is responsible for all but verses 4*b*-5 (the Priestly Writer), the pivot upon which history turns. That history concerns not just Israel but, ultimately, all of humankind, and it is a history of salvation.

Chapter 12 marks a change in both the subject matter of the book of Genesis and in literary genre. Genesis 1–11 is the primeval history, the account of beginnings, long ago and far away. Genesis 12–50 contains the stories of the patriarchs of Israel, narratives that focus on family life. Verses 1-3 of Genesis 12 in particular are the turning point in history, for up to this point the Yahwist has written a history of sin. After the creation of the first pair (Gen. 2), there was the initial disobedience in the garden followed by its dire effects. Then follows a case of fratricide (Gen. 4:1-16), the disruption of the order of creation by the intermarriage of divine and human beings (Gen. 6:1-3), and eventually the corruption of the race leading to the flood (Gen. 6–9). Even after that new beginning human hubris leads to the dispersion and division of people into different races and tongues (Gen. 11:1-11).

But a new history begins with the call of Abraham, identified as salvation history by the promises that accompany the call. We can recognize at the outset what becomes more and more clear as the story unfolds, namely, that God sets history on a course that leads to blessing. The promise, reiterated to each succeeding patriarch, unfolds in three movements.

The first is directed to Abram himself: "I will make of you a great nation, and I will bless you, and make your name great, so that you will be a blessing" (verse 2). While addressed to the patriarch himself, the blessing is a promise for the future, that one day his descendants will be a mighty and renowned nation. Implicit here and explicit elsewhere in the patriarchal traditions is the promise of progeny and land (verse 7), both prerequisites for nationhood. The reader familiar with the preceding report—Genesis 11:27-32 is a transition into the Abraham story—will find the promise of a future for Abraham's progeny all the more remarkable, for Sarah was barren (Gen. 11:30).

The second movement concerns God's solidarity with Abraham in his relations with others: "I will bless those who bless you, and [those] who curse you I will curse" (verse 3*a*).

The final development goes even further to include all peoples in the divine blessing expressed to this individual: "And by you all the families of the earth shall bless themselves" (verse 3*b*). There are no clear grammatical grounds for deciding whether the final verb should be read as reflexive ("shall bless themselves") or passive ("shall be blessed"). In either case, however, the universal goal of the divine blessing through the descendants of Abraham is clear.

We should bear in mind that this text was originally heard by a people who, in the monarchical period, experienced their national life as the fulfillment of this blessing. The Yahwist believed that the "great nation" of which he was a part was the result of the divine blessing uttered in antiquity. Built into this promise are two factors to temper any nationalistic pride that might arise. On the one hand, according to the genealogical scheme Abraham had other descendants besides Israel. On the other hand, the purpose of the blessing that Israel receives is the blessing of all human families.

If verses 1-3 are the turning point for a history that reaches from creation to the settlement of the land and even beyond into the monarchy, verses 4-9 introduce both Abraham and the patriarchal stories as a whole. They report how the ancestor responded to the divine instructions. The word of the Lord in verse 1 is less a call than a command. There is no drama in the patriarch's response, no question of his obedience to the command. We hear simply that Abraham set out on his journey in response to the Lord's instructions. Then verses 6-9 present an itinerary, the list of the places where Abraham stopped, along with a few important notes, mainly concerning altars he built. His movement is from north to south through the land of Canaan.

Abraham, like his parents before him (Gen. 11:31-32), was a migrant. Thus, the Lord's command to leave his country and kindred, while involving both separation and adventure, is not a call to abandon a settled existence for that of a nomad. Note also that he is not alone. With his wife Sarah, his nephew Lot, all their property, doubtless including livestock, and "the persons that they had gotten in Haran" (verse 5) he sets out. Along with the narrator we know more than Abraham and Sarah knew, that they would never find a place they could call home, but would travel as resident aliens in a foreign land. In the end, when Sarah dies, Abraham has to buy a burial place from one of the present legal owners of the land promised to his heirs (Gen. 23).

Abraham's obedient and courageous response to set out on such an adventure, especially in view of his advanced age (verse 4), is an important dimension of the passage. However, it is not so decisive as the promise of blessing. We are given here a picture of God's salvific purpose, and it finally is global in its direction and scope. In that context, Abraham's response in faith is a gift to the generations that follow.

Psalm 33:12-22

The Old Testament lection for this Sunday begins the semicontinuous reading of the Pentateuch. This reading begins with the narrative of the call of Abraham, a story which inaugurates Israel's account of its special history as the people of Yahweh.

A privotal verse in Psalm 33 is verse 12 which, like the call of Abraham, focuses on the particularity and pecularity of the chosen people. This verse contains two affirmations. The first declares that the nation which has Yahweh as its God is blessed. One might expound this half of the verse as a view of sacred history from the "inside." That is, it affirms Israel's special status on the basis of the nation's worship of Yahweh. What gave Israel its uniqueness was its worship of Yahweh. Other nations had their gods or god but Israel served Yahweh whom they, of course, understood as the real Deity. As worshipers of the true divinity, Israel could thus rest confident in the superiority of its religion.

The second half of this verse—"Blessed is . . . the people whom he has chosen as his heritage"—makes the same affirmation but attributes Israel's special status to divine initiative rather than to the correctness of the nation's religion. (Although the term "blessed" only occurs once, it governs both halves of the verse.) The election theme, of course, is given its fullest expression in the narrative of Abraham's call.

Over against the idea of Yahweh's election of Israel, the people also spoke of Israel as the people assigned to Yahweh. One can see this view in the song of Moses, a text that may be older than the present version of Genesis 12:1-9.

> When the Most High [Elyon] gave to the
>   nations their inheritance,
> when he separated the sons of men,
> he fixed the bounds of the peoples
>   according to the number of the sons of God.
> For [Yahweh's] portion is his people,
>   Jacob his allotted heritage. (Deut. 32:8-9)

This old presentation of world and national ordering assumes that Yahweh is one of the members of the divine pantheon of gods, headed by Elyon, who is given Israel as his domain. Other deities would have been assigned other territorial states and people. Psalm 33:12*b* has moved beyond the idea of assignment to the idea of election. Yahweh has picked Israel; the people belong to Yahweh by choice.

Verses 13-22 play on two themes: the might and greatness of God, on one hand, and the attitudes and sentiments of the people, on the other. In exegeting and preaching this text, these two issues can form the poles for discussion and proclamation.

What is said of the Deity?

1. God is first of all depicted as the sovereign of the universe who, from an exalted position, looks over and oversees the affairs of all the humans on earth (verses 13-14). This is no longer a Deity who shares in the governance of the world but one who is the sole governor of the world. All the human world is under his supervision and observance.

2. Yahweh is the one who has shaped the hearts of people (who therefore should have an innate knowledge of God and the divine will) and observes all their deeds, that is, God assesses what they do in terms of what they should do (verse 15). Here the Deity is depicted as the author of the human

instincts (the heart) and the judge of what is done on the basis
of that knowledge of the heart (their deeds).

3. In comparison to the Deity, a king with his army, a
warrior with his strength, and a horse with its might are
really nothing (verses 16-17).

Human attitudes that are noted in the text as the proper
posture before the Deity are referred to in the terms "fear,"
"waits for," "trust in," and "hope in." Fearing, waiting,
trusting, and hoping are what humans, and especially the
chosen people, must do and what they confess they are
doing (verses 18-22). These attitudes, which certainly can be
related to the picture of Abraham the migrant, are seen as the
basis of the human-divine relationship, especially in times of
need and want (verse 19).

Romans 3:21-28

With today's epistolary reading, we begin the semicontinuous reading of the Epistle to the Romans that runs for
sixteen weeks through Proper 19. This is an appropriate text
with which to begin since it serves as the thesis statement of
the epistle. It is a tightly conceived summary of Paul's gospel
and arguably one of the most difficult sections in the letter.
Here are introduced themes that will be elaborated,
unpacked, pursued, and explicated throughout the rest of
the letter.

It well serves as an outline of Pauline theology, and we
may delineate the following major themes:

First, *God's righteousness manifested apart from the law.* A key
word here, of course, is "righteousness" *(dikaiosune)*,
rendered by NEB as "justice" (verse 21). A major debate is
whether "righteousness of God" refers to an aspect of God's
character or to God's saving work, that is, whether it refers to
a passive quality or to an active work, to an attribute of God or
to an activity of God. It is probably more the latter than the
former, since the term is fairly consistently used in the Greek
Old Testament in contexts that also speak of God's work of
deliverance and salvation (Ps. 18:24; 71:2, 15-16; Isa. 46:13;
51:5-6). This dynamic dimension is captured effectively by
NEB: "It is God's way of righting wrong" (verse 22).

But perhaps the crucial point for Paul is that "God's way of righting wrong" now occurs "quite independently of law" (NEB, verse 21). The "now" is emphatic, referring to the eschatological turn of the ages. A new era in God's dealings with human beings has been ushered in. An old way of understanding God's relationship with us has gone by the board. A new way has been opened up. This has occurred in the public domain: "God's justice has been brought to light" (verse 21). What God has done has been done before the eyes of all. It is now universally visible.

If at one time, Paul saw (the) law as the singular statement of how God acts to reconcile sinful humanity, this is no longer the case. Torah can no longer be seen as the only window through which to see God's justice at work. A repository of divine revelation it might have been, but it can no longer lay claim to exclusive revelatory status. A new way of conceiving and experiencing God's justice has now been opened up, and it no longer has a "legal" texture.

Even though this new way of conceiving the divine-human relationship is radically new, it was not unforeseen. Rather it conforms to scriptural expectations: "The Law and the prophets both bear witness to it" (NEB). As noted above, Scripture had already spoken profoundly of God's "righteousness." The psalmist envisioned God as providing deliverance and rescue "justly" or "righteously" (Ps. 71:2). God's work was seen as "righteous acts" (Ps. 71:15-16). As the epistle unfolds, we see Paul expounding his theology of justification and defending it as compatible with the "law and prophets." In Romans 4, for example, he presents Abraham as the supreme paradigm of someone whose faith commended him to God and cites Old Testament chapter and verse to substantiate his argument.

But the point is clear: God's new way of "righting wrong," though foreshadowed in Scripture now occurs "quite independently of law." Something has happened that has now superseded, and thus relativized, Torah.

Second, *faith in Christ as the new way of experiencing God's righteousness* (verse 22). The phrase might be rendered literally as "righteousness of God through faith *of Jesus Christ*" (cf. Gal. 3:26). Some scholars have pressed the

31

significance of the genitive to mean that we are able to appropriate God's righteousness because of the faith displayed *by* Jesus Christ (subjective genitive), that is, Christ's own fidelity or faithfulness shown in the face of the temptation to disobedience. This is a clear alternative to the more traditional rendering, "faith in Jesus Christ" (objective genitive), followed by RSV, NEB, JB, NIV.

Whether Christ is regarded as agent or locus of "God's way of righting wrong," what is clear is the new texture of this relationship. God's reordering of human existence is no longer construed apart from the Christ-event. Neither can we participate in this reordering apart from Christ. This is the act of Christian faith: to believe that now God "rights wrong," both *our* wrong and *all* wrong, in a new way—no longer through Torah but through Christ. Christ thus becomes the new point of entry into God's reconciling love as well as the lens through which it is focused. When refracted through the Christ-event, God's righteousness is newly exposed to us.

Third, *the universal applicability of God's new way of righting wrong.* The picture sketched here is not one that is narrowly applicable to one segment of humanity or to one geographical region. Its effects reach across the board of all humanity. Entering God's righteousness is now available for "all who believe" (verse 22). Faith is no longer genetically construed. Being faithful is no longer a matter of ancestry. Jews are no longer privileged because of God's election of Israel and their role in salvation history, as distinguished as this history might have been. The way of faith is now a way "without distinction" between Jews and Gentiles. It is literally a gift available to every single person on earth.

And why is this the case? Why is God's grace universally available? Because sin is a universal experience (verses 23-24). Here Paul insists that every one of us, regardless of our presumed status before God or our presumed exclusion from the presence of God, is flawed by sin. We are "deprived of the divine splendour" (verse 23, NEB). The "glory" or "splendor" with which Adam was originally clothed (Gen. 1:26–3:24) was lost in the Fall. We have continued to exchange God's glory for a flash in the pan (Rom. 1:23).

The universality of human guilt is the basis for the universality of divine grace (cf. 1:16-17).

Fourth, *the death of Christ as the effective event of redemption* (verses 24-25). Two metaphors are introduced here: redemption and expiation. The first signifies liberation and may recall the practice of manumitting slaves or even God's deliverance of Israel in the Exodus (cf. Mark 10:45). The other is cultic and regards death as a sacrifice in which blood is shed and through which ritual purification occurs (cf. Lev. 16). One exegetical question here is whether expiation *(hilasterion)* is to be understood as an act aimed at placating an offended, angry God, or as an act of purification in which God is the actor rather than the object. Probably the latter.

In either case, the death of Christ is seen as the pivotal event in God's act of righting human wrong (cf. Rom. 5:6; 8:3).

Fifth, *justification by faith* (verses 27-28). The way of salvation is through faith not by our "success in keeping the law" (verse 28, NEB). The crucial question here is whether salvation is construed as gift or achievement. If the latter, we have reason to boast. It is ours because we earned it. If the former, "boasting . . . is excluded." To receive a gift is to participate in an act of generosity in which the only proper response is to say, "Thank you."

To be justified by faith is to see God's righteousness no longer as a *quid pro quo,* something God does to reward our efforts, as something we earn. It is rather God's generous response to our sinfulness, an act of grace that sets right our wrongs by canceling their effects. And how do we appropriate this righteousness? The short answer is, "in faith." Indeed, the gospel reveals God's righteousness from faith to faith (Rom. 1:17). Our entry into this sphere of divine grace is an act of faith through and through. Faith is being responsive to an unwarranted favor, receptive to an undeserved gift. "Faith is the opposite of any kind of earning or achievement. It is the correlative of sheer grace—utter receptiveness, bringing absolutely nothing in your hand, simply making room for God and his action, acknowledging there is nothing you can do or contribute" (J. A. T.

Robinson). Since faith is response to something unearned, it is "basically human receptivity, as actively as it may express itself in obedience" (Käsemann).

Any one of these themes deserves extended thought and careful homiletical treatment, although there will be occasion over the next several weeks to explore various aspects of the message of Romans. Perhaps a few words of caution are in order here. We should distinguish between the underlying theological principles at stake here and the concrete religious issues through which they come to expression. Paul's immediate task is to address the Jew-Gentile question, but the issues are of much wider import. He in fact addresses questions that lie at the heart of every religious system: How do we construe our relationship with God? How is this relationship properly initiated? How is it sustained? These are questions that are part of every genuine religious quest, and Paul's answers are unequivocal: faith not works, grace not law, all humanity not just some.

Matthew 7:21-29

Now that the liturgical year has ended, the lectionary offers during this "ordinary time" semicontinuous readings in the biblical texts. This means that, except for the few special days, we will be reading through Matthew until Advent. The benefits to the listeners and the preacher are many. Among them are: getting a sense of the narrative of Jesus' life and work, attaining some understanding of the theological perspective and literary skills of a single writer, building a series of messages on themes too large for single sermons, and experiencing the cumulative effect of proclamation with continuity. We begin with the conclusion to the Sermon on the Mount, earlier portions of Matthew having been read during the Christmas, Epiphany, and Lenten seasons.

Matthew 7:21-29 consists of three units: the first two (verses 21-23, 24-27) conclude the Sermon proper with a double emphasis on obedience to what has been taught, and the third (verses 28-29) is Matthew's conclusion to the

Sermon in which he remarks upon the nature of Jesus' teaching and the response of the crowds.

The twofold conclusion to the Sermon on the Mount addresses two audiences: those who might deceive themselves into thinking that extraordinary religious activity is an acceptable substitute for obedience to the will of God (verses 21-23) and those who might deceive themselves into thinking that there is saving merit in having heard Jesus preach (verses 24-27). The former group is characterized as saying, "Lord, Lord," but without accompanying obedience. It is clear that Matthew intends by the title "Lord" in both verses 21 and 22 to refer to Jesus as exalted Lord of the final judgment, "that day" (Joel 2:1; Amos 5:18, 20; Luke 17:24; I Cor. 3:13; Heb. 10:25). Inasmuch as "Lord" can also mean "Sir" in the sense of addressing one's teacher, Luke's form of Matthew 7:21 (6:46) may be more nearly the original, set in the context of the ministry of the historical Jesus. But Matthew's perspective is that Christ is enthroned and calling his followers to account, and the issue is, Did you obey what I taught you during my ministry among you? If any in the church assumed that "every one who calls upon the name of the Lord will be saved" (Joel 2:32; Rom. 10:13) did not involve obedience, then verses 21-23 shatter that assumption. And if anyone assumed that an impressive ministry of prophesying, exorcising demons, and performing miracles would dazzle the Lord and effect a suspension of the demand for moral and ethical obedience, then verses 21-23 shatter that assumption. These are addressed as "evildoers" (RSV) or persons with "wicked ways" (NEB), the words of the Lord's judgment being drawn from Psalm 6:8. Literally the word means "lawless," a translation that might better capture the emphasis of Matthew on doing what Christ instructed. Prophecy, exorcism, and miracle-working are not evil in themselves; the evil is the disobedience, the lawlessness.

The second group addressed in our text (verses 24-27) is a more familiar one: those who have heard great preaching, even that of Jesus himself, but whose lives exhibit no evidence of obedience. To these there need be no direct word of judgment as upon the first group; life itself will in time reveal the folly of hearing without doing. When the storms

35

hit, the difference between the life of obedience and the life of listening alone will be dramatically evident. (The preacher may want to look at Luke 6:47-49 to see the different imagery that makes the same point. Luke's builders place their houses by a river which rises.) Verses 24-27 are reminiscent of James 1:22-25 in which, by means of a different image, doing and not hearing only is heavily underscored.

Matthew concludes the Sermon (verses 28-29) with the phrase, "And when Jesus finished these sayings," which is the formulaic conclusion to all five of the major bodies of teaching in Matthew (7:28; 11:1; 13:53; 19:1; 26:1). The crowds of 5:1 are reintroduced and the description of Jesus as an authoritative teacher is taken directly from Mark 1:22, although in Mark the content of his teaching is not given. Jesus does not teach by passing along the interpretations of generations of rabbis but by providing a direct, unmediated interpretation of God's will for human behavior and relationships. Obedient attention to his teaching, says Matthew, is the key to life in the Kingdom.

Proper 5

Sunday Between June 5 and 11 Inclusive (If after Trinity Sunday)

Genesis 22:1-18; Psalm 13; Romans 4:13-18; Matthew 9:9-13

In the Old Testament reading the story of Abraham continues with the account of the near sacrifice of Isaac. Since Paul refers in Romans 4:13-18 to the promise to Abraham and his descendants, the first and second readings focus on the common theme of faith. The psalm is one of the infrequent instances of the inclusion of an individual complaint or lament psalm in the *Common Lectionary*. It is a prayer for help from enemies that becomes rejoicing because God heard the one who trusted in him. The Gospel lection is the account of Jesus' controversy with the Pharisees because tax collectors and sinners followed him and ate with him. The citation of the prophetic saying, "I desire mercy, and not sacrifice," suggests connections with Genesis 22.

Genesis 22:1-18

Our assigned reading contains two closely related but quite distinct units. The first, verses 1-14, is doubtless one of the most powerful and troubling passages in the Old Testament, the story of Abraham's near sacrifice of his own son Isaac. The second, verses 15-18, is the reiteration of the promise of blessing to Abraham, heard already in last week's reading from Genesis 12. At the time of his call the promise was given to Abraham as an act of grace without qualification; here it is repeated and strengthened precisely because the patriarch has demonstrated his faith in God.

The story of Abraham and Isaac, momentous in itself, takes on particular theological meaning when viewed in its context as a whole. Abraham and Sarah had set out to a

37

strange land with the promise that their descendants would become a great and powerful nation, possessing the land in which the patriarchs would only be resident aliens. The report of the fulfillment of the promise begins in the book of Exodus and is not concluded until the books of Joshua and Judges. Thus this pithy narrative is a chapter in the history of salvation, including Exodus, covenant on Sinai, wilderness wandering, and settlement of Canaan. Awareness of this larger story heightens the drama, as if there were not drama enough already, for it is not only the life of a single child that is in jeopardy, but the life of the future people as well.

More directly, the immediate prelude to this chapter is the story of the birth of Isaac (Gen. 21:1-7). Long after the aged pair had given up hope for a son, and therefore for the fulfillment of the promise of descendants, Isaac is born to Sarah. Not only is his birth a blessing in itself, but it is also the necessary first step in the fulfillment of the promise.

The story begins with an explanation of what it is about: "God tested Abraham" (verse 1). As is so often the case in biblical narrative, the readers and hearers know more than the characters do. Abraham, not having been told that he is being tested, hears only the horrifying command to take Isaac to the land of Moriah and offer him as a burnt offering. The narrator, who knows everything, gives us virtually no description but only action and dialogue, and that with great restraint. There is no speculation on the emotions or feelings of the characters, but the language and pace lead us on. The repetition in the command, "Take your son, your only son Isaac, whom you love" (verse 2), stresses the deep affection and strong ties between father and son, as does the image of the two going on foot to the mountain with the instruments of death in their hands (verse 6).

Although we have heard the story many times and know how it turns out, to hear it again is to become engaged in its poignancy and power. Will the angel of the Lord arrive in time? We know that it is a "test," but quickly we also realize that it is a matter of life and death. The question, Will Abraham pass the test? soon becomes less significant than the other one, Will Isaac live? At the climax both questions are answered at the same time. Abraham, who had never hesitated, is willing to obey, but God will not require the life of Isaac (verses 10-12).

The story has evoked so much reflection in the history of both church and synagogue, because of the seriousness of the issues it considers and because of all that is left unsaid. When the boy asked the obvious question, "Where is the lamb for the burnt offering?" (verse 7), Abraham's answer (verse 8) was a foreshadowing of what would happen. But did he know, did he hope, or was the response a ruse to keep Isaac quiet, to end the conversation with a religious platitude? Why, we may ask but find no satisfying answer, did God need to test Abraham in the first place?

It would be a serious mistake to reduce this rich narrative to a single point or meaning, for there are many. In one sense the story is an etiology of a place and its name (verse 14). At some stage in the oral tradition, the story probably dealt with the question of child sacrifice, which was not unheard of in the surrounding cultures. Early Israelites could well have asked, "Does our God require that we sacrifice our children?" Failure to do so does not mean lack of faith, for our ancestor was willing but God did not, and will not, require it. The sacrifice of a ram will be sufficient.

Central to the story is the issue of faith. It is Abraham's faith that is tested, and in the process the biblical tradition leaves us with a profound understanding of what faith is. It is not defined by means of a theological treatise or a set of propositions, nor are we left with admonitions to be faithful. Rather, the question is answered by means of example, with a story. It is the story of Abraham who trusted in God even when God appeared to be acting against his promise. Faith is like that. Faith is commitment, the directing of one's trust toward God. It entails the courage and risk of action. Whether Abraham knew that the God he worshiped would not require the life of his son we cannot know. However, as we reflect on this passage in teaching and preaching, and consider the difference between faith and fanaticism, it is well for us to remember how the story ended: the biblical God does not require such sacrifices.

Abraham's obedience becomes the occasion for the repetition and elaboration of the original promise (verses

15-18). There is an almost ironic note: because you have not withheld your son "I will multiply your descendants as the stars of heaven and as the sand which is on the seashore" (verse 17). As in Genesis 12:1-3, this is a promise of blessing for the future, including the great and powerful nation, and the blessing to "all the nations of the earth" (verse 18).

Psalm 13

This is a psalm of individual lament. The following is the structure of the composition: (1) complaints addressed to the Deity (verses 1-2), (2) an appeal addressed to God for help (verses 3-4), (3) an affirmation of faith and confidence as the motivation for divine help (verse 5), and (4) a statement of optimistic confidence about the future (verse 6). Except for verse 6, all the material in the psalm is addressed to Yahweh. The final and exceptional verse was perhaps addressed by the worshiper to some human audience, perhaps the cultic leader who officiated at the ritual in which the psalm was employed.

Generally, the psalms of lament contain a section describing the plight and distress from which the worshiper wished to be saved or redeemed. This lament contains no clear statement of such distress but intermingles this with the complaints and appeal. Presumably the person who used this psalm was one suffering severe pain and facing potential death.

The opening verses of the psalm are clearly complaints lodged against the Deity. These consist of four questions beginning with "how long." The NJPSV provides a better translation than the RSV:

How long, O Lord; will You ignore me forever?
How long will You hide Your face from me?
How long will I have cares on my mind,
   grief in my heart all day?
How long will my enemy have the upper hand?

The form of these questions indicate that the worshiper is willing to lay the blame for the condition of distress at the feet of Yahweh. At least God is the one assumed to know the answers to the questions and to be able to rectify matters. The distress of the worshiper is spoken of in terms of threefold relationships.

1. The human-divine relationship is described as one in which the worshiper feels forgotten by God who hides his face (verse 1). In ancient court etiquette, a person was not allowed to look directly at the face of the king until the king indicated this was all right. Such a procedure was followed to show respect and also to protect the king from evil influences. If the monarch wished to show displeasure, he would simply never have face-to-face contact with a supplicant. Thus, to hide one's face was to show displeasure. The worshiper in this text depicts the divine not only unresponsive but also hostile. As we have noted from time to time in this lectionary series, worshipers were encouraged or even forced in the cult to give vent to their anger toward the Deity.

2. The person-to-self relationship is noted in verse 2*ab*. Here the situation is one of constant cares (the Hebrew term is "counsels") on the mind or in the soul and sorrow in the heart. The worshiper acknowledges the deep problems and troubles that upset and burden the health of the personality.

3. Finally the relationship to the outside world is one of alienation and enmity (verse 2*c*). The sense of alienation and trouble is not merely experienced as an enemy out there but as an enemy who has the upper hand, an enemy to whom one is subservient. Who the enemy is is never clarified and it does not need to be since it could be either the problem itself or whatever is causing the problem.

The appeal in verses 3-4 is introduced by three imperatives. "consider, answer, lighten my eyes" (or "restore my strength"; see I Sam. 14:27-30; Ps. 38:11; Ezra 9:8). These three requested actions include a plea that God subject the worshiper's life to an examination, hear the worshiper's case, and then give aid to the petitioner that will result in the restoration of health.

If God does not aid, then two consequences could result: (1) the worshiper could die (verse 3*b*) and (2) the enemy would be able to rejoice in having triumphed over Yahweh's servant (verse 4).

In verse 5, the worshiper expresses to the Deity a confidence in being heard and responded to affirmatively. The basis of the confidence is having trusted in Yahweh's love or faithfulness (verse 5*a*). Although the psalmist never admits sin or any wrongdoing as the cause of the distress, there is no appeal to innocence as a motivation for divine help. In the last analysis, the hope for grace and help rests on divine favor.

In verse 6, we encounter a confident worshiper who vows to sing praise to Yahweh for the help God has granted. This verse is no longer addressed directly to God but rather to a human audience since God is spoken of in the third person. Perhaps in worship the temple official in charge of the ritual proclaimed a positive word of assurance to the worshiper who then responded with confidence and hope, with a new perspective on life. No mention is made of the enemy's destruction, just a statement that the worshiper can now rejoice on the basis of God's bountiful dealings. The reassertion of faith (verse 5) itself may have been sufficient to alter the outlook of the worshiper.

Romans 4:13-18

In Romans 4 we have Paul's extended treatment of Abraham, whom he regarded as the classic Old Testament example of one who was justified by faith. Indeed, of all the Old Testament figures who informed Paul's understanding of faith, Abraham was the most formative and influential. In him, Paul saw foreshadowed what life before God means— implicit trust in a God who promises the impossible and does it!

Today's epistolary text is one section of this extended exposition. It should be read and studied as part of the entire chapter.

Even before Paul's time, the case of Abraham had presented a problem for Jewish exegetes who saw the law of Moses as the sum and substance of God's revelation. If God's will is embodied in Torah and if obedience to God means being obedient to Torah, how could they explain those prominent figures of Jewish history whose lives were regarded by God as praiseworthy but who antedated the giving of the Law at Sinai? This would include such men as Enoch and Noah and most especially Abraham, for to him God had made the well-known promise of people and land (cf. Gen. 12:1-3; 15:5-6; 17:7-8).

Various explanations were offered. One suggestion was that even though Abraham antedated the giving of the Law, he actually embodied the Torah in advance. He was, as it were, an instance of "en-souled law," even before it was actually revealed to Moses and written down. Other interpreters, apparently without sensing any anachronism, actually asserted that Abraham kept the Law: "He kept the law of the Most High, and was taken into covenant with him" (Sir. 44:20*a*).

Paul opted for still a third line of interpretation. As he read the Hebrew Scriptures, he saw that God's promise to Abraham (Gen. 12) and God's "reckoning" Abraham as righteous (Gen. 15:6) actually *preceded* the covenant of circumcision (Gen. 17:1-27). It was all too clear: Scripture itself attested that God's righteousness was extended to Abraham, that is, Abraham was justified before God, prior to, and thus apart from, circumcision, the quintessential mark of admission to the people of God. Thus, whatever else this signified, it meant that Abraham was "father" in a redefined sense. He could only be regarded as "father of the faithful" not as "father of the circumcised" (Rom. 4:11-12). The legitimate heirs of Abraham, then, are those whose faith resembles his, not those whose initiation rite resembles his.

From this, Paul concluded that Genesis 17:5, "I have appointed you to be father of many nations" (NEB), must have wider import than normally understood. Abraham was not to be regarded merely as the father of the Jewish nation, but of *many* nations, which could only include Gentiles as well. His real progeny are the faithful not the properly circumcised.

This reading of the story of Abraham recorded in Genesis made it possible for Paul to set "law" over against "faith" as two mutually exclusive ways of appropriating God's righteousness. Granting the way in which he drove a sharp wedge between Abraham and the Law, we can understand his insistence that "the promise to Abraham and his descendants . . . did not come through the law but through the righteousness of faith" (verse 13). The way of law, which involved transgressing a clearly understood prescription and incurring God's wrath as a result of such infraction (verse 15; cf. Rom. 1:18; 5:9; also 3:20; 5:13, 20; 7:8, 10-11; 13; Gal. 3:19), all came later. This was not the way in which God's relationship to Abraham was initially defined, at least according to Paul's reading of Genesis 12–18.

What's more, Abraham served as the classic example of one who believed in a particular kind of God, namely, the creator God. Abraham placed his faith in "the God who makes the dead live and summons things that are not yet in existence as if they already were" (verse 17, NEB). This, of course, is a reference to God's enabling Sarah to conceive even when she was well beyond the age of childbearing. This was the essence of Abraham's faith: he received a promise from God that was palpably absurd—that he would become the "father of many nations" (verse 18, NEB)—yet he acted *in faith*, as absurd as this action seemed. And in doing so, he caught and exemplified the true essence of biblical faith, as Paul saw it: implicit trust in God's promise, however irrational or ephemeral it seems; and, more than this, leaning into this promise with the full weight of our lives so that our trust becomes God-oriented action.

In Abraham, Paul saw foreshadowed the essence of Christian existence and faith. To believe in Christ, after all, is to entrust ourselves to a God who has brought life from death in the resurrection and who can and will do so again (Rom. 4:24-25). In this respect, Abraham serves as the true paradigm of Christian faith.

Matthew 9:9-13

Although today's Gospel reading does not follow immediately the text for last Sunday, the central theme is the same: doing the will of God. In Matthew 9:9-13, the will of God has to do specifically with human relationships; that is, does the will of God call for separation from sinners or association with sinners?

In a rather lengthy section consisting primarily of miracle stories, Matthew inserts two conflict stories, one with Pharisees (9:9-13) and one with the disciples of John the Baptist (9:14-17). Only the controversy with the Pharisees is our concern today. The story is found also in Mark 2:13-17 and Luke 5:27-32, but with noticeable differences in the identification of Jesus' critics and the name of the tax collector. In addition, Matthew alone includes Jesus' use of Hosea 6:6 in his response to the critics.

According to Matthew, the tax collector who follows Jesus is named Matthew. Mark calls him Levi, the son of Alphaeus (2:14), and in Luke he is simply Levi (5:27). The reason for the different names is unclear: different sources, different events (very unlikely), and a change of name after becoming a disciple are all possibilities. In all the lists of the Twelve (Matt. 10:2-4; Mark 3:16-19; Luke 6:14-16; Acts 1:13) a Matthew is named, but there is no Levi. When Jesus called him, Matthew was sitting at the booth or table near the city gate or in the marketplace. He was collecting taxes for the Romans and for their puppet tetrarch, Herod Antipas. Taxes on the people were many and burdensome: road taxes, bridge taxes, tax on trade goods passing by caravan, and at times personal or household tax. The taxes alone were enough to alienate the collector; the fact that the taxes went to a foreign government multiplied the hostility toward the collector.

The conflict with the Pharisees was prompted by the presence of Jesus and his disciples at a dinner in Matthew's house (Luke 5:29 makes clear what is implied in Matthew, that the meal was in the tax collector's house). Matthew's other guests are tax collectors and sinners; that is, tax collectors and others who had been labeled "sinners" and put out of the synagogue. Mark says they were followers of Jesus (2:15), but Matthew leaves us with the assumption that they were friends and business associates of Matthew. The occasion and the nature of the group caught the attention of the Pharisees. (By the time of Matthew, Pharisees are treated as a group in conflict with the church. A more careful distinction, such as "some Pharisees," has now been lost.) The issue is clear: Jesus is having table fellowship with persons morally and ritually unclean (verse 11).

The response of Jesus consists of two parts. First, Jesus recites a well-known maxim about the physician: his place is with the sick not with the well. Second, Jesus uses a rabbinic formula, "Go and learn" (verse 13) to send his critics back to their Scriptures and to Hosea 6:6 in particular. Matthew quotes from the Greek translation of Hosea 6:6, "I desire mercy." The Hebrew word translated "mercy" is *hesed*, an extraordinarily rich and significant term meaning steadfast love, righteousness, loyalty. The Old Testament uses the word to describe God, God's relation to Israel, and the quality of life expected of Israel. Hosea 6:6 became a favorite verse for Israel in exile and away from the sacrificial system of the temple. It continued to be important for the synagogue and its leaders, the Pharisees, especially after the fall of the temple.

Jesus, then, cites a central text to his critics (used again at 12:7 in response to the charge of sabbath-breaking) and sends them back to learn what it means. And what does it mean? Do the character of God and the will of God call for a response of distancing oneself from all whose lives are tainted with sin and compromise or does it call for a response of drawing near in love and forgiveness? The issue is not solely between the synagogue and the church of Matthew's day, but within the church, then and now.

Proper 6

Sunday Between June 12 and 18 Inclusive (If after Trinity Sunday)

Genesis 25:19-34; Psalm 46; Romans 5:6-11; Matthew 9:35–10:8

The texts for today introduce us to very different worlds, from birth and conflict in a patriarchal family to images of the world at peace because God is king to the proclamation of the Good News of the kingdom. Genesis 25:19-34 contains the stories of the birth of Jacob and Esau, the twin sons of Isaac and Rebekah and of Esau's sale of his birthright to Jacob. The psalm is a hymn praising God as the king of all the world who establishes peace, and doubtless is used here because of the refrain, "the God of Jacob is our refuge" (verses 7, 11). In Romans 5:6-11 Paul argues that through the death of Christ, "while we were yet sinners Christ died for us" (verse 8), we are reconciled to God. The Gospel lection reports how Jesus taught and preached the Good News of the kingdom and how he began to commission the Twelve.

Genesis 25:19-34

The patriarchal stories extend over four generations, those of Abraham, Isaac, Jacob, and the children of Jacob. For reasons that are not obvious, the four generations do not receive equal attention. Abraham, through whom the history of salvation was initiated, is the model of faith; Jacob, who becomes Israel, is the ancestor of the chosen people, and the twelve sons of Jacob are the patronymic ancestors of the tribes. There is remarkably little material in which Isaac is the central character (Gen. 26). He appears, of course, in the Abraham story and figures in important incidents in the life of Jacob. Thus while the events reported in today's reading transpire in Isaac's household, Genesis 25:19 actually marks the beginning of the Jacob story.

47

Genesis 25:19-34 contains three relatively distinct parts, verses 19-26, 27-28, and 29-34. There is evidence that various elements of the material once circulated independently in the oral tradition, but in the final written form, the first two sections provide the background and setting for the third. The first two of these parts are not stories at all, but basically reports of events; that is, they do not attempt to create interest by developing the tension of a plot, but simply list what happened. In the context, however, they prepare us for the anecdote in verses 29-34. The theme shared by the entire passage is that of conflict between the two brothers, a theme that will continue to recur in the rest of the Jacob narrative.

Verses 19-26 are framed by the genealogical and chronological notices common to the Priestly Writer (verses 19-20, 26*b*), by which the connections are drawn, eventually from creation to the establishment of Israel as a nation in the land. The lengthy report of Isaac's marriage to Rebekah in the more ancient document (Gen. 24) here becomes a brief notice (verse 20). There follows the observation that Isaac prayed to God because his wife was barren and she conceived. She is troubled by the struggle within her womb so she inquires of the Lord. The oracle in response takes us far beyond the family situation to a prophecy of struggle between two nations, the descendants of the yet unborn twins (verse 23). The account of the birth of the boys is full of humor, made of plays on words, puns, and ridicule. The hand of the narrator is heaviest on Esau. The firstborn is red (the Hebrew is a play on the name Edom) and hairy (a play on "Seir," where the Edomites lived). The narrator and his audience were laughing at the Edomites by ridiculing their ancestor, but they did not leave their own patriarch unscathed, for he came out of the womb grasping the heel of his brother. There is a pun on his name as well, for "Jacob" is here explained as "heel," perhaps a double entendre. (Actually, the name means "God protects," or "may God protect.")

Verses 27-28 provide the transition from the birth of the twins to the story in verses 29-34, setting the scene by characterizing the sharp differences between the two brothers. One is a hunter, living out in the open; the other is more civilized, living in the tents of the shepherd. One is loved by his father and the other is loved by his mother.

The humor of caricature and ridicule continues in the story of Esau's sale of his birthright to Jacob (verses 29-34). The former is drawn as a rough, impetuous man, more concerned about his stomach than his future. "Give me some of that red stuff to gulp down, for I am famished" (verse 30, NJPSV), he says. In the end he impolitely "ate and drank, and he rose and went away" (verse 34). Jacob is shrewd, calculating, and mistrustful, demanding an oath before handing over the food. The plot turns on the transfer of the birthright from the older to the younger, but the story is silent on the meaning of this right. Deuteronomy 21:17 specifies that the firstborn is to receive a double share of the inheritance, but it seems unlikely that our story has such a specific meaning in view. Beyond the story, in the wider patriarchal narrative, we must think of the promise of blessing that has been passed down from Abraham to Isaac and will now pass through Jacob.

Except for this last feature, which, after all, belongs not to our passage but to its context, theological concerns are almost completely missing from this passage. There are, of course, the religious matters of prayer (verse 21) and inquiry of the Lord (verses 22-23), but these are hardly developed at all. The anecdote about the brothers does have a "moral," explicit in the narrator's criticism of Esau, "Thus Esau despised his birthright" (verse 34). The strangeness of the biblical world is patently obvious here, and we must resist the temptation to moralize. Nevertheless, two issues emerge for serious reflection.

1. There is the theme of the reversal of expectations in general the last shall be first—and of the triumph of the "lesser" or younger brother in particular. Whatever the specific inheritance rights, in patriarchal societies the firstborn son had the advantage. However, the stories of Israel's ancestors, like most of the Bible stories, are told from the perspective of those who did not have the advantage, but still were chosen. Thus the oracle announces what will begin to be fulfilled in the story, "the one shall be stronger than the other, the elder shall serve the younger" (verse 23).

2. The leading motif of these paragraphs, present in each of them and persistent in the entire Jacob narrative, is conflict.

Conflict and competition are seen to exist at every level of human society. It is in the family, for the brothers struggle with each other even before they are born, and even the affection of parents is divided (verse 28). Its existence on the cultural or socioeconomic level is reflected in the ridicule of the hunter by the bearers of the tradition, who identify with the shepherd. Finally, it is present on the political, national, and international level, for the two brothers are ancestors of the states of Israel and Edom. Immediate neighbors, their rivalry persisted from earliest times until the end of the Old Testament era and frequently broke out into violence. Ancient Israel was neither sentimental nor sanguine about "brotherhood," but knew that conflicts at all levels are as old as the race and as persistent as time. Thus for all its exaggeration and caricature, the story presents a realistic view of human life and calls our attention to realities that we ignore only at our peril. It offers no solution except to poke a little fun at human frailties and foibles.

Psalm 46

The association of this reading with the Old Testament lection from Genesis is based on the psalm's refrain: "The Lord of hosts is with us;/the God of Jacob is our refuge." The mention of the God of Jacob ties the text, although very loosely, to the stories of Jacob's birth and his acquisition of the birthright. Although this refrain now only occurs twice in the psalm (verses 7 and 11) one would expect it to have once appeared between verses 3 and 4, thus clearly dividing the psalm into three three-verse stanzas.

This psalm gives expression to some of the beliefs held about the city of Jerusalem (or Zion) by the ancient Judeans. This psalm, like 48 and 76, celebrates Zion as the city of God and proclaims divine protection for the city. The earth and existence may be threatened but Zion is declared steadfast and divinely protected.

Originally Psalm 46 was probably utilized in the great autumn festival, the Feast of Tabernacles, which celebrated the end of the old year and the beginning of the new year. One of the functions of the fall festival was to put the old year behind and to greet the new year. One way in which this was done was through the celebration of God's power to overcome chaos and the forces of disorder. (Note how this is a theme of our political campaigns and part of the promises of each new administration.) As part of the ritual celebration, the world was described as temporarily returning to chaotic conditions (the Good Friday motif). In reaffirming divine rule over the universe, God reenacted the original creation. Thus every new year or autumnal celebration was, as our new year's days are, a new beginning.

Psalm 46 shares in this thinking about chaos and order but presents the city of Zion as so divinely protected that whatever the chaotic conditions are Zion will remain an unshaken refuge.

In verses 1-3, the text speaks of chaos in the world of nature. The NJPSV translates verses 2-3 as:

God is our refuge and stronghold,
  a help in trouble, very near.
Therefore we are not afraid
  though the earth reels,
  though mountains topple into the sea—
  its waters rage and foam;
  in its swell mountains quake.

The second stanza speaks of chaos and uncertainty in the historical realm—"nations rage, the kingdoms totter"—but the people of Yahweh have no need to fear (verse 6). Verse 4 refers to a river whose streams make glad the city of God. Jerusalem, of course, had no major stream nearby. What then does this refer to? Three options suggest themselves:

1. The ancient high gods, such as El in Canaanite thought, were assumed to live on a sacred mountain (like Olympus in Greek mythology). This sacred mountain was also considered the source of one or more rivers. Thus it is possible that language originally used to speak of some other deity and some other sacred site have been transferred to Yahweh and to Zion.

2. The Garden of Eden was assumed to be located on a mountaintop in some texts (see Ezek. 28). Since streams

flowed from the garden (see Gen. 2:10-14) and if Zion was identified with the Garden of Eden, then one could expect talk about streams in regard to the site.

3. Maybe the stream referred to was the spring Gihon which supplied Jerusalem with its source of water. Interestingly, one of the streams flowing from the Garden of Eden was called Gihon (Gen. 2:13).

At any rate, water, the source of life and such a precious commodity in Palestine, is here associated with Jerusalem. The prophet Ezekiel later built on this imagery of water and Zion and predicted a time to come when a stream would flow from under the temple and water the land of Palestine transforming it into a paradisical state (Ezek. 47:1-12).

Verses 8-9 invite people to behold the works of Yahweh, namely, how he works desolation in the earth, brings wars to an end, and destroys the weapons of war—the bow, the spear, and the chariot. Thus we have in the schematic framework of the Zion theology the idea of chaos followed by divine intervention followed by universal peace or at least the destruction of the weapons of war (see Isa. 2:2-4). War dances, war games, and the symbolic destruction of the enemy may have been a part of the ritual of the fall festival.

In verse 10, a divine oracle occurs, probably spoken in worship by a cultic official. The RSV translates the opening word as "be still." This assumes that the divine word is addressed to the people of Yahweh. The term basically means, "leave off," "abandon," or "stop." Perhaps the oracle is here assumed to be addressed to the enemies, the nations of verse 6. If so, it demands that they recognize Yahweh and halt their aggressive actions, probably against Zion.

Throughout this psalm, the emphasis falls not only on the inviolability of Zion, where to live was considered a special privilege (see Isa. 4:3), but also on God as the protector of the city. The refrain in verses 7 and 11, as well as verse 1, praise God as the source of the city's security. Zion was a secure fortress because Yahweh was a sure refuge.

Romans 5:6-11

We are so accustomed to think of God as one who acts generously in our behalf that we overlook the radical paradox of Christ's death. In today's text, Paul probes this paradox, trying to expose the interior of this central mystery of our faith. Death and dying are perhaps the prominent motifs of the first half of our text, occurring four times in verses 6-8.

We speak so glibly of "the death of Christ" that it comes to have a certain obviousness. No scandal here. Part of God's eternal plan. Foreordained. Inevitable, given the circumstances. Not so, according to Paul. In fact, the enigma of God's Messiah dying on behalf of helpless, ungodly, sinners is perhaps reflected in Paul's broken, even tortured syntax. It is not something about which he can write with absolute clarity, so we find him struggling in verse 7 to get at the heart of the matter—introducing one thought, stopping in mid-sentence to replace it with a more fitting example. Even with this start-and-stop syntax, the flow of his argument is clear—there is something inexplicable, even inconceivable about the death of Christ.

Paul insists that it is one thing for a person to die in behalf of a "righteous man" (verse 7a). This has a certain logic about it even though it is a rarity; it "hardly" occurs. But what if you raised the ante? What about dying on behalf of "a good man"—not someone who is "just," or hard-nosed, but "good," or fair-minded and generous? The case is more compelling, and one could doubtless think of instances where this might "perhaps" occur.

In either case, dying for someone who is just or good can be defended. It has some redeeming value. One life is given up so that another life is extended. Society will benefit from a "righteous" or even "good" life preserved and extended.

But there is no social defense or explanation for the death of Christ. Those benefited are "weak . . . ungodly . . . sinners" (verses 6-8). There is no clear rationale as to why Christ should act in our behalf, nor it is clear why the extension of our life will be of any demonstrable benefit. Why help the helpless? Even more to the point, why help the morally bankrupt?

Surely this is the force of the opening verse: not "at the right time" or "at the right moment" (RSV, TLB, NIV; cf. Gal. 4:4), but "at the very time when we were still powerless"

(NEB). It is not so much that the death of Christ was good timing on God's part; rather it was morally inexplicable. "The point is that Christ did his saving work at an unexpected and, morally considered, even inappropriate moment. Unworthy, genuinely ungodly people benefited from it" (Käsemann following Furnish).

God's action through Christ is logic-shattering. It can only be seen as a visible, forthright expression of divine love: "God's own proof of his love towards us" (verse 8, NEB; cf. John 3:16; 15:13; I John 4:10; also Rom. 8:32). To die for a righteous or good person may be an act of bravery; to die for a morally bankrupt person can only be an act of love.

To be sure, Paul does not treat the matter at a safe, objective distance. Note how pervasive the first person plural is. Clearly, he is existentially involved: the death of Christ is in *our* behalf.

On the one hand, there is the objective reality of justification: "we are now justified by his blood" (verse 9), or "at the cost of his blood" (Barrett). Here Christ's death is regarded as sacrificial, his blood effecting purification like that of the sacrificial animal (cf. 3:25; Lev. 16:13-15; I John 2:2).

This is reinforced when Paul introduces the language of reconciliation (verses 10-11). It is, of course, a different metaphor—enemies brought together again and reconciled (cf. 11:15; II Cor. 5:18-20; Eph. 2:16; Col. 1:20-22; also I Cor. 7:11). It is a process through which hostile forces, notably flesh and Spirit, are neutralized (Rom. 8:7; cf. James 4:4).

In both cases, the death of Christ is the common meeting ground between us and God. In the one instance, God "makes things right" through Christ's death. The shedding of Christ's blood becomes the grounds for our acquittal before the righteous Judge. In the other instance, God "makes peace" through Christ's death. It becomes a peace-treaty event, where two sides, formerly at odds, are reconciled to each other.

The effects are both present and future. Justification and reconciliation are objective realities of the present, but their thrust is future: we shall "be saved . . . from the wrath of God" (verse 9); we shall "be saved by his life" (verse 10). We can now be delivered from God's eschatological wrath that was unfurled in the New Age (Rom. 1:18-32; 4:15; also Matt. 3:7; I Thess. 2:16), and Christ is the agent of deliverance (I Thess. 1:10; 5:9). The resurrection life that he now enjoys will be ours eventually (verse 10; cf. II Cor. 4:10; Phil. 1:20). The focus of our rejoicing, literally our "boasting" (verse 11) is God, who acted through Christ in effecting our reconciliation (cf. I Cor. 1:31; II Cor. 10:17; Gal. 6:14; Phil. 3:3; also Jer. 9:23-24).

Homiletically, we might note how existentially identified is Paul with the death of Christ. The language of the first person plural is pervasive. Note the frequency of "we" and "us" in our passage. He is not discussing the death of Christ from a safe, objective distance. He is rather standing in the eye of the storm, looking at justification and reconciliation from the interior, as one who is himself "weak . . . ungodly . . . sinner," yet the inexplicable object of God's love.

Also, the preacher's task with today's text may be to break through the barrier of the obvious to expose the radical paradox of Christ's death. Paul himself will be instructive here. As we examine the text closely, we see the apostle struggling to articulate this essential mystery of the faith.

Matthew 9:35–10:8

In the Gospel reading for last Sunday we saw that the followers of Jesus found in his word and example their authority for inclusive table fellowship. Today our lesson reveals that the church understood its own mission in and through both the command of Jesus and the model of his own ministry. The summary description of Jesus as teacher, preacher, and healer is offered by Matthew as foundational for his description of the mission of the Twelve.

Matthew 9:35 virtually repeats Matthew 4:23, forming what is termed in literature an inclusion. By concluding a section of material with the words of its introduction, a writer gives unity to the whole. In other words, between 4:23 and 9:35 Matthew has given teachings and miracles of healing, the whole of which not only characterizes Jesus' ministry but will now characterize that of his disciples as well.

Verse 36 provides us with the motivation for Jesus'

ministry, again implying that his followers will be likewise motivated. Jesus had compassion on the people in their state of oppression, confusion, fear, and frustration, much like sheep without a shepherd (Num. 27:17; I Kings 22:17; Ezek. 34:5). So great was the need that Jesus could not, even with the help of his disciples, meet it. He calls upon his followers to pray that God will send more laborers (verse 37; see also John 4:35). The analogy of harvest, used elsewhere in Matthew to refer to the last judgment (3:12; 13:8, 39-40), here includes the present and urgent work which will, of course, have its final consummation and revelation on the last day.

Matthew has now laid the foundation for the call and commissioning of the Twelve. The structure of 10:1-8 is quite clear: Jesus calls the Twelve, he gives them power to exorcise demons and to heal, the Twelve are named, and then Jesus gives specific instructions for their work. Slight variations occur in the four lists found in the New Testament (Matt. 10:2-4; Mark 3:16-19; Luke 6:14-16; Acts 1:13), but all begin with Simon Peter and end with Judas. The only time Matthew calls them apostles is here at 10:2. Most of them are known only by their names; the church looks to tradition for any word about their subsequent work.

Jesus' instructions to the Twelve define the arena of their work and the work they are to do. That they are to restrict themselves to Israel, going neither to Gentiles nor Samaritans (10:5-6), is without parallel in the other Gospels and difficult to reconcile with other passages in Matthew, such as 8:11 and 28:18-20. Some take the statement to refer to the chronology of the Christian mission: to the Jew first, then to the Gentile. Others see the passage as the reflection of a very conservative Jewish Christian community which confined itself to the circumcised. We know from Acts 15 and Galatians 2 that such groups existed in the early church. As to the work the Twelve were to do, the list fits the contours of Jesus' own ministry as recorded by Matthew: preaching, healing the sick, raising the dead, cleansing lepers, and casting out demons. In Luke's account of the ministry of the church (Acts), all but cleansing lepers are recorded. Jesus' word that they were to give without pay just as they had received without pay (verse 8) is without parallel in the other

Gospels but found its most conscientious practitioner in the Apostle Paul (I Cor. 9:3-18; II Cor. 11:7).

This final word to the effect that the church freely received and should freely give returns the instruction to the description of Jesus' own tireless ministry: "When he saw the crowds, he had compassion for them" (9:36).

Proper 7

Sunday Between June 19 and 25 Inclusive (If after Trinity Sunday)

Genesis 28:10-17; Psalm 91:1-10; Romans 5:12-19; Matthew 10:24-33

Although specific links between the readings for the day are difficult to discern, the combination of texts leads to the interpretation of history as a history of salvation. The Old Testament lection is the report of Jacob's dream at Bethel, in which he receives the promise that his descendants will become a nation through whom all peoples will be blessed. The psalm is a meditation on divine protection and the blessings of living in the shelter of the Most High. Continuing where last week's reading ended, the epistolary text considers sin, death, and the law, pointing out that death reigned from the time of Adam to Moses, even before the law was given. In Matthew 10:24-33, Jesus continues to instruct the disciples and to tell them whom to fear or not to fear.

Genesis 28:10-17

In the story of his dream at Bethel, Jacob will experience divine revelation and receive the promise originally given to Abraham. It is one of the two high points in the Jacob tradition; the other is next week's Old Testament reading, Genesis 32:22-32. Given our usual expectations about those whom God calls and blesses, this story is all the more remarkable when we consider the character of Jacob as presented in the rest of the tradition. From his very birth he was a grasper (Gen. 25:26), and in his early manhood he took advantage of his hungry and less civilized brother, buying his birthright for a bowl of soup (Gen. 25:29-34). Then when his father was on his deathbed, and with the assistance of his mother, he deceived his father to gain the blessing that he had bartered from Esau. In that process he played upon his father's weaknesses. Although he was initially tricked by his father-in-law Laban, eventually he outwitted him on two occasions, once to obtain wealth (Gen. 30:37-43), and once to flee from Laban's homeland (Gen. 31:17-42). When he returns to meet his brother, he is afraid of him, in spite of God's promise of protection, so he hides behind the women and children (Gen. 32:6-8). He is nowhere presented, like Abraham, as a hero of faith. He is the shrewd and successful shepherd who can get the best of anyone he encounters.

Jacob's experience at Bethel comes at a critical point in the story. The patriarch is leaving the land of Canaan in which his father Isaac and his grandfather Abraham had lived as resident aliens to return for a while to the territory of their ancestors in northwest Mesopotamia. There he will eventually acquire wives and children before returning. The encounter with God takes place during his trip from one land to the other. It is not a simple journey, however, but an escape. On the advice of his mother, Jacob is a fugitive, fleeing for his life from the wrath of his brother. He is at great risk from the known behind him and the unknown before him.

Genesis 28:10-17, while a coherent unit, includes only the first part of the story of Jacob's dream at Bethel; the complete account includes verses 18-22 as well. The unit is the interweaving of material from the two older Pentateuchal sources, the Yahwist and the Elohist. Different divine names, Yahweh ("Lord") and Elohim ("God") appear in consecutive verses (12-13 and 16-17), and verses 16 and 17 are repetitions. In verse 12 the revelation is a dream of angels (E), while in verse 13 (J) Yahweh himself addresses Jacob. Characteristic theological interests of the different writers have been merged into a single story. The Elohist (verses 10-12, 17-18, 20-22) understands revelation in terms of dreams and angels while the Yahwist (verses 13-16, 19) is interested in the promise to the patriarchs.

Skillfully the narrator reports that Jacob stopped to spend the night at an unnamed "certain place" (verse 11). The designation of the name, of course, is reserved for the conclusion, and there is already a distinct sense of the location as a place of destiny. The ancestor did not plan to spend the night there, but stopped where he was when the sun went down. Thus the events that follow take place at night.

The remainder of the narrative consists of the account of the revelation (verses 12-15) and of Jacob's reaction to it (verses 16-22). The revelation occurs in a dream of a ladder—"stairway" (NJPSV) is a more accurate reading—connecting earth and heaven, and "the angels of God were ascending and descending on it" (verse 12). Commentators since the late nineteenth century have recognized here connections with the Mesopotamian ziggurats, temple towers, where the divine and human met. Then Yahweh, identifying himself as the God of Abraham and Isaac, spoke to Jacob and proclaimed the by-now familiar promise. Jacob's reaction upon awakening is awe, acknowledgment of the meaning of the revelation, and acts of piety.

At more than one level, the passage is concerned with explaining the origin of a sacred place and rituals associated with it. The story explains the name Bethel ("house of God") in terms of Jacob's exclamation when he awoke (verses 17 and 19). In fact, this is not the first time the place name has been encountered in the patriarchal stories. Abraham had built an altar there (Gen. 12:8) and returned to it later (Gen. 13:4). Bethel was well known during the era of the Israelite monarchy. More important than the origin of the name is the story's understanding of holy places. One does not simply choose a place and make it holy, e.g., by building a sanctuary or an altar. Its sacredness must be either discovered or disclosed, and then recognized.

Theologically, the heart of the story is the Lord's promise to Jacob. It begins with only a slightly modified form of the promise initially given to Abraham (Gen. 12:1-3), that the patriarch's descendants would possess the land (verse 13), would become a great nation both numerically and geo-graphically (verse 14a), through whom all nations would be blessed (verse 14b; see the comments on Gen. 12:1-9 for Proper 4 in this volume). In addition there is a special promise appropriate for the specific occasion. Jacob is leaving the land and Yahweh promises to be with him and bring him back (verse 15). Behind this promise is the uncertainty that stems from the ancient idea that gods are attached to particular lands. Yahweh, however, will be where he chooses to be.

The biblical text does not make specific connections between the patriarch's character and the promise. We cannot help but note, however, that the grace of God comes to the fugitive fleeing for his life, the one who is no model of faith. What is manifest here is the Lord's will, and not human design. The Lord wills to bless a particular people and through them all families of the earth.

Psalm 91:1-10

In the Old Testament reading, Jacob has set out to return to the old homeland. He is venturing out into the unknown, an unknown fraught with dangers and uncertainties. He is on a mission of faith and obedience.

Psalm 91 is a psalm of assurance written to offer support and to instill confidence in someone facing an uncertain future. The psalm consists of two speeches. The first, in verses 1-13, addresses the supplicant with words of great assurance. The second, in verses 14-16, has the Deity speak words of support about the supplicant.

If this psalm was written for some service of worship, then how are we to understand its usage? This question is bound up with other questions. Who was the person seeking some words of promise and assurance from the Deity? Who addressed the worshiper in verses 1-13? Why is the Deity's speech in verses 14-16 not addressed directly to the worshiper? Unfortunately, such questions often must be left unanswered since we do not have sufficient evidence to answer them.

The military imagery in the text suggests that it was used as part of the ritual preparation for battle. Before the troops marched off to war, supplications, prayers, and sacrifices were made to God for success in battle. This psalm reads as if the soldiers or perhaps the king himself (as military commander) is being addressed with promises of protection.

The psalm opens with statements about the one who could expect protection from God (verses 1-2). First of all, the person is one who lives under the protective canopy of the divine. The terms used for God in verse 1 are old names for the Deity (Elyon = Most High and Shaddai = Almighty). Why these names rather than Yahweh are employed in this verse is uncertain, perhaps they are to be taken as epithets now applied to Yahweh to emphasize his power and transcendence. If one takes the phrases, "dwells in the shelter" and "abides in the shadow," literally, then they could refer specifically to the king who living in Jerusalem near the temple "dwelt" in a special proximity to the Deity. (Note Isa. 4:2-6 which speaks of God enclosing Zion under a shelter and canopy of special protection.) If the phrases are used metaphorically, then they could refer to anyone who relied on Yahweh for care and protection. The terms "shelter" and "shadow" suggest, first, a place of refuge from storms and rain, and, second, a cool place where one gains relief from the oppressive heat.

A second characteristic of the person aided by Yahweh is that of confessing faith in God. Confession places one in the camp and under the protection of Yahweh. Both "refuge" and "fortress" are terms drawn from military imagery and suggest a place of safety from assault.

In the remainder of the lection (verses 3-10), a speaker notes the care and protection that God will offer. The expressions used to describe the protection of the divine are drawn from various facets of life. The "snare of the fowler" draws upon the imagery of hunting birds while "deadly pestilence" reflects the imagery of communal sickness (verse 3). In verse 4a, God is depicted as a protective bird that guards its young under its wings while verse 4b again uses military terminology. In verses 5-6, contrasts are made—night-day, darkness-noontime—in order to express totality. All the time is what is meant. "Terror," "arrow," "pestilence" (or plague), and "destruction" (or scourge) probably refer to those communicable diseases that so often plagued ancient armies. The use of four terms again stresses the sense of inclusiveness. (Note that we still use the terms "strokes" and "attacks" to speak of physical maladies.)

Verses 7-8 promise that although the slaughter may be great, the one granted protection will escape it all and will only see the fall of the wicked, that is, the enemies. Again, the imagery is that of warfare.

Verse 9-10 provide a summarizing assurance. The NJPSV provides a slightly better translation of the verses than does the RSV:

> Because you took the Lord—my refuge,
> the Most High—as your haven,
> no harm will befall you,
> no disease touch your tent.

Romans 5:12-19

Today's text also serves as the epistolary lection for the First Sunday of Lent in Year A. The reader may wish to consult our remarks in *Lent, Holy Week, Easter, Year A.*

Today's epistolary lection is one of the classic statements of Paul's Adam Christology (cf. I Cor. 15:20-28). As Paul read Genesis 1–3, he saw Adam as "a type of the one who was to come" (verse 14). Through this typological reading of Scripture, he came to see Adam and Christ as prototypical representatives of two essentially different aeons. Indeed, each inaugurated a new reign not only as the first figure of his respective era but as the one through whose work the reign came to be defined.

One of the first points Paul presses home is this: the act of one person can affect the destiny of many persons. This is obvious enough in one sense. Citizens are affected directly by the decisions and actions of their leader. But more than this is being said in our text, for here we have a claim to universality. Adam's deed had universal effect: "sin came into the world through one [person] . . . so death spread to all" (verse 12).This should not be understood in the sense that sin is genetically transmitted from Adam to every succeeding generation, even though this has been a consistent way of interpreting this passage. Rather, Paul insists that sin is a universal reality because all have sinned (verse 12). Rather than saying that each of us is born with the taint of sin, Paul is suggesting that sin is a universal disease that is endemic to the human condition. His basic point, however, at least at the outset (verses 12-14), is that the nature and destiny of every human being has been affected, directly or indirectly, by the actions and deeds of the one man Adam. Through the actions of the one, the destiny of many has been affected.

In similar fashion, Paul argues for the pivotal role of Christ (verses 15-19). If one grants his reading of Genesis 1–3, one must at least grant the theoretical possibility that the work of the one man Christ can have universal effects on every other person, dead and alive. And this is the point he argues: through the disobedience of the one man Adam death entered the world (verse 15), but through the obedience of the one man Christ a new form of life entered the world, one characterized by the free gift of grace (verse 15) and righteousness (verse 17). In each case, Adam and Christ are doors opening into different worlds. Adam ushered in a world, an aeon; its essential features were sin and death, and in one sense law (verses 13-14). By contrast, Christ ushered in an era of righteousness and life, in every sense an era of grace.

Quite obviously, Paul insists on the incomparable superiority of the era of Christ over the era of Adam. Note the use of "much more" (verses 15, 17). The inner structure of the argument is one of comparative advantage. Any way you look at it, according to Paul, what God achieved through Christ exceeds by far what happened through Adam.

We might note some of the points of contrast:

1. Just as Adam is identified with disobedience, so is Christ identified with obedience (verse 19). Adam comes to stand as a shorthand expression for "sin," "transgression," "trespass," "judgment," and "condemnation." Everything the disobedient Adam was not, the obedient Christ was. Accordingly, the work of Christ taken as a whole becomes the avenue through which the "grace of God" as "free gift" becomes manifested to the world (verses 15-16). Adam and Christ thus come to represent not only two aeons, but two

ways of living before God—one as resistance, the other as obedient response. In this sense, Christ is "much more" than Adam.

2. The effects of the work of Adam and Christ may be similarly contrasted. If God's treatment of Adam demonstrated divine justice, God's treatment of Adam's successors through Christ displays divine generosity. In Adam's case, there is a single transgression, which resulted in condemnation (verses 16-17). In our case, there have been multiple transgressions, yet these have been met with grace and forgiveness (verse 17). Thus in Adam we saw a display of divine justice; in Christ we see a display of divine love. What makes this remarkable is that the accumulation of sin over time might normally have prompted God to increase the punishment, to condemn in return for sin, indeed to give up on humanity. Yet the cumulative force of "many trespasses" (verse 16) was met with the most unexpected of responses: justification as a free gift (verse 16). Adam comes to symbolize condemnation, while Christ comes to symbolize acquittal and life (verse 18).

3. The era of Adam is an era of death; the era of Christ is an era of life. The one thing we all know is that death is inevitable for us. As someone has put it, we are all terminal. Death, Paul insists, is the great universal (verse 12). If anything characterizes the entire period from Adam until Moses, it is death (verse 14). This was true even in those cases where persons did not flagrantly violate God's command as Adam did (cf. Gen. 2:17; 3:19; also II Esdras 3:21-22, 26; 6:23).

It is important for Paul to stress that both sin and death are prior to the Law, even law (verse 13). If sin is understood as transgression of the Mosaic Law, or of some universal law, what does it do to our understanding of sin if law is removed? Even though we recognize that putting a prohibition in words makes it concrete, we also know that the reality precedes the codification. This is Paul's point. The tendency and capacity for doing wrong exist even before we are able to formulate precisely what it is we have done wrong. Sin precedes law, even though law may serve as the way of articulating sin.

Just as this capacity for doing wrong afflicts all of us as

human beings, so does it bring death. Human experience teaches us that wrongdoing is ultimately, if not immediately, destructive. Its effects are both personal and social, affecting us as individuals and others with whom we associate. According to the creation story in Genesis 1–3, the sin of Adam resulted in physical death, the expiration of life. Yet as the story is told, we clearly see that more is at stake than this. Ultimately, it meant separation from God's presence. This is the real meaning of death. The Genesis story depicts existential death.

But Paul insists that this is precisely what was reversed in Christ. Through this one man's "act of righteousness" occurs "acquittal and life for all" (verse 18). If the era of Adam was the era of alienation and separation, the era of Christ is the era of reconciliation (verse 11). If death is the ultimate separation from God, eternal life is the ultimate form of reunion with God that has been achieved through Christ (verse 21).

Homiletically, our text offers numerous possibilities. We should remember that it has had a profound influence on the history of doctrine and still informs the way many of us understand the nature of sin and humanity. The preacher's task may be to address some of these perceptions directly. In what sense, if any, are we basically inclined toward sin? Is it an inborn tendency or something acquired? To what extent is it a matter of our own human responsibility?

Matthew 10:24-33

We continue today the instructions of Jesus to his disciples prior to sending them on a mission. This instruction began in last Sunday's reading and will continue through next Sunday. In fact, the formulaic ending at 11:1, "and when Jesus had finished instructing his twelve disciples," identifies this section as one of the five major bodies of teaching in Matthew, all of which are concluded in this way (7:28; 11:1; 13:53; 19:1; 26:1).

If one takes the view that Matthew is here giving to his church, which is living under social, economic, and political as well as religious pressure, the word of Jesus for their situation, then two benefits follow. One, we are better able to understand how the words of Jesus functioned for the early Christians. Here in 10:24-33 we have sayings of Jesus found in partial and modified parallels in the other Gospels, but which are now gathered into a single body of instructions for the mission. Collecting and editing these sayings for a church in a particular situation is Matthew's gift to his church and to us. Second, having seen how the church appropriated Jesus' teachings for a given time and place, we are not only permitted but obligated to hear those teachings afresh and anew in our own situation. To read Matthew and come away with an appreciation for the trials, difficulties, and faith of early Christians is laudable, but not enough. To call Matthew Scripture is to be addressed by it.

Even though Matthew 10:24-33 is a body of collected sayings that probably existed originally in other contexts, thematic unity is not absent and the preacher need not despair. Jesus both charges and encourages the church to face opposition without being paralyzed by fear. That overall theme unfolds in the following units: verses 24-25, verses 26-27, verse 28, verses 29-31, verses 32-33.

In verses 24-25 Jesus tells his followers they surely can expect opposition because he, their leader, faced it and the servant is not greater than the master. Expect no exemptions. John 13:14-16 and 15:18, 20, elaborate on this theme. As an example of abuse to himself, Jesus refers to his being called Beelzebul, an Aramaic word and one of many names for the devil. Matthew will relate the Beelzebul controversy in chapter 12. Here the point is simply that Jesus' followers should expect to be called names and to be misrepresented. To be called a servant of Satan when one is seeking to share the love of God is not casually dismissed with, "Sticks and stones may break my bones, but words will never harm me."

Verses 26-27, unlike the partial parallels in Mark 4:22 and Luke 12:2-3, carry the force of the imperative. What Jesus has told his disciples privately, and therefore safely, must now be proclaimed publicly, and therefore, dangerously.

Verse 28 is difficult to understand because of the reference to destroying both body and soul in hell. Luke 12:4 radically alters the saying to make it clearer. Surely the point is not to offer a new theory about hell, to the effect that in hell the wicked are totally annihilated. The point seems rather to be in the contrast: you will stand before judges who can execute you, but you also stand before a God whose power is not physical only or confined to the world only. In view of the difference, which will most affect your behavior?

Verses 29-31 do not convey warning but encouragement. God will never, in all that you endure, abandon you. God knows and is concerned about the fall of a sparrow, worth only a half-penny. God is so attentive to your life that even the number of hairs on your head is known to God. Can anyone doubt, then, the attention and care of God for those who love and serve faithfully?

And finally, verses 32-33 lift the theme to the final and ultimate level. Before earthly tribunals, pressure to be silent, to deny Christ will be very strong, but remember, those who acknowledge the lordship of Christ will have their names spoken in advocacy before the throne of God. Conversely, silence or denial of faith under duress will have its recompense in the removal of one's name when Christ presents his own to God. And confession/denial crises have not ceased among the followers of Christ.

Proper 8

Sunday Between June 26 and July 2 Inclusive

Genesis 32:22-32; Psalm 17:1-7, 15; Romans 6:3-11; Matthew 10:34-42

Themes of struggle, conflict, and transformation run through the texts for today. In the Old Testament lection Jacob struggles all night to realize that he has been wrestling with God, who gives him a new name. Psalm 17 is a complaint or lament song of a righteous individual crying for help against his adversaries. In the epistolary reading Paul says that those who are baptized in Christ are baptized into his death and then raised to newness of life in him. The Gospel lesson contains Jesus' troubling announcement that he has come not to bring peace but a sword, to set persons against one another, for anyone who follows him must take up a cross.

Genesis 32:22-32

In terms of context, Genesis 32:22-32 is the counterpart to last week's Old Testament lesson, Genesis 28:10-17. That story of Jacob at Bethel took place as he was leaving Canaan for northwest Mesopotamia, and the events in today's reading take place on the boundary of the land as he is returning. Both are at key turning points in the life of the patriarch, and in both instances he is the object of divine revelation at a dangerous time, and at night. Fear stands in the background of both accounts. In the first instance he was fleeing from Esau; here he knows he is about to meet his brother, so the immediate context of Jacob's nocturnal struggle at the Jabbok is his conflict with his brother. A story of struggle with superhuman powers is framed by a confrontation between brothers.

Brief as it is, the story of Jacob at the Jabbok is strange and complicated. Some of its strangeness and complexity can be explained in terms of the history of its transmission and development. There is strong evidence that the story was passed down in the oral tradition in various forms. We begin to recognize that evidence when we attempt to identify Jacob's opponent. Initially we are told that "a man wrestled with him until the breaking of the day" (verse 24), but later it appears that the opponent has the power both to put Jacob's thigh out of joint with a touch and to bless him. This confusion, along with the facts that the opponent fears the daylight and refuses to divulge his name, suggest a nocturnal demon. In the struggle the opponent declares ambiguously that Jacob has "striven with God and with men" (verse 28), and in the end the patriarch says he has "seen God face to face" (verse 30). It seems clear, then, that the narrator has taken over an ancient, pre-Yahwistic tradition that once talked of a nocturnal demon or deity and reinterpreted it as a confrontation between Israel's God and her ancestor.

The complex history of tradition is also revealed in the fact that the story has so many distinct resolutions or conclusions. Some of these points seem almost trivial when compared with the others. There are two distinct etiological conclusions: (1) explaining the name of the place as Peniel, "face of God," because Jacob saw the face of God there and lived (verse 30), and (2) explaining the origin of a ritual practice. The Israelites do not eat "the sinew of the hip," because the opponent touched the ancestor's thigh at the sinew of the hip (verse 32). This latter point is particularly curious, not simply because the taboo is unattested elsewhere, but because it was a man's thigh that was touched and animal sinews that are therefore not to be eaten.

The two other resolutions to the story are more integral to the plot and to each other. One concerns the change of the ancestor's name to Israel or, more likely, the giving of an additional name. This emerges directly from the struggle. On the one hand, Jacob demands to know his opponent's name but he refuses to disclose it. In the old oral tradition, to know the name of the nocturnal demon or deity was to obtain a measure of control over it. On the other hand, when the adversary asks, Jacob identifies himself and in turn receives the new name, Israel ("one who strives with God," or "God strives"). The other point concerns the blessing, a direct result of the conflict. The opponent demands to be released because daybreak is approaching, but Jacob refuses to release him until he is blessed (verse 26). This is the hinge upon which the drama turns. Who will win the contest? Jacob received his blessing (verse 29), but he did not escape without injury.

In all levels of the tradition this is a story of strife and struggle. Our author, the Yahwist, and his audience would not have missed the corporate implications of the story and its results. The people of Israel, like their patronymic ancestor, had striven with powers both human and divine and, in the time of the monarchy, knew that they had prevailed and been blessed. Moreover, although the ancient tradition may have viewed the conflict as one with some demon, our narrator finally knows that behind the hidden visage is the face of God. As the old traditions have been incorporated into a theological interpretation of Israel's past, there is a skillfully developed ambiguity in the identity of the opponent.

Those who know struggle—and who does not?—will find it easy to identify with both the protagonist and the storyteller. Life entails strife, conflict, and struggle. Often we can neither see the face nor know the name of what confronts us in the night. The struggle may even be with the unfathomable mystery of God. The passage, however, goes further than holding up a mirror to life as struggle. By example it says: do not let go, but continue to struggle, even when God is experienced as threatening. Furthermore, by its resolution it concludes that struggle—even with God—may end with a blessing, even though one may limp on afterward with the scars of the battle.

Psalm 17:1-7, 15

Psalm 17 is a psalm composed for use in legal hearings at the temple when a person felt or was falsely accused of some wrong. Old Testament laws concerned with the administra-

tion of justice allowed for cases to be appealed to Yahweh and
the temple personnel when it was impossible to decide a case
in the normal fashion, that is, when a jury of elders could not
reach a verdict (see Exod. 22:7-8; Deut. 17:8-13; 19:15-21; I
Kings 8:31-32). Failure of the normal process might be the
result of a lack of witnesses, the particularity of the case, or
other reasons.

In the temple ritual or ordeal, the litigants in a case would
appeal to God for a verdict, assert their innocence, and place
themselves under an oath or curse. The priests sought to
determine guilt and innocence and where they could not the
participants' self-imprecation was assumed to bring condemnation upon the guilty. Frequently the litigants spent the
night in the sanctuary under the observation of the cultic
officials. Apparently verdicts in a case were declared in the
morning.

The reason for selecting Psalm 17 for reading with Genesis
32:22-32 is its reference in verse 15 to seeing God's face which
bears some analogy to Jacob's experience at the ford of the
Jabbok.

The following is an outline of the contents of the psalm: (1)
opening appeal to God for a hearing (verses 1-2), (2) a
statement of innocence (verses 3-5), (3) a second appeal
(verses 6-9), (4) a description of the accusers (verses 10-12),
(5) a final appeal (verses 13-14), and (6) a statement of
confidence (verse 15). Note that the entire psalm consists of
prayer addressed to the Deity. (The lection for this Sunday
breaks off in the middle of the second appeal.)

In the initial appeal to Yahweh (verses 1-2), legal and court
terminology prevail: "just cause," "lips free of deceit,"
"vindication," and "the right." The case of the supplicant is
laid at the feet of Yahweh with an appeal that Yahweh would
hear, give heed, and look upon (favor) the right or innocent
one in the case. The specifics of the case are not laid out. Such
psalms as this one were composed to be used over and over
again by different persons as the need arose. Thus the
statements about the case are made in general terms in order
to cover a particular type of situation rather than a specific
situation per se.

In verses 3-5, the worshiper, as a defendant, offers to the

Deity a statement of innocence. If the psalms were written by temple personnel, as I assume they were, then this statement could have served two purposes. On the one hand, it allowed the innocent person to affirm innocence in the strongest of terms. On the other hand, for one who was actually guilty but pretending innocence, this statement forced the litigant to lie in a strong fashion. Such statements of innocence may have forced the guilty into a crisis of conscience and thus confession. At any rate, it would have greatly intensified the sense of guilt and perhaps served to engender a reevaluation of one's status before God. The worshiper, in other words, was forced, in the context of a solemn service in the temple in the presence of Yahweh, to confront the reality of guilt and innocence. The worshiper was confronted with telling the truth or lying with a high hand. The cult was as committed as any other institution to truth telling!

Innocence is asserted in several ways in verses 3-5. References to the heart and testing at night (when asleep) indicate the total commitment of the person and the conscience to truthfulness. Reference to the mouth indicates a claim not to have participated in slanderous gossip or unsubstantiated accusations. Commitment to "the word of thy lips" is a claim to have lived by the divine teachings as made known in the community. The supplicant claims that knowledge of God's will has kept him/her from participation in the ways of the violent. The paths of God have been where the supplicant's feet have trod.

In the appeal, the worshiper asks God to incline the ear, hear the words of appeal, and answer (verse 6). The matter however is not left at the level of a legal hearing and verdict rendering. There is also a request for divine mercy and love.

Romans 6:3-11

This same text also serves as the epistolary lection for the Easter Vigil in all three years, and the reader may wish to consult each of the *Lent, Holy Week, Easter* volumes for additional comments.

Here we have an extended discussion of Paul's baptismal theology. We should remember that this act of Christian initiation is variously understood and interpreted in the New Testament. In the Johannine church, it was understood as a new birth (John 3:1-15). This metaphor allowed it to be seen as the beginning of a new life of organic growth. The metaphor of circumcision is also used to interpret it (Col. 2:11-15). Here the image is one of stripping away "fleshly" desires and actions, a way of emphasizing that baptism marks a shift in behavior—away from the life of the flesh toward the life of the Spirit (cf. Rom. 8:1-8). It could also be interpreted in light of the story of Noah and the flood, with emphasis placed on the salvific effects of water (I Pet. 3:18-22).

But in today's text, baptism is interpreted by Paul in light of the Christ-event—as a death and resurrection. To make sense of Paul's remarks here, we must remember that early Christian baptism, so far as we can gather, was an act in which adult believers were immersed in water—literally "buried" under water and "raised" out of the water (cf. Acts 8:36-39). Similar initiation rites were known in certain ancient Graeco-Roman religions, where the initiate's immersion in water was seen as a reenactment of the dying and rising of the pagan deity. How much Paul's thinking here is indebted to these contemporary practices has been long debated; but the source of his thinking is less important than its contours and significance.

Our text speaks of being "baptized into Christ Jesus" (verse 3). This is probably traditional language arising from early Christian worship and teaching (cf. Gal. 3:26). It suggests that Christians are *incorporated* into Christ through baptism. Such language makes sense in light of Paul's understanding of the Body of Christ (I Cor. 12). In the resurrection, the corpse of the crucified Jesus took on new form—the resurrected and exalted body which no longer was confined to a human frame. It rather became cosmic in scope, something in which others could share and into which they could be incorporated. Accordingly, Paul insists that the church is the Body of Christ—not a body of Christians. The former suggests a corporate union with a living figure, the latter a collection of persons with common interests. In our text, baptism is seen as that moment of entry, that act of

PROPERS AFTER PENTECOST

incorporation, in which the person and identity of the believer are welded to that of Christ.

One way of seeing this is to note the "with" language throughout our passage (verses 4, 5, 6, 8). By stressing that the believer in baptism actually dies *with* Christ, is buried *with* Christ, and rises *with* Christ, Paul underscores the union of the believer with Christ (verse 5). What is being claimed here is union and participation, not mere reenactment and imitation. In the one, the believer and Christ are actually co-participants in an event that can only be described as a death and coming again to new life. In the other, the believer goes through a ritual action *like* that of Christ. It is a difference between lines that converge and lines that remain parallel.

Obviously, in one sense when we "die and rise" in baptism, we do so in a way that is unlike Christ's own death and resurrection. On the cross Christ expired physically, which we do not do when we are baptized; but Paul is really not thinking of Christ's death in this physical sense. True, Christ *died* on the cross, but it was a double death: expiration of physical life, but more important a death to sin: "the death he died he died to sin, once for all" (verse 10). He died "to sin" in the sense that his death culminated a life resistant to sin and victorious over it. He also died as the result of others' sin against him. Indeed, he died "for sin." The cross must be seen, then, as more than Christ's last breath. It was also sin's last breath. In the cross, Christ died, but sin died as well, and in this sense both Christ's death on the cross and our death in baptism are alike: they signal the death of sin, in his case in a cosmic sense, in our case in a personal sense. This is what it means to say that "our old self was crucified with him so that the sinful body might be destroyed" (verse 6).

But if something died, something also came to life: resurrection life. For Christ, the resurrection meant entering a new plane of existence, one in which "death no longer has dominion" (verse 9). It also launched a new level of life before God, what our text calls "living to God" (verse 10). This dimension of our existence, though begun in baptism, still lies in the future. Eventually, "we shall certainly be united with him in a resurrection like his" (verse 5; also verses 4, 8, and 11). This is the "not yet" part of Christian existence. Even

75

so, to the degree to which we put sin behind us, no longer yielding to its dominion, to that degree we are participating in resurrection life. These ethical implications Paul spells out further in the following verses (verses 12-23).

All of this may seem obvious and all too familiar to us, and yet Paul introduces his remarks by asking, "Have you forgotten . . ." (verse 3, NEB). The preacher's task is often that of unfolding the implications of the familiar as much as it is introducing the unfamiliar. Especially is this the case when the clue to our true identity lies as close to us as our own experience of baptism.

Matthew 10:34-42

Matthew's second major section of Jesus' teachings (9:35–11:1) concludes with today's reading. These teachings are not to the crowds but to Jesus' disciples; that is to say, to the church. Even though Matthew has gathered these sayings of Jesus under the rubric of "instructions prior to a mission," there is no report of the disciples actually going on or returning from such a mission. Both Mark (6:12-13) and Luke (9:6; 10:17) report both the mission and its successful completion. Apparently, then, Matthew has subordinated any historical interest in a mission journey of the Twelve to a prior concern with what Jesus says to the church for its life and ministry in a context of hostility and suffering. In fact, the mention of cross-bearing in verse 38, coming as it does prior to Jesus' introduction of the subject of Caesarea Philippi (16:13-26), indicates that the text before us is Matthew's reflection on Jesus' demands for discipleship after the fact of the crucifixion and resurrection. We may so hear it and appropriate it for ourselves.

Matthew 10:34-42 falls naturally in two parts: verses 34-39 and 40-42. The first part pictures scenes of domestic strife created by loyalty to Christ but claims that separation from family is not to be compared with the possibility of separation from Christ. In the background of the passage is Micah 7:6. The statements are stern, to be sure, but the reader may be aided in understanding by three observations. First, verses 34-36 are presented in the Semitic perspective that views result as purpose. That is to say, the result of an action is then stated as having been the purpose of the action. For example, the result of Isaiah's preaching was the hardening of hearts, and so Isaiah 6 says that Isaiah preached *in order to* harden hearts. So here in our text, commitments to Christ divided some persons from their families, and so the writer says that the purpose of Christ's call to faith was to divide families. Those in Matthew's church who have experienced such domestic strife can be encouraged to know that such pain was and is no surprise to God. Strangely enough, the words of verses 34-36 are words of encouragement to those already divided rather than a call to alienation from one's family.

Second, these words were addressed to cultures, Jew and Gentile, which possessed strong family connections. Whatever religion the head of a household held, all the family and servants embraced the same. For one in the family to become a disciple of Jesus had serious personal, domestic, social, political, and economic consequences.

And finally, the call to love Christ more than one's family is an indirect way of paying honor to the family. Jesus gave his call for loyalty over against the strongest, not the weakest claim a person otherwise knew, the claim of family love. Jesus never offered himself as an alternative to the worst but to the best in society. As Paul would put it, when one counts life's good, life's gain, as loss, then the real test of discipleship has been passed.

Verses 38-39 change the imagery to cross-bearing and losing one's life, but do not really alter the accent of the preceding verses. Bearing a cross and losing/finding life are sayings joined in the tradition here, at 16:24-25, and at Mark 8:34-35.

The second part of our text, verses 40-42, does shift the focus to speak of those who are hospitable to Christ's disciples. The reward of discipleship goes not only to those followers who have lost their family ties but also to those who welcome such disciples, knowing who they are and what their loyalties are. It is, of course, clearly implied that while receiving Christ's disciples brings a disciple's reward, it also brings upon one the threat and hostility that the disciples themselves bear. Verses 41-42 are structured on three parallel expressions: receiving a prophet, receiving a righteous man, and receiving a little one. All three may be taken as referring to the extension of hospitality to Christians. This text gives one an increased appreciation for the significance of the frequent biblical injunctions to practice hospitality.

Proper 9

Sunday Between July 3 and 9 Inclusive

*Exodus 1:6-14, 22–2:10; Psalm 124; Romans 7:14-25a;
Matthew 11:25-30*

As the readings from the Pentateuch continue, the book of Romans and the Gospel of Matthew each takes its own direction. The Old Testament lesson sets the scene for the Exodus by characterizing the Egyptian oppression of the Israelite people and reporting the birth of Moses. The psalm is a corporate thanksgiving song, an appropriate response to the anticipated deliverance from Egypt. The epistolary text is part of Paul's reflection on the relationship between the law and sin, leading to his cry to be delivered "from this body of death" (Rom. 7:24). In Matthew 11:25-30 Jesus asserts his authority and calls for all who are heavy-laden to come to him and he will give them rest.

Exodus 1:6-14, 22–2:10

It is important to set these verses into their broader Old Testament context, for a great deal has transpired between last week's account of Jacob at the Jabbok (Gen. 32:22-32) and today's reading. Momentous events are yet to come. Jacob returned to Canaan with the sons who would be the ancestors of Israel's tribes. The lengthy and sophisticated account of Joseph and his brothers (Gen. 37–50) finally served to show how Jacob's family ended up in Egypt. Our reading for today describes the circumstances of Israel in Egypt and begins the preparation for their Exodus under the leadership of Moses.

The lectionary has selected verses from three distinct but closely related units. The first paragraph of the book (1:1-7) provides the transition from the book of Genesis. When the book of Exodus begins, that family of Jacob in the time of Joseph has "increased greatly . . . so that the land was filled with them" (Exod. 1:7). Thus the first part of the promise originally made to Abraham (Gen. 12:1-3) and reiterated to his son and grandson has been fulfilled, the promise that their descendants would become a people great and numerous. The second unit (Exod. 1:7-22) reports the Egyptian oppression, the dark background for the Lord's rescue of his people. The third section (Exod. 2:1-10) is the story of the birth and deliverance of the baby who will grow up to lead Israel to freedom. A jealous and foolish tyrant fears a little baby and, it turns out, for good reason. Except for verses 1-7 and 13-14, which come from the Priestly Writer, this material comes from one of the older Pentateuchal sources, most likely the Yahwist.

The account of the Egyptian oppression (1:8-22) provides the necessary narrative preparation for the Exodus in general and for the birth story of Moses in particular. The new (unnamed) Egyptian king fears the now numerous Israelites for hypothetical reasons—in case of war they might join the enemy. He takes two steps to deal with the problem, and both of them defy logic. First, he enslaves them and sets them to work on his construction projects, but mysteriously they thrive all the more and the Egyptian fears increase (verses 11-12). Second, he takes one and then another step to kill the Israelite male babies. This was hardly the best way to assure himself of a good slave population, but tyrants are not known for their wisdom and good judgment. After the Hebrew midwives refuse to cooperate by killing the males (1:15-21), Pharaoh commands that all the male babies be thrown into the Nile (1:22).

The story of Moses' birth and rescue, like that of the Hebrew midwives, is a woman's story. Chapter 2 begins abruptly as the report of perfectly ordinary events, marriage and birth, but by verse 2 the reader knows that the death threat stands in the background. The unnamed baby's mother manages to conceal him for three months but then must take other steps. What follows is a historically improbable sequence of events and full of irony. With great care the mother prepares a waterproof basket for the baby (verse 3), and the very river in which he was to be drowned bears him to safety. Now the central character appears on the scene, the boy's older sister. (The report of the baby's birth implied that he was the firstborn, but obviously he was not.) She and the mother watch while the princess and her attendants come to bathe in the Nile and discover the child. The princess has compassion on the baby, and remarkably knows that "this is one of the Hebrews' children" (verse 6). Boldly the sister comes forward and offers to find a nurse to care for the baby, her offer is accepted, and she brings out the child's mother.

One purpose of the story is to report how Moses got his name. Ordinarily, children would have been named at their birth, but here it comes later to serve as the narrative conclusion. The princess named him Moses *(mosheh)* because she "drew him out" *(mashah)* of the water. The etymology, like most such biblical accounts, is a popular, nontechnical one based on similarity of sounds. As many commentators have noted, our narrator probably did not know that the name "Moses" is actually the Hebrew form of a common Egyptian word meaning "son."

A second concern is revealed by the story's style and tone, and especially its irony. It is ironical that the future leader of the people is the adopted son of the princess—that is, he grows up in the very court of the one who sought to kill him—and at the same time is nursed by his own mother. The instrument of that reversal, that defeat of Pharaoh's scheme, is a simple slave girl. Doubtless, later children of those slaves must have laughed or at least smiled to hear how a girl and her mother outwitted the tyrant. Moreover, one way that slaves survive tyranny, and sometimes even overthrow it, is through ridicule. Note that the tradition is not unqualified in its criticism of foreigners, for success depended on the compassion of the Egyptian princess.

Above all, this passage is a chapter in the story of the deliverance of Israel from slavery in Egypt. It sets the stage and introduces the central human character, Moses, and reports that he was on the one hand educated in the Egyptian court but on the other hand was nursed and guided by his Israelite mother. Although the name of God is not mentioned in the story of Moses' birth, we are to understand from the context that the will of God is being worked out in history, and in opposition to the will of the foreign king. God will save a people through human instruments, eventually Moses, but here through a girl and her mother, and even though unwittingly, a compassionate foreign princess.

Psalm 124

Psalms 120–134 are called "Songs of Ascents." Perhaps a better translation would be "Songs of Pilgrimage." This collection or booklet of psalms was put together to be sung by pilgrims as they made their way from various towns throughout Palestine to Jerusalem for the great festivals. According to Exodus 23:14-17, every male was required to participate in the three great festivals held every year. These festivals were the Feast of Unleavened Bread (also called Passover) in the early spring, the feast of harvest (our Pentecost) in early summer, and the feast of ingathering (also called Tabernacles) in the early fall. These were great national celebrations. The most important of these was the fall festival which marked the end of the old year and the beginning of the new. It also celebrated the creation of the world and Yahweh's establishment and preservation of order in the universe.

The Mishnah, a collection of rabbinic materials from the days of the early church, tells us a bit about how pilgrims made their journey to Jerusalem. People from a district would assemble in the main city of the district. The pilgrims spent the night in the district capital. The night was spent sleeping outdoors to avoid any contamination that would make them unclean and thus unable to make the pilgrimage. For example, sleeping outside avoided being in a house when someone died. Everyone in the house became unclean for seven days when a death occurred.

The pilgrims left town early in the morning under the direction of a pilgrim leader. The journey to Jerusalem might take several days, depending on the distance. Psalms 120–134 were sung as the pilgrims made their journey toward Jerusalem.

Psalm 124 is a thanksgiving psalm which offers thanks for God's care during the past. Thus, it is the type of psalm that would have been appropriate for the occasion when pilgrims looked back over the past year.

Probably the opening of the psalm was sung by the pilgrim leader who then calls upon all the pilgrims to join the song. This explains why verse 2*a* repeats verse 1*a* and why verse 1*b* says, "Let Israel now say." The remainder of the psalm may have been sung by the leader line by line and then repeated by the pilgrims.

The psalm offers thanks for having survived the past. We would say for having survived the alienation and anarchy of life. Two main images are employed to give expressions to the concepts—overwhelming waters (verses 3-5) and bird traps (verses 6-7). The opponents of the worshipers are simply described as "men" (verse 2*b*) and "their" (verse 6*b*). The actual opponents are not as significant as the sentiments expressed. The psalm allows the worshipers to express their feelings and give vent to their emotions.

The sense of alienation and being overwhelmed by life are described with strong pictures: swallowed up, anger kindled, floods sweeping over one, torrents overcoming, and "raging waters." Obviously, the idea is that of people struggling to retain their bearings and some stability in life. The threat is that of absolutely losing control. The minister could preach on this psalm and deal with the human effort required to stay in control of life. Much of every person's life is spent fighting anarchy. Paying bills, meeting schedules, and a whole range of activities are undertaken merely to clear a little space in which we feel at home. Sickness, and in this case, the actions of others, always are potential "waters" that threaten to engulf life.

Verses 6-7 pay tribute to God's care. Just as verses 1-5 proclaim that having God on one's side gives life some tranquility so God is here blessed for having offered rescue in the time of need. Again strong metaphors appear. The NJPSV translates these verses:

> Blessed is the Lord, who did not let us
> be ripped apart by their teeth.

We are like a bird escaped from the fowler's trap;
the trap broke and we escaped.

Here as is so frequently in the Psalms, the speakers seem to be paranoid to a certain extent. Whether or not this seems to reflect a situation bordering on the psychotic or not would depend on how one experiences and interprets life. There is a legitimate extent to which all people occasionally experience the world as a very hostile place, as if life were lived on a beachhead. At least, ancient Israel allowed its worshipers to give expression to this sense of life as enemy territory.

The psalm, of course, does not begin or end on a pessimistic note. At the beginning, one encounters the word Yahweh before meeting a description of life's problems. At the end the psalm concludes with a strong affirmation. After all, if God who made heaven and earth is on our side, then one has hope. In the psalm, people offer thanksgiving for this bedrock of faith in the divine.

Romans 7:14-25*a*

There are two questions interpreters of this passage have consistently debated: (1) whether these remarks are primarily autobiographical, and thus depict primarily Paul's own moral struggle, and (2) whether what is in view is the struggle *before* becoming a Christian, or *while* living as a Christian.

The answer to the first question will turn on how we understand the "I" that is repeatedly used in the passage. Is Paul the fundamental referent, or is "I" used in a generic sense, as an equivalent of "one," or "everyone"? Or, is it the "I" of the religious person, or more specifically, of the Jew striving to be faithful to Torah? The preacher will need to consult other passages where Paul uses "I" in an ambiguous sense (cf. I Cor. 8:13; 9:15-27; 13:1-3, 8-13).

To answer the second question, we must look carefully at the tenses of the verbs used in the chapter. We should note especially that the past tense dominates the first part of the chapter (7:1-13), while the present tense dominates the latter part of the chapter (7:14-24). What is striking about today's text is the way in which the moral struggle is envisioned as a present reality, as something ongoing.

Obviously, how one answers these questions will affect how it can be appropriated homiletically. If, for example, we read the text as the agonized struggle of the religious person, indeed as a mature Christian, it may address the perennial Christian question, If I am already a Christian, why do I continue to sin? Does not being Christian mean that I should be able to do what I know is right and avoid doing what I know is wrong? Pursued this way, the text can be explored as a set of profound, and chillingly honest, insights directed to those who are already religious but who nevertheless continue to know and experience the tension between is and ought.

If, however, the text is taken to describe pre-Christian existence, it will lend itself to a different form of homiletical interpretation. Among other things, it will be read as depicting a life that was left behind and transformed through our union with Christ (verses 24-25).

Even so, several observations are in order. First, these remarks are made in the context of defending the law, in this case the law of Moses (verse 14; also cf. 7:12). A sharp distinction is made here between sin as an overarching, cosmic principle, and the law as the articulated commandment of God. Devout Pharisee that he was, Paul found it difficult to concede that Torah, as God's revelation, was somehow deficient. Indeed, it had positive value in giving expression to wrongful acts, such as coveting (7:7-12). It should be regarded as "spiritual" (verse 14), since it comes from God. The real culprit is something else, a force far more sinister—Sin. It takes on personified form and can be conceived as a force lurking within the self that distorts our best intentions and keeps the law from achieving its desired purpose.

The force of Paul's remarks here is clear: we cannot explain our moral dilemma by harping on the deficiencies of law. The place to begin is with honest introspection, with a true understanding of the human self. He places the locus of moral responsibility within the human heart, "in my inmost self" (verse 22), not somewhere else—not with God, nor with the law. For him, contrition is the beginning of morality, and in this respect he echoes the sentiments of the Quman *Community Rule* 11:7-8: "As for me, I belong to wicked mankind, to the company of ungodly flesh. My iniquities, rebellions, and sins, together with the perversity of my heart, belong to the company of worms and to those who walk in darkness" (cf. Ps. 51:5).

Second, our text sketches the tension between willing and doing in a most unforgettable fashion: "I fail to carry out the things I want to do, and I find myself doing the very things I hate" (verse 15, JB). Naturally, others besides Paul knew, and wrote about, this conflict between knowing and doing. The Roman poet Ovid, an earlier contemporary of Paul (d. A.D. 18), wrote, "Desire persuades me one way, reason another. I see the better and approve it, but I follow the worse" (*Metamorphoses* 7.19-20).

But we miss an important Pauline insight if we read these words as the soliloquy of the quintessential negative thinker, of one who simply has not thought positively long enough and hard enough. It is more than an inward human struggle. It is rather a war between the cosmic powers being carried on within the self—the "law of God" pitted against the "law of sin" (verses 22-23; cf. Gal. 5:17; James 4:1, 5; I Pet. 2:11). The struggle depicted here is not merely the failure of the individual to realize his or her full human potential; it is rather the hopeless struggle of the person who is "sold under sin" (verse 14). What is being described here is a form of savage enslavement (verse 23) from which we must be rescued.

It is on this note of spontaneous thanksgiving at the thought of being rescued that our passage concludes (verse 25; Rom. 6:17; I Cor. 15:57; II Cor. 2:14; 8:16; 9:15).

As we think about preaching from this text, we are reminded that it is one of those texts where our own human experience may be as illuminating as reading commentaries. To be sure, we must understand the contours of Paul's thoughts, but equally important, we must know the contours of our own hearts. Doing so will allow our own "I" to identify with the "I" of the text, both in its moments of desperation and in its moments of hope.

Matthew 11:25-30

The listener and perhaps the preacher will welcome this lection as a break from a series of statements about the very heavy demands of discipleship. Matthew 11:25-30 puts discipleship into the context of revelation and grace. This is not to say that the passage is easy to understand. On the contrary, it is difficult, and primarily for two very different reasons. First, the text is unique in the Synoptics, being based on Wisdom Christology and, as we shall see, more at home in Johannine thought. Second, this passage is very popular, being claimed by every reader who feels burdened and heavy-laden. That the original audience very likely were Israelites burdened under the yoke of the law is for many readers no longer a pertinent historical item: Jesus' promise of rest and a light burden is heard and appropriated by all whose lives are pressed down, for whatever reason. Once a text is owned by all who hear it, it is the historical interpreter who seems the intruder.

Matthew 11:25-30 consists of three parts: a thanksgiving (verses 25-26), a proclamation (verse 27), and an invitation (verses 28-30). The first two parts are found in Luke 10:21-22 in a different context but seem already to have been joined in the tradition common to Matthew and Luke. Some commentators speculate that these two parts were joined because they are both sayings about revelation or sayings about "the Father." More likely, however, they are joined not only to each other but also to the third, verses 28-30 (found only in Matthew), because all three draw upon the Wisdom tradition of Judaism.

One meets the desirable but elusive figure of Wisdom (Sophia) in many places in the Old Testament, most noticeably in Job 28:12-28: "But where shall wisdom be found?"; Proverbs 8:22-36: "The Lord created me at the beginning of his work . . . then I was beside him, like a master workman"; Ecclesiasticus 24:1-24: "The one who created me assigned a place for my tent. And he said, 'Make your dwelling in Jacob' "; and Wisdom of Solomon 7:22-30: "For she [Wisdom] is a reflection of eternal light, a spotless mirror of the working of God, and an image of his goodness."

Even a casual reader of these passages can see how some early Christians saw in Jesus Christ the incarnation of God's eternal Wisdom, or in its masculine form, eternal Logos. One finds in I Corinthians 1:20, 26-29, Paul's way of saying Matthew 11:25-26. And Matthew 11:27 is so much like John 1:18; 6:35-59; 7:25-30, and many other such passages, that the German scholar von Hase called the verse "a meteorite from the Johannine heaven."

And finally, verses 28-30, Christ's invitation to the weary and burdened, clearly echo Ecclesiasticus 51:25-27 in which Wisdom calls out to an Israel bent low beneath the heavy yoke of the law. Wisdom says, "Come, take my yoke, and find for yourselves rest." In our text, Jesus is God's eternal Wisdom making that offer of refreshment and release.

In summary, then, two statements need to be made. First, in the immediate context, Jesus has just finished upbraiding certain Galilean cities in which his mission failed (verses 20-24). Jesus, however, understands their rejection in terms of the concealed/revealed Wisdom of God. In their own vaunted pride and wisdom they have missed the revelation God grants to the humble and receptive. Second, in the larger context of Jesus' moral and ethical demands on all who would follow him, these verses come as a clear reminder: apart from the twin gifts of God's revelation and God's grace, we would all be bent low beneath the burden of those very demands. However, Christ's offer is not permissiveness but that of a shared yoke, of love, and of forgiveness.

Proper 10

Sunday Between July 10 and 16 Inclusive

Exodus 2:11-22; Psalm 69:6-15; Romans 8:9-17; Matthew 13:1-9, 18-23

Each of the readings for today raises its own distinctive issues. The Old Testament lesson's account of Moses killing the Egyptian and fleeing to Midian raises questions of morality and leadership. Psalm 69:6-15, part of a prayer for deliverance from enemies, is an appropriate response to the situation depicted in the Exodus story, especially because the psalmist, like Moses, has become a stranger and an alien. In the epistolary lection Paul contrasts the life of the flesh with the life of the spirit and testifies that the Spirit is bearing witness to our spirits that we are children of God. The gospel reading is the parable of the sower and its interpretation, a lesson concerning the response of those who hear the word of the kingdom of God.

Exodus 2:11-22

Within the structure of the story of the Exodus as a whole, the main purpose of the two episodes that comprise today's reading is to show how the future deliverer came to be in the land of Midian where he received his call to lead his people out of bondage. In what amounts to a narrative aside, the verses that immediately follow our passage (Exod. 2:23-25) draw the explicit connections with the Exodus in particular and the broad sweep of the history of salvation in general. There the Priestly Writer indicates that while Moses was away, the pharaoh who enslaved Israel died but the people continued to suffer. When they cried out for help, God heard them and remembered his covenant with their ancestors. The reader is not allowed to forget for long that within all these human events God is patiently at work.

The two stories in our text for the day (verses 11-15*a* and 15*b*-22) must have once circulated independently in the oral tradition before they were incorporated into the Yahwist's narrative. Each is a self-contained anecdote. In themselves, they focus on the early life and, to some extent, the character of Moses. In both tales the stress is on action and dialogue, with little or no explicit reflection on the motives or personalities of the characters, and only implicit moral evaluations. The storyteller contracts time in the transitions and expands it in the body to relate the sweep of events to specific incidents. Thus verse 11*a* includes all the years that it took for Moses to grow up, and verses 11*b*-15*a* cover the events of two days. Likewise, verses 15*b*-20 tell what happened in a single day, and verses 21-22 quickly pass over several years.

When the first story begins, Moses is a young man living in the royal court but when it ends he is a fugitive on the run from the same pharaoh who had earlier sought to kill him. The course of events that leads to this conclusion is transparent and involves two scenes with three violent confrontations, one between an Egyptian and a Hebrew, one between Moses and the Egyptian, and another between two Hebrews. Observing an Egyptian beating "one of his [own] people," Moses takes action. He is not impetuous but purposeful. The narrator is careful to point out that he took pains to do the deed in secret. He looked around, saw no one, killed the Egyptian, and buried him in the sand (verse 12). On the very next day he interceded in a struggle between two Hebrews and quickly discovered that they would not acknowledge his authority and that the deed he thought he had concealed is known. Not for the last time, the authority of Moses is challenged by those he seeks to rescue. Rebellion against his leadership is a common motif in the stories of the wandering in the wilderness (Exod. 14:10-12; 16:1-3).

Note how many important questions are left unanswered by the story. Presumably Moses knew from his mother that he was one of the Hebrews, but this is not stated. What were his motives and feelings as he went out and "looked on their burdens" (verse 11)? How did the secret become public? Above all, was the murder justified or not?

The second episode (verses 15*b*-22) begins at a well in the land of Midian. At the outset Moses is a fugitive but in the end he is at home with a family and with a livelihood. In the process he is again involved in violent conflict. Seeing the shepherds bully the seven daughters of the priest of Midian, Moses intervenes and helps them water their flocks (verse 17). When the girls return home and report what happened, their father chides them for not showing proper hospitality. Moses happily comes to live with the man, who gives him Zipporah as a wife. Although he has settled down, the name of the first child, Gershom (beginning with Hebrew *ger*, "sojourner"), emphasizes that Moses is in a foreign land (verse 22). This note serves on the one hand to associate Moses with his ancestors and on the other hand to foreshadow the future.

One set of issues in the passage concerns the character and authority of Moses. While there is a certain heroic element in the actions of the future leader, it would be a mistake to overemphasize this point. It is stronger in the second episode than the first, but in any case it is not unambiguous. He commits murder by stealth, and then, understandably to be sure, runs away in fear. Moreover, the secret act of violence does not strengthen but rather undermines his authority with his own people. Those he tried to help neither understood nor accepted him.

Above all, these stories evoke reflection on questions concerning the relationship between justice and violence. In both episodes Moses acts violently in response to injustice. One could take the first act as one of solidarity with his own people, but the more fundamental concern is with the oppressed. That is even more explicit in the second story, where he acts on behalf of the weak foreigners against the strong, who also are foreigners. That clearly anticipates the major theme of the Exodus story, the rescue of a people from slavery. In neither case does Moses act on behalf of himself, but for others, putting himself at risk. Both acts, however, arise out of a complex matrix of entirely human events. The first act bears no fruit, neither in solidarity with the people nor in lasting success. We are not even clearly informed that Moses' murder was righteous anger, justified or not. Thus no direct answer to the question of violence in opposition to injustice emerges, but only a description of human realities.

Psalm 69:6-15

Psalm 69 is an individual lament composed to be used in worship during a time of personal crisis. The structure of the entire psalm should be noticed so that this Sunday's lection can be seen in its context. The following elements make up the psalm: (1) an opening address to the Deity which already makes an appeal and speaks of the worshiper's trouble (verses 1-3); (2) a short description of the distress (verse 4); (3) a plea incorporating an acknowledgment of wrongdoing (verses 5-6); (4) further description of the distress (verses 7-12); (5) a further appeal to God for assistance (verses 13-18); (6) a fourth description of the distressful trouble (verses 19-21); (7) a fourth appeal to the Deity, this time asking for the destruction of the enemy (verses 22-28); (8) a final short description of the distress and an appeal (verse 29); (9) a vow to praise God addressed to a human audience (verses 30-31); (10) admonition addressed to a human audience (verses 32-33); and (11) a statement of confidence (verses 34-36).

This psalm has been selected to be read in conjunction with the Old Testament text because it presumably describes a person's plight that is analogous to that of Moses in Exodus 2:11-22. The author of Psalm 69 certainly does not seem to have had the Moses story in mind when composing the psalm. On the other hand, the passion narratives in the Gospels certainly drew upon the image of this psalm in depicting the events of the Crucifixion.

This Sunday's lection commences with an appeal to the Deity, requesting that the supplicant not be the cause of others' shame and dishonor. Presumably, some group was associated with the one offering prayer to the extent that persons faced shame and dishonor if the supplicant were not favorably responded to by God. Was the original user of the psalm the Jerusalem king whose people's status depended on his status? Perhaps some other leader, such as a prophet whose reputation was at stake, was the worshiper. Or is the person merely referring to friends and family? We may simply be confronted with stereotypical and metaphorical language whereby the supplicant associates others with his cause. By referring to the associates as "those who hope in thee" and "those who seek thee," the worshiper tends to lay a greater responsibility on God for a favorable hearing since the standing of God's other devotees are involved as well.

The posture of those referred to in verse 6 should be noted. They hope in and they seek after God. At the same time, those who look to God fear being put to shame and suffering dishonor. That is, they fear a loss of personal and social status because of the situation of the supplicant.

In verses 7-12, the psalm again picks up on a description of the distress. Two factors are the central motifs in this section. On the one hand, references are made to religious actions performed by the worshiper as signs of service "for thy sake" (verse 7). On the other hand, there is noted the alienation and ridicule that these acts of religious devotion produced. Verse 7 may be seen as a summarizing statement about both of these. The worshiper claims that it is devotion to God or some act undertaken for God that has resulted in personal dishonor and shame which, as verse 6 notes, threatens to spill over onto others. The religious acts and pious devotion noted are zeal for the temple (verse 9), weeping and fasting (verse 10), and the wearing of sackcloth (verse 11). The last two of these refer to actions one would take while in grief, suffering, and repentance. (For a case of wearing sackcloth, see Isaiah 20, where the prophet is lamenting over the participation of his people in plans for revolt. The subsequent removal of his clothes was a more drastic demonstration!) What zeal for the house of God means is uncertain. There are a number of options: a desire to have a case heard by God in the temple (note that the end of verse 3 suggests that a charge of theft may have been involved), a desire to worship, general concern for the temple, and so on. The shame and reproach are reflected in a number of statements: becoming a stranger to friends, being alienated from family (verse 8), suffering insults and reproach (verses 9-10), becoming the butt of jokes and gossip (verse 11), and even the subject of barroom songs (verse 12). Obviously, the descriptions here are intent on making matters seem as bad as possible.

Nonetheless, they are at least honest expressions of a feeling of alienation, a sentiment better expressed than suppressed.

In verses 13-15, the worshiper expresses complete reliance on God. In this appeal, one again finds the terminology of anarchy and of being overwhelmed: sinking in the mire, my enemies, deep waters, flood, deep, and the pit. Appeal is made, not in the name of just deserts, but to Yahweh's love and faithful help. For solace and salvation, the soul turns to God.

Romans 8:9-17

Parts of today's epistle reading are also used elsewhere in the Common Lectionary. For Trinity Sunday in Year B, the epistolary text is 8:12-17 (cf. *After Pentecost, Year B*). For Pentecost in Year C, the first option for the New Testament reading is 8:14-17 (cf. *Lent, Holy Week, Easter, Year C*).

One thing that distingiushes today's text from its other uses in the Lectionary is that in the Season After Pentecost in Year A it occurs as part of the semicontinuous reading of the Epistle to the Romans. The first move, then, is to place it in its literary context, above all to read 8:1-8 as a crucial middle link between last week's lesson from chapter 7 and today's text.

In one sense, verses 1-8 provide the organizing structure for the two parts of today's text: verses 9-11 and verses 12-17. Without undue oversimplification, we might note that the opening verses introduce us to two fundamental perspectives: living "in" and living "according to." Accordingly, the first part of today's text especially stresses the locative: where we live, our participation *in* the Spirit, ourselves as the residence of the Spirit. In the second part, we detect a shift from life "in" to life "according to," from is to ought, from indicative to imperative, where the concern is not so much on *where* we live but *how* we live. This distinction provides one scheme for treating our passage.

The World We Live In (verses 9-11). Paul speaks of "in the flesh" and "in the Spirit" as though they are two worlds, two realms of existence in which we might live, or two spheres of influence that pose options by which we can establish our identity. His thought in this respect is dualistic: flesh and Spirit represent two antithetical forces (8:5).

But Paul recognizes that deciding on the world in which we live is part of a reciprocal process. Where we live is actually determined by another, perhaps even prior, decision: who, or what, we allow to live within us. What we inhabit is determined by what inhabits us. The way we shape our world results from what we allow to shape us. Living "in the Spirit" is predicated on the Spirit "living within us" (verses 9, 11). Moral transformation may occur within us so that our existence may be said to be "in Christ Jesus" (8:1, 2), but the vital complement to our being in Christ is Christ's presence within us (verse 10).

This close association between our being in God's presence and God's presence within us is reflected in the psalmist's prayer: "Cast me not away from thy presence, and take not thy holy Spirit from me" (Ps. 51:11). For the psalmist, to be "in God" is to be indwelt by God's divine Spirit. To have God's Spirit taken away is to be banished from the divine presence. Not to have God's Spirit within is to be evicted from life in and before God.

To be sure, divine presence in our text is understood christologically. "Spirit of God" and "Spirit of Christ" are all but indistinguishable, and yet the presence of Christ within us is a clear sign of identity, possession, and ownership (verses 9-10). Moreover, our own resurrection hinges on Christ's resurrection (verse 11; cf. I Thess. 4:14; I Cor. 6:14; 15:20-21; II Cor. 4:14; 13:4; Rom. 6:5; Eph. 2:6; Col. 1:18; 2:12-13; II Tim. 2:11). It is the Spirit of God who demonstrated the capacity to bring life from death in the resurrection of Christ that now provides the energizing, life-giving force to Christian existence—but not *in absentia*, not remotely, but by its indwelling presence "within us" (verse 11).

For Christ to be "in us" does not ignore the reality of our moral struggle (verse 10). We still experience the presence of Christ within our mortal existence, within our bodies that are "dead because of sin." When Christ comes into the house, it is not as if all the inhabitants immediately evacuate (cf. Mark 3:27). Sin still occurs. When we sin, we still place ourselves on a collision course with death. But while our "bodies," our "selves," still work under normal, human constraints and weaknesses, our "spirits" begin to experience a new life. The Christ-event of death and resurrection begins to play itself out within us. We go through the cycle of death, and in doing so, experience the effects of sin, yet we also go through the cycle of resurrection, and in doing so taste God's righteousness as we experience God's "righting" action. Death in us still? Yes! But Life emerging too? Yes! Death in conflict with Life, but gradually giving way to Life and Righteousness—eventually realized fully when God bestows on us resurrection life (verse 11).

How We Live in the World (verses 12-17). Here the emphasis shifts to moral obligation: "Therefore," that is, in light of how your existence is defined—by living in the "world" of God, Christ, and the Spirit, and by having all Three "live in" us—"we have an obligation" (verse 12, NIV). This is the language of ought, of ethical imperative.

We should first note the correlation between "living in" and "living according to." Where we live has norming effect on us. Context does affect behavior. Two norming possibilities are held out: flesh and spirit. The one is associated with death, the other with life. Indeed, death and life not only set the contours of existence within each, but define the *teloi*, the ends toward which each inexorably takes us.

More is envisioned in life "with Christ" than divine presence. It is not simply that the Spirit indwells us, but actively directs us: we find ourselves being "moved by the Spirit of God" (verse 14, NEB, JB). So powerful is this pull that its effect is transforming: slaves become transformed into children. To be a slave is to be without freedom, under oppression and tyranny from forces or persons over whom we have no power (8:2). The natural corollary of slavehood is fear (verse 15).

But being a child means becoming an heir (verse 17). As "children of God" we share in Christ's own cherished status as "child of God," thereby becoming co-participants with Christ of God's blessing of resurrection life, and with it genuine freedom before God and the world.

But to be God's child in the sense that Christ was should not be idealized or romanticized: it entails suffering and scandal (verse 17). Yet God's Spirit bears witness to our true identity precisely in those moments when we not only question who we are, perhaps even forget who we are, but also when we may desert who we are. In those moments, we feel the tug of God's Spirit, reminding us, "You are God's child. Now behave like one!"

Matthew 13:1-9, 18-23

We have today the first of three lections drawn from Matthew 13, a collection of parables with some explanations. This constitutes the third major body of Jesus' teachings in Matthew (ending at 13:53), the Sermon on the Mount and the Mission Charge being the first two. Because three Sundays will focus on parables, the preacher will probably want to study verses 10-17, omitted from our lection, and read one or two commentaries on the nature of parables and methods of interpretation. Verse 9, "He who has ears, let him hear," certainly implies a weight of importance and a burden on the listener beyond that which would accompany simple stories or illustrations, as some have supposed parables to be.

The entirety of Matthew 13:1-23 consists of four parts: the parable of the sower (verses 1-9); Jesus' explanation of why he speaks in parables (verses 10-15); Jesus' blessing on the disciples (verses 16-17); and the interpretation of the parable of the sower (verses 18-23). Our present concern is only with the parable and its interpretation.

All three Synoptics have the parable of the sower and its interpretation (Mark 4:1-9, 13-20; Luke 8:4-8, 11-15). Both Mark and Matthew locate the parable teachings beside the sea. Matthew has Jesus going out of the house (13:1), perhaps vaguely referring to the house in Capernaum, but Capernaum has not been mentioned since 9:28. Perhaps it is more helpful to take the sea as the public side of Jesus' teaching in parables and the house (13:1, 36) as the private, since the parables both reveal and conceal. Efforts by Prof. Jeremias and others to recover the original locations and audiences of the parables have never been very successful.

On the face of it, the parable of the sower is a simple story drawn from ordinary life. A sower scatters seed in a field prior to plowing, as was the custom in Palestinian farming. Naturally the seed fell indiscriminately among weeds, on rocks, on the path worn by passersby, as well as in the good soil. And again quite naturally, the yield at harvesttime was largely determined by the differences in the soil. Verse 9 implies that the story is very important but not everyone will understand it. Verses 10-17 give the clear impression that the crowds are confused by this and other parables while the disciples discern the meanings. However, such was not the case apparently, since the parable had to be explained to them.

The interpretation of the parable of the sower (verses 18-23) presents a number of problems for the reader. In the first place, it is doubtful that Jesus explained his own parables. The explanation seems to lie in the Christian tradition between Jesus and the Gospel writers. Second, the interpretation is allegorical; that is, each item of the story (sower, seed, weeds, rocks, good soil) is said to represent something else. To allegorize is to say something other than what one is saying. Once a popular method of biblical interpretation, allegorizing is today viewed with suspicion; it allows meanings to run rampant. Third, the wording of the interpretation is confusing. Matthew improves upon Mark, but the phrasing leaves it unclear whether the various hearers are what is sown (although the seed is the word of the kingdom, verse 19) or the soil or both.

Even so, the preacher can safely assume the parable deals with the variety of ways listeners respond to the word. For different reasons different hearers fail to become fruitful Christians while others respond so positively as to make the enterprise of witnessing and teaching worthwhile. We cannot know for sure whether Jesus' intent was to explain why there is some failure in the mission or to encourage his disciples by pointing to the good soil and the abundant yield. Both perspectives are valid since they are two sides of the same coin. Certainly in Matthew's context, and in the context of many communities since that time, doubt, criticism, rejection, and disappointment make the parable a welcome word not simply of explanation, but of assurance to Jesus' followers.

Proper 11

Sunday Between July 17 and 23 Inclusive

Exodus 3:1-12; Psalm 103:1-13; Romans 8:18-25; Matthew 13:24-30, 36-43

The Old Testament reading is the narrative of Moses' commission to return to Egypt and lead the Hebrews out of bondage, free them from Egyptian oppression, and lead them to the land of promise. The psalm offers a description of the character and work of God who "made known his ways to Moses, his acts to the people of Israel." The Epistle reading, like the Old Testament lection, plays on the themes of human suffering in the present and divine redemption in the future. The Gospel reading, the Matthean version of the parable of the sower, speaks too about salvation, redemption, and judgment.

Exodus 3:1-12

This passage and next week's reading (Exod. 3:13-20) form only the first parts of the report of the vocation of Moses. When the account begins Moses is settled down in the land of Midian with a family and a livelihood, but when the account ends he is headed for Egypt as the Lord's agent to rescue his people. The passage forms the essential prelude for Moses' confrontation with Pharaoh and the Exodus from Egypt. Careful study of the first two parts of the vocation report during these two weeks enables us to address questions important to all who reflect on their divine vocations.

It is a long account, reflecting both the combination of literary sources and a complex history of tradition. The report of Moses' call is the combination of the older Pentateuchal sources J (the Yahwist) and E (the Elohist) which in turn rest on oral traditions. In addition there is the Priestly Writer's parallel (Exod. 6:2–7:7) which reports that the vocation took place in Egypt. Evidence for the composite character of the account here includes the different divine names, God and Yahweh (read "Lord" in most translations except the Jerusalem Bible), repetitions of contents (verses 7-8 parallel verses 9-12), the different names for the sacred mountain ("Horeb" here but "Sinai" in other texts), and the manner of divine revelation (through an angel or by direct address). Modern scholarship has rightly recognized that at least two old oral traditions have been combined in the written sources. One focused on the theophany and accounted for the sacredness of the place. It would have been similar to the story of Jacob at Bethel (Gen. 28:10-22). That place was the mountain remembered as the site of the covenant (Exod. 19–24). In addition to the designation as "Horeb, the mountain of God" (verse 1), the Hebrew name for the burning bush (*sin*, verse 2) probably contains an allusion to "Sinai." The other tradition, that of the vocation of Moses, now dominates the record.

Within a slender narrative framework our reading consists mainly of dialogue between God and Moses. The solitary shepherd finds himself in the wilderness at Horeb, which he probably does not know is "the mountain of God." Verse 2 serves as a general heading for what is to follow: "The angel of the Lord appeared to him." Seeing an astounding bush that burns but is not consumed, he approaches, only to hear the voice of God speaking first with a warning that he is on holy ground (verse 5), then with self-introduction (verse 6), and finally with a call (verses 7-10). Moses' response (verse 11) is only the first of a series of objections, but God reacts with words of reassurance and promise (verse 12).

Two major themes are sustained in this passage, corresponding to some extent to the old traditions behind it. The first is the divine self-revelation in the form of a theophany to a particular individual. How does God make himself known? According to a great many Old Testament accounts, it is by means of a dramatic appearance at a holy place. Here that place is on or near "the mountain of God." As in most other such reports, the individual who witnesses the theophany did not choose the place, nor did he even set out to find such a place or such an experience. It is almost providential or fortuitous that Moses strayed where—it is clear—God wanted him to be.

Often reports of theophanies indicate that God "came down" (cf. Exod. 19:20), but in any case the Lord's appearance is accompanied by a dramatic natural phenomenon or some "marvelous sight" (verse 3, NJPSV) such as the bush that burns but is not consumed. The theophany at Mount Sinai included smoke and fire and the quaking of the mountain (Exod. 19:18; cf. I Kings 19:9 ff.). Some of the prophetic vocation reports include allusions to such dramatic phenomena (Isa. 6:1-4; Ezek. 1-3). Furthermore, theophanies hardly ever are simple demonstrations of the awesome presence of God; they include direct address, words.

Moses stands in the presence of the Holy One, and the encounter is awesome and frightening. It is dangerous to approach the boundary between the divine and the human. Obeying the command to remove his shoes because he is on holy ground, he hears God speak and hides his face. No one can see God directly and live (Isa. 6). God, however, deigns to identify himself as the personal God of the ancestors. If the theophany stresses God's transcendence, the words stress his identification with a particular people.

The second major theme is carried by the dialogue between the two parties, God's call and Moses' response. In fact, the major narrative tension of the report as a whole concerns whether or not Moses will accept his vocation to lead the people out of Egypt. The full substance of the call is stated at the very outset: God has heard the cries of his people in Egypt and will bring them out to a land of their own. Moses is to be the instrument of that will (verses 7-10). Moses resists, not once but several times, and God patiently responds to his objections. Finally, armed with reassurance, the name of God, signs and wonders to perform, and the help of his brother Aaron, Moses obeys.

The reluctance of Moses requires special attention. Readers of this passage find it difficult to resist the temptation to analyze the personality of Moses or even speculate on physical limitations that might have made him a poor public speaker. This resistance, however, is not specific to Moses, but is found in virtually all of the other Old Testament vocation reports. Gideon (Judg. 6), Isaiah (Isa. 6), and Jeremiah (Jer. 1:4-10) all resist the call on the grounds of unworthiness or inadequacy. Consequently, it is clear that a sense of unworthiness or inadequacy is inherent in being called by God. The resistance to the call is related to the experience of the Holy. One need not be especially timid, shy, or cowardly to express reluctance.

Another aspect of the biblical understanding of vocation and the will of God is transparent here and in other reports of calls. It is God who will bring the people of Israel out of Egypt, but it is taken for granted that a human agent is required to effect that will. Moreover, the will of the one called is not subsumed completely into the will of God. Rather, he has—and is allowed to have—autonomy to continue to question, resist, or to choose to obey the One who called him.

Psalm 103:1-13

This hymnic psalm of thanksgiving comes very close to a theological catechism enumerating the personal qualities and behavioral characteristics of the Deity. In expounding this psalm, the ancient rabbis, however, were interested in what it had to say about the human, that is, its anthropological dimensions. In speaking about "all that is within me," the midrash (rabbinic commentary) on Psalms notes ten things within a person: "the windpipe for voice, the gullet for [swallowing] food, the liver for anger, the lungs for drink [to absorb liquids], the gall for jealousy, the maw [when full] for sleep, the stomach to grind the food, the spleen for laughter, the kidneys for counsel, and the heart for decision." Of interest here is the way various organs are associated with particular human emotions.

In speaking of the expression "bless the Lord," one ancient rabbi noted the following as the distinction between God as artisan and all other artisans: "A sculptor makes a statue; the sculptor dies, but his sculpture endures. But with the Holy One, it is not so. For the Holy One made man, and man dies, but the Holy One lives and endures. This neither the sculptor nor the silversmith can do. The silversmith casts an image; the silversmith dies; the casting endures. But the Holy One made man, and it is man who dies; it is the Holy One who lives and endures for ever and ever."

Although a thanksgiving, this psalm contains no direct address to the Deity, thus it is not a prayer of thanksgiving. In fact, the composition begins as a self addressing the self (verse 1). In the final stanza, the range of vision is greatly expanded, arching out to include the angels, the heavenly hosts, and all the works of creation.

The verses selected for the lection are fundamentally theological affirmations; their content is composed of descriptive statements about God. If we include verse 6 with verses 1-5, and this is a possible although not an obvious division, then the first six verses speak of seven deeds of the Deity:

> forgives iniquity
>   heals diseases
> redeems from the Pit
>   crowns with steadfast love and mercy
> satisfies with good as long as one lives
>   renews youthful vigor like that of an eagle
> works vindication and justice for all oppressed

All of these actions are expressed through participial forms of the verbs. One might take such formulations, like participles in English, as describing states of being. Thus the actions denoted are taken as descriptions characteristic of the Deity.

Verses 8-13 has a second series, containing this time six items that describe the character of Yahweh, particularly with regard to the divine reaction to human error, wrongdoing, and rebellion. Verse 14 should be considered in conjunction with these verses since it offers anthropological insight and rationale for divine behavior, offering reasons anchored in human existence for God's grace and mercy.

Throughout this section, descriptions of God's treatment of the sinner and explanations of divine behavior are interlaced. Each verse makes independent but interrelated points. (1) God's nature is oriented to mercy and grace; he is not easily upset and when he is, there is mercy abounding (verse 8). (2) God does not perpetually torment or nag incessantly since his anger does not abide forever. The text does not deny that God has anger and that he does react in wrath; however, the divine is willing to let bygones be bygones (verse 9). (3) God does not operate on a tit-for-tat basis. The punishment is not made to fit the crime. God is free to reduce the penalty, to soften the shock of human actions (verse 10). (4) Divine mercy is compared to the greatness of the heights of the heaven above the earth (verse 11). (5) The vertical dimension used in verse 11 is replaced by a horizontal dimension in describing the removal of transgressions. East and west, or literally the rising and setting (of the sun), is a way of stressing the radical separation (verse 12). (6) The parent-child relationship and parental pity form an analogy by which to understand divine love. It should be noted that such pity is granted to those fearing (= obeying the will of) God (verse 13; note verses 17-18). The human condition helps incline God to mercy: God knows the weakness of the human condition; people's dusty origin and their dusty destiny.

Romans 8:18-25

Part of this passage overlaps with the first option for the New Testament reading for Pentecost in Year B (8:22-27). The reader may wish to consult our remarks in *Lent, Holy Week, Easter, Year B.*

Today's text is a clearly defined unit of thought that follows directly on last week's epistolary reading which ended on the note of suffering: "sharing [Christ's] sufferings so as to share his glory" (8:17, JB). If it was Christ's lot to suffer, so does it appear to be ours, who are co-heirs with him (cf. Mark 10:39-40; Luke 22:28-30; Rom. 5:3-5). How, then, can we cope with the reality of suffering and its inevitability?

The answer of today's text: "live in hope." The thrust here is forward: suffering in this life is contrasted with "the splendour, as yet unrevealed, which is in store for us" (verse 18, NEB). Suffering and splendor, pain and glory—these are the two poles of the Christ-event. They correspond to death and resurrection. Christ suffered death, to be sure, but God raised him to new life, a life of splendid glory. His fate and destiny charts the course for everyone who enters his story, lives in it and by it, thus is said to be "in Christ" (II Cor. 4:10-11; Col. 3:3-4).

What keeps Paul's response here from being artificial and hollow is to recall that Christ himself suffered "in hope." Since we read the gospel story from this side of Easter, we tend to think of Christ knowing in advance that glory would be his automatically and that this somehow diminished the impact of his suffering. Yet the Gospel accounts of Christ's passion and death suggest otherwise. They show him suffering and facing death in a way that tested his faith and refined his hope. To think otherwise is to suppose that Christ lived by sight rather than by faith. Experiencing the splendor of divine salvation is "something we must wait for with patience" (verse 25, JB), even as Christ did (Heb. 5:7-10).

There is something else besides the example of Christ that makes it possible to cope: to realize that our own suffering is part of a much larger process. This is more than simply saying that other people suffer like we do, even though realizing that what we endure others have endured often helps us cope.

Rather, Paul envisions "the whole creation" (verse 19, JB), or "the created universe" (NEB), as having been launched on a course of suffering with the sin of Adam. Behind his remarks in verses 19-20 are clear allusions to the creation story, especially Genesis 3:17-19. We are told that the created order "was made the victim of frustration, not by its own choice, but because of him who made it so" (verse 20, NEB). The crucial exegetical question here is, Who is "him"—God or Adam? Was it God who subjected the created order and set it on its course of pain and suffering, as punishment for Adam's sin? So suggests JB: "It was not for any fault on the part of creation that it was made unable to attain its purpose, it was made so by God" (verse 20). Or, if this sounds too vindictive and incompatible with our conception of God, we might prefer to fault Adam, the one whose sin was ultimately responsible for things going awry.

105

In spite of its predicament, however, the created order still lives "in hope" (verse 20). Here, we face another exegetical choice: whether "in hope" concludes verse 20 or introduces verse 21. If the former, it would appear that God subjected the created order to an existence of frustration, yet did so "in hope" that such punishment would be redemptive (so RSV). If the latter, the hope of creation is that it might someday be freed "from its slavery to decadence" (so JB, NIV). This may even be a hope that is seen from our vantage point, looking back: "yet always there was hope" (verse 21, NEB).

In spite of exegetical difficulty, the point is clear: the created order, taken in the most comprehensive sense, is viewed as living in hope. To be sure, it has been shackled with mortality, encumbered with all the pain and suffering that accompany earthly existence. Yet it looks for a better day and faces the future with hope rather than despair.

To make his point even more vividly, Paul uses the metaphor of child birth. He envisions the created universe as engaged in "one great act of giving birth" (verse 22, JB). In its attempt to usher fresh, innocent life into the world, it is afflicted with severe labor pains. Thus to give birth to life inevitably entails pain and suffering. We are asked to imagine the whole cosmos crying out with groans and labor pains as it tries to bring forth new life. It is a vivid image and one we do well to ponder.

What happens in the cosmos also happens in the person. Macrocosmic pain and suffering have their counterpart in the microcosm of individual suffering. In Christ, we have experienced the "first fruits of the Spirit" (verse 23; cf. II Cor. 1:22; 5:5; Eph. 1:14); that is, God has given us the Spirit as payment in advance of the life to come. New life has entered us through the insemination of God's Spirit, and now we too "groan inwardly as we wait for our bodies to be set free" (verse 23, JB, cf. II Cor. 5:2, 4). The metaphor shifts slightly here, but the point is clear: like the cosmos in general, we too experience the painful groaning that accompanies our mortal existence, and we await that moment of birth to a new existence where our salvation becomes complete.

Few of us are accustomed to thinking of the created order in terms as personalistic as this. For us, the created order consists of animate and inanimate existence. Humans and animals may squeal with pain but not rocks, trees, and stars. Yet, for Paul the whole created order is engaged in a painful process of cosmic transformation that will culminate in the Eschaton, when suffering gives way to splendor. To think this way might give us greater pause as we plunder the earth, and now space. It may help shatter the illusion that we can do as we please with the inanimate and lifeless, as if no pain can be inflicted on it. Yet we are gradually learning that the fate of the earth, and of space, is also our fate, that our destiny is indissolubly connected to the destiny of creation.

Matthew 13:24-30, 36-43

We continue today with the second of three lessons from Matthew 13, a chapter devoted to Jesus' parables and comments about them. A quick review of the statements introducing last Sunday's lection might be helpful. As was true of that lection, today's text consists of a parable and its interpretation.

The parable of the weeds growing in the wheat replaced the parable of the seed growing secretly in Mark's sequence (4:26-29), a story with which Matthew's replacement has very little in common. In fact, Matthew's parable of the weeds is different from most of Jesus' parables in one important respect. While its story line is based on a common fact of experience: weeds grew in wheat fields; weeds were gathered in bundles and burned for fuel while the wheat was preserved in "barns"; and some weeds resembled the wheat in early stages so that wheat was lost in the removal of weeds, still there are elements in the story that call unusual attention to themselves. These elements do not serve to make the story natural and normal but alert the reader to anticipate special meanings. In other words, the reader is "set up" by the story to receive an interpretation, almost as though Matthew began with the interpretation and worked back to the story. For example: the seeds are sown, not by the servants as one would expect, but by the owner, and the weeds by "his enemy." Who would assume common weeds were sown by anyone? A conflict situation is created. Or again, twice it is said the householder sowed "good seed." What other kind would he sow? The word "good" prepares us for its counterpart, evil. Or again, the servants are not to separate the weeds until the harvest when, in fact, farmers of that day more than once during a growing season would remove weeds from a grain field. We are prepared to anticipate a day of reckoning.

This parable and its interpretation, found only in Matthew, is clearly Matthean in its perspective. The interpretation is again allegorical and needs little comment. However, a few elements call for attention. The parable presupposes a church situation in which Jesus' disciples are tempted to become involved in purging evil. Since "the field is the world" (verse 38), it is unclear whether the desire of Jesus' followers is to remove evil from the world or, as is more likely, from within the church. Matthew's church certainly contained undesirable elements (7:21-23; 18:15-20), and in that church as in many others, the desire to achieve purity and perfection was in tension with the obligation to accept, forgive, and restore.

The master's injunction against efforts to expunge evil had three reasons behind it. One, such attempts now are premature. Two, such attempts have as their usual result the disturbance and loss of the faithful in the process of seeking to eliminate the unfaithful. And three, the task of judging between good and evil belongs not to us but to Christ. We are not to judge (7:1) but rather to work at reconciliation (18:15-16) and to forgive without limitation (18:21-22). Christ will come in the end-time as judge of all people (16:27; 25:31-46). Once the weeds (evildoers) have been separated forever, then the wheat (righteous) will be gathered into the kingdom of God (verses 42-43; I Cor. 15:24-28).

However Matthew's frequent theme of a final judgment may sound to subsequent readers, to the church originally addressed it spoke two words clearly: one, do not fret over evildoers for neither their present nor their future is your responsibility; and two, God will bring history to a close with justice and the saints will finally be freed from abuse and oppression. The parable of the weeds in the wheat is therefore not a threatening but a comforting word.

Proper 12

Sunday Between July 24 and 30 Inclusive

Exodus 3:13-20; Psalm 105:1-11; Romans 8:26-30; Matthew 13:44-52

The Old Testament lesson presents a dialogue between Moses and God in which the Deity makes known to Moses his name which he is to use in encouraging the Hebrews to leave Egypt and in confronting Pharaoh. The psalm is a hymn of thanksgiving which narrates the great events of salvation and celebrates the realization of the promise made to Moses and the fathers. In the Epistle lesson, Paul assures his audience of the divine help available in living the Christian life and in shaping the community of the predestined. The Gospel lesson contains three parables about the nature and life of the kingdom. All four texts are concerned with the creation and shaping of the life of redemption.

Exodus 3:13-20

These verses from Exodus 3 continue directly where the reading for last week ended and contain a second part of the report of the call of Moses (Exod. 3:1–4:17). The unit as a whole is structured as a dialogue between God and Moses. Following the dramatic appearance of God revealed through the burning bush, God calls Moses to bring Israel out of Egypt; Moses offers one objection after another: God deals with each objection in turn; and then finally commissions Moses to bring about the release of the people. The vocation report is quite similar to others in the Old Testament, especially those of the prophets (Isa. 6; Jer. 1:4-10; Ezek. 1–3).

In its immediate context, Exodus 3:13-20 functions to present Moses' second objection and the Lord's response to

109

it. Note how indirectly Moses objects and poses the question, as if it is not his own query but that of the people: "If I come to the people of Israel [he has not yet agreed to go!] and say to them, 'The God of your fathers has sent me to you,' and they ask me, ' What is his name?' what shall I say to them?" (verse 13). The question is by no means a trivial one, Who is God, and how shall I address him? Such questions may be asked for a wide variety of reasons. Moses suggests a pragmatic and political concern—will the people listen and follow? The question can come from the heart of faith: one wants to know how to begin a prayer of praise or thanksgiving. It can also come from the fundamental human desire to control—to call down the power of the heavens into one's own service. The intrinsic importance and urgency of the question explains why Jewish and Christian commentators and theologians from the earliest times have fastened upon this unit of scripture. They wanted it to yield an answer to Moses' question, but the Christian preacher might very well make the question itself the focus of homiletical reflection.

The divine response to Moses is, to say the least, enigmatic: "I AM WHO I AM" (verse 14). This appears to be a popular etymology for the name Yahweh. Grammatically, "I am' ('ehyeh) is a first person singular imperfect form of the Hebrew verb "to be," and could with equal reliability be translated with a future tense, "I will be what I will be" (RSV footnote). "Yahweh" could be a third, not first, person singular imperfect form of the same verb. It is not possible to determine whether or not the divine name itself actually originated from this verb, as a confession of faith in the God "who is," or "who will be," or even "who causes to be," but that seems unlikely. What we have here is a similarity of sounds and some reflection upon the meaning of the name, but only after it had been in use for centuries.

The specific connection of the expression, "I am who I am," with the name Yahweh comes only in verse 15, which in itself would have been a direct answer to the question posed by Moses. It seems likely that the response to Moses reflects more than one stage of development. In its present form, Moses' question is answered, but in an earlier stage it seems likely that God refused to answer directly. The answer, "I am who I am," is similar to the answer a parent hears when he or she asks a child where she is going, "Out," or "I am going where I am going."

Particular concern with the disclosure of the name in the time of Moses comes from the Elohistic source, according to which the name was not known earlier. That interest is shared by the Priestly Writer, who also considered it anachronistic for the name to be mentioned before the time of Moses (Exod. 6:2-9). The Yahwist, on the other hand, obviously believed that God was known by that proper name even to the first human beings (Gen. 2:4b ff.). Thus the sources presumed different doctrines of history and revelation. According to E and P, knowledge of the name Yahweh was not general, and was revealed to Israel only in the time of Moses, just before the Exodus.

What does it mean that God refuses to disclose his name directly, or at best gives an enigmatic response? A similar ambivalence is seen in the story of Jacob at the Jabbok (Gen. 32:22-32), in which the patriarch asks for the name of the one who struggles with him but he gets no answer (see also Judg. 13:15-20). Refusal to answer is an expression of the divine freedom and at the same time raises questions about the human temptation to control God. Ancient Israel knew that temptation well and tried to guard against it with the third commandment: "You shall not take the name of the Lord your God in vain" (Exod. 20:7); that is, no one shall use the divine name to manipulate God. Throughout Old Testament times the divine name Yahweh was both known and used, forming part of a great many proper names (e.g., Elijah, "my God is Yah[weh]"). But the concern to obey this commandment and thus to honor the freedom of God was so great that Judaism eventually would not allow the name to be spoken aloud, even in the reading of scriptures.

In this text, however, God finally does reveal himself as Yahweh, and Yahweh announces to Moses what he has done and will do. God's self-identification is fundamentally in terms of a continuity of graceful acts in history. The God who turns himself to Moses is "the God of your fathers, the God of Abraham, the God of Isaac, and the God of Jacob" (verse 15; cf. verse 6), who now declares his intention to fulfill the promise to those patriarchs. This very one has heard the cries and seen the affliction of the people in Egypt and reveals himself in order to rescue them from slavery (verses 16-17). The only appropriate response is to acknowledge that good news and remember that name and those deeds "throughout all generations" (verse 15).

Psalm 105:1-11

This hymn thankfully praises Yahweh for his guiding the course of Hebrew history from the time of the patriarchs to the inheritance and settlement in the Promised Land. After the initial call for the community to give thanks (verses 1-6), the psalm rehearses the sacred history of the people's past.

In many ways, the psalm follows the outline of the Hexateuch, that is, the biblical books from Genesis to Joshua. The following is the general outline of the hexateuchal scheme, minus the material on human prehistory in Genesis 1–11:

The Patriarchs—Genesis 12–50
Moses and the Exodus—Exodus 1–15
The Stay and Wandering in the Wilderness—Exodus
   16–Deuteronomy 34
The Settlement in the Land—Joshua 1–24

The following is an outline of the psalm along the same division of material:

The Patriarchs—verses 7-25
Moses and the Exodus—verses 26-38
The Stay and Wandering in the Wilderness—verses 39-43
The Settlement in the Land—verses 44-45

A few details in the psalm differ from the depiction in the Hexateuch. (1) In the psalm, Joseph is described as suffering severely while imprisoned. There is no reference in Genesis to his feet being hurt with fetters and his neck being put in an iron collar (verse 18). This emphasis reflects the tendency to depict the ancestors as undergoing hardships, pains, and temptations on behalf of later generations. In later rabbinic Judaism this was understood as the ancestors' accumulating merits that could be passed on to the benefit of subsequent generations. (2) Joseph is depicted as instructing the leaders and wise men of Egypt (verse 22). Again this is a tendency seen also in later non-biblical Jewish writers. The Hebrews are understood as the source of the wisdom of the Egyptians. (3) In describing the plagues in Egypt, the psalm speaks of only eight and not quite in the same manner as the opening chapters of the book of Exodus. Here the plagues are darkness (verse 28), water into blood (verse 29), frogs (verse 30), flies and gnats (verse 31), hail and lightning (verse 32), smiting of vines and fig trees (verse 33), locusts (verse 34), and the slaughter of the firstborn (verse 36). Ten plagues can be obtained if one takes the fish dying (verse 29b) and the gnats (verse 31b) as separate incidents.

This psalm may be seen as a sung version of Israel's sacred past. Probably they sung songs and celebrated the events in worship services long before they wrote books about their past.

The events of the past could be used in diverse ways. Psalm 105 rehearses the past to create a sense of praise and thanksgiving. Psalm 106 uses a similar version of past history but with the desire to create a sense of guilt and repentance (see Proper 14, page 130).

In the psalm lesson for today, verses 1-11, two things are prominent. First of all, verses 1-6 call the people to respond both to God and to the events of their sacred past. Toward God they are to give thanks, sing praises to, glory in, rejoice in, seek him. With regard to the sacred past, the people are called to make these known, tell about them as testimony, and remember them. Second, in verses 7-11, the theme is the promise/covenant of the land. In the patriarchal narratives of Genesis 12–50, the theme of the Promised Land ties together the narratives and the generations. Here too the affirmation is made that the land was promised and covenanted to Abraham, Isaac, and Jacob as an everlasting covenant. What Moses is commissioned to carry out in Exodus 3:1-12 is part and parcel of what was promised to the earlier ancestors.

Romans 8:26-30

There is a slight overlap between today's epistolary reading and the first option for the New Testament reading for Pentecost in Year B (8:22-27). The reader may wish to consult *Lent, Holy Week, Easter, Year B,* for further comments.

Today's text, with its introductory word "likewise" (verse 26, RSV; or "in the same way," NEB), recalls verse 23, with its mention of the "groaning" that is experienced both by ourselves and by the created order. Yet creature and creation have been infused with God's Spirit, the "first fruits," an advance payment of God's presence. It is, after all, the God present among us who has launched creation toward ultimate redemption. But because this salvation is still unfolding and not fully realized, we experience it as suffering and pain mingled with patience and hope. The one is giving way to the other but not without the agony that accompanies every meaningful transformation.

But the Spirit is more than mere representative of God's presence in this process of painful change. Today's text assures us of the Spirit's active role in relating us, as fellow participants in this transformation, to God: "the Spirit helps us in our weakness" (verse 26). We look about us and see forces at work that are truly cosmic. They are larger than life, hidden from our view, difficult even to identify. Yet we are victims and our utter weakness is exposed.

So overwhelmed are we that words escape us. Our loss of words leaves us feeling helpless. In spite of having Jesus' model prayer (Matt. 6:9-13), even an abundance of prayers in both the Old and New Testaments that reflect the whole spectrum of human experience, we nevertheless find ourselves speechless. We find ourselves not knowing *what* we ought to pray, or perhaps not knowing "*how* to pray as we ought" (verse 26, italics added, RSV, NEB). Awkward confusion abounds: what to say? how to say it? Such sighs may be reminiscent of Jesus' own experience (Mark 7:34; 8:12). In any case, anxious sighing characterizes existence of this aeon (II Cor. 5:2, 4).

Since Christian prayer is prayer in the Spirit (I Cor. 14:15; Eph. 6:18-19; Jude 20), and since the presence of the Spirit within us is an axiom of Christian existence (Rom. 5:5; 8:14-16), the Spirit comes to our rescue. It is the Spirit who acts as the intermediary presence between us and God to put our inarticulate thoughts into words. In Johannine terms, the Spirit is the Paraclete, who advocates our case before God (John 14:15-17, 26; 15:26; 16:7). This intercessory work the Spirit also shares with Christ himself (8:34; Heb. 7:25; I John 2:1).

One exegetical question that arises in verse 26 is whether the *Spirit's* intercessory remains inarticulate, or whether the Spirit takes *our* inarticulate concerns and interprets them before God. RSV opts for the former: "the Spirit . . . intercedes for us with sighs too deep for words" (also NIV). NEB opts for the latter: "through our inarticulate groans the Spirit himself is pleading for us." JB represents a happy compromise: "the Spirit . . . expresses our plea in a way that could never be put into words."

In either case, we stand before God "who searches our inmost being" (verse 27, NEB). It is the sentiment of the psalmist who acknowledges that the Creator has full, intimate knowledge of the creature (Ps. 139:1; cf. Jer. 11:20). Just as the Spirit knows the inner recesses of the mind of God (I Cor. 2:10), so does God know "what is the mind of the Spirit" (verse 27). Theirs is a reciprocal relationship in which unobstructed communication occurs. Yet what commends the Spirit's appeal to God is that "he pleads for God's people in God's own way" (verse 27 NEB).

If participating in God's cosmic transformation can leave us feeling helpless, it can also test our own sense of calling as well as the fidelity of the God who called us. To this concern the second part of today's text is addressed.

Again we face a crucial exegetical question in verse 28. One manuscript tradition, which is followed by KJV, reads, "All things work together for good." Another manuscript tradition, followed by RSV, NEB, JB, NIV, reads "in everything God works for good." The former implies a process of impersonal providence, while the latter more directly involves God in history. Indeed, our text posits God in a *cooperative* role with us: "By turning everything to their good God co-operates with all those who love him" (verse 28,

JB; also NEB; cf. RSV). One of the remarkable features of Paul's theology is the dramatic involvement of the human in the work of God (I Cor. 3:9; II Cor. 6:1).

But here the stress lies on God's dramatic involvement with us. Again, we should note the context: suffering (8:18, 35). When we suffer, the lingering question is, where is God? How can this possibly be for our good? The question becomes even more pressing when it is asked by those who love God.

Our text is quite explicit in locating God's cooperation among "those who love him" (verse 28). Only rarely does Paul speak of the Christian's relationship with God in this way (I Cor. 2:9, 8:3), but when he does so it is significant. Quite clearly, loving God is the crucial complement of knowing God, in fact is the more primary of the two. Yet our love for God is axiomatic in Christian teaching (James 1:12; 2:5; Matt. 22:37).

To live in the love of God is to be responsive to the call of God (verse 28). Through the gospel the call of God is issued and there our election becomes formally initiated (I Thess. 2:12; 4:7; II Thess. 1:15; 2:13-14; I Pet. 5:10). Yet we are assured that this is part of a much longer process that stems from the beginning of time (Eph. 1:5, 11; 3:11; I Pet. 1:2): foreknowledge, predestination, election, justification, and glorification (verses 29-30).

These verses have obviously been formative in the history of doctrine, and questions still abound concerning divine foreknowledge and election. The emphasis here, however, is less on the particular "doctrine" suggested by each of these terms than it is on the overarching assurance of God's purposeful activity in the whole of history (cf. II. Tim. 1:9). From start to finish, God's active concern has been shown for those who live in loving response to the divine call. Even when the purposes of God seemed hidden and when human forces were ostensibly at work thwarting the divine will, God was still actively at work. As in the case of Joseph, evil seemed to threaten the divine purpose, but what his conspirators meant for evil, God meant for good (Gen. 50:20).

Today's text begins with the recognition of human weakness. It may take the form of abject speechlessness or absolute despair in not being able to recognize the presence of God in the midst of our own pain. As to the one, Paul assures us that when we know neither what to say nor how to say it, when circumstances make us dumb struck before God, the Spirit who knows us as well as God, brings to appropriate expression what life has left us unable to say. As to the other, we are asked to believe in God's capacity to be present with and among us when our love has responded to the divine call. But not only to be present but to be *at work with us in everything*, even if human circumstance blinds us to the presence and work of our Collaborator.

Matthew 13:44-52

This reading concludes this series of three Sundays on the parables of Jesus and is also our final lection from the third of the five major bodies of teaching in Matthew (the Sermon on the Mount and instructions for mission were the first two). Matthew 13:44-52 consists of four parables, if indeed the fourth unit (verses 51-52) can be called a parable. Each parable is brief, self-contained, without an informing context, and virtually unrelated to the other three. The preacher will be a bit pressed to find thematic unity for one message on these four units. Perhaps the fact that they are spoken to the disciples and not to the public (verse 36) will provide focus. Or possibly the phrase "kingdom of heaven," common to all four will be sufficient to gather under one topic these four glimpses into the kingdom life which Jesus offers. One should keep in mind that "kingdom of heaven" in Matthew is synonymous with "kingdom of God" in the other Gospels. "Heaven" is a pious way of avoiding use of the holy name and is not intended to point the reader beyond here to the hereafter.

The treasure hidden in a field (verse 44). The one who discovers the kingdom, even accidentally, is so full of joy and anticipation that everything else is sold in the prospect of that one treasure. Let the interpreter avoid getting entangled in the legalities of hiding the treasure until the field can be bought. Likewise talk of sacrificing for the kingdom should be eliminated. The highlights are the surpassing worth of the kingdom and the joy of finding it.

The pearl of great value (verses 45-46). The message here is essentially the same. It is a judgment call as to whether this parable was intended to convey a small contrast with the preceding one. In the one case, the kingdom was discovered as though accidentally; in the other, the kingdom was found by one on a search. Whether or not such a distinction was intended, faith experiences confirm the difference.

The fish net (verses 47-50). In several respects the passage is similar to verses 24-30, 36-43: both the fish net and the weeds in the grain field are parables about the final judgment; both carry their own interpretations; both parables have an element of unreality in order to accommodate the interpretations. Some students of the parables are persuaded that Jesus' original parable consisted only of verse 47: "Again, the kingdom of heaven is like a net which was thrown into the sea and gathered fish of every kind." Were such the case, then the parable would be similar to that of the sower in which the word was sown indiscriminately with no intention of being selective. Or perhaps more exactly it would correspond to Luke's parable of the banquet (14:16-24) in which all kinds of people were invited. However, the fish net is Matthew's parable, and we know Matthew's frequent reminders of a separating judgment. In fact, in Matthew's account of the parable of the banquet (22:1-14), both good and bad are invited but the king tosses out the one without a wedding garment.

The householder's treasury (verses 51-52). The comparison here is not with the kingdom but with "every scribe who has been trained for the kingdom." The disciples of Jesus say they have understood all these parables (verse 51; quite unlike Mark's portrait of them, 4:13, 34). In the statement that follows, Matthew has Jesus comparing his disciples to scribes, or perhaps implying that they should be as scribes trained for the kingdom. This favorable view of scribes is found elsewhere in Matthew (23:34: "Therefore I [Jesus] send you prophets and wise men and scribes") and has led some to speculate that Matthew was himself a scribe. Given this Evangelist's emphasis on teachings and the careful observance of them, it is reasonable to assume a Christian scribal tradition would develop in this circle of Christianity. In any case, the kingdom scribe draws upon a rich treasure of the old and the new. Specifically, what is meant is unclear. Law of Moses (old) and Christ's word (new)? Christ's teachings (old) and Matthew's interpretations (new)? Perhaps both; at least the church has carefully preserved the tradition while continuing to hear and understand it anew.

Proper 13

Sunday Between July 31 and August 6 Inclusive

Exodus 12:1-14; Psalm 143:1-10; Romans 8:31-39; Matthew 14:13-21

The Old Testament lesson contains Yahweh's speech to Moses and Aaron which gives directions about the preparations to be made in anticipation of the coming Passover. Just as the celebration of Passover recalls the Hebrews' escape from oppression in Egypt, so Psalm 143 recalls the memories of earlier days. In the Epistle lesson, Paul affirms that nothing in time or space can separate Christians from the love of God in Christ. Eating together—sharing memories and hopes—forms a basic ingredient of celebrations such as Passover. It is no wonder then that Christians recalled Jesus' feeding the multitude in the Gospel reading.

Exodus 12:1-14

Between the call of Moses, reported in last week's reading, and the passover night recorded in today's lection, the story has reported a series of confrontations between Moses and Pharaoh, and nine plagues upon the Egyptians. Exodus 12 brings us very close to the center of the Exodus story, for the Passover was believed to have been instituted in the very night that Israel was brought out from Egypt. Each time the Passover was celebrated in Israel the people of God remembered that they were slaves set free by their God.

While the section before us is relatively straightforward, it is part of a very complex section in the book of Exodus. Since it is the climax of the Exodus traditions, it has attracted a great many diverse elements. The unit, which reports the events immediately surrounding the departure from Egypt, begins in Exodus 11:1 and ends in Exodus 13:16. One can identify four distinct motifs within this section. The most important is, of course, the departure from Egypt itself. Although this is noted quite briefly (12:37-39), it is the focal point of all other motifs. Second is the report of the final plague, the killing of the firstborn children of the Egyptians. This plague is quite distinct from those that preceded it, both in the fact that it was effective and in the extensive preparations for it. The third and fourth motifs are the religious ceremonies connected with the Exodus, the celebration of Passover and the Feast of Unleavened Bread. Passover is linked to the final plague because it entailed a procedure for ensuring that the Israelite firstborn would not be killed, and it is connected in very direct ways with the immediate departure from Egypt. The final plague is what motivated Pharaoh to release Israel, and the Passover was to have taken place just before they left.

It is important to keep in mind that this passage is part of a narrative, a story more of divine actions than human events. Its setting is the history of salvation, the account of Yahweh's intervention to set his people free. In that context, Exodus 12:1-14 is a report of divine instructions to Moses and Aaron concerning the celebration of the Passover. Thus everything except verse 1 is in the form of a speech by Yahweh, a direct address to Moses and Aaron. These instructions have the tone and contents of rules established for perpetuity, and thus reflect the perspective of Israelites centuries after the events. On the basis of the style and the technical terminology, this passage, with the possible exception of verse 14, comes from the Priestly Writer.

The instructions are precise and detailed with regard to both time and actions. The month in which the exodus takes place is to become the first month of the year, and the preparations for the Passover begin on the tenth day of the month (verses 2-3a). It is a family ceremony, with a lamb chosen for each household—that is, unless the household is too small for a lamb, in which case neighboring families are to join together to make up the right number to consume the lamb (verses 3b-4). A lamb without blemish is to be selected, and then killed on the fourteenth day of the month (verses 5-6). Blood is to be smeared on the lintels and doorposts of the houses, the meat is to be roasted and eaten with unleavened bread and bitter herbs (verses 7-9). The meal is to be eaten in haste, and anything not consumed by morning is to be burned (verses 10-11).

After the instructions follows an explanation of the meaning of the meal and of the practices associated with it. The Lord will pass through the land of Egypt to destroy the firstborn, but will see the blood and "pass over" the Israelites (verses 12-13). Verse 14, which comes from another writer, stresses that the day is a "memorial day," and forever, whereby later generations will remember the Exodus.

In both the present text and later practice, Passover was combined with the Feast of Unleavened Bread. The former was a one-night communal meal and the latter was a seven-day festival. The combination was quite ancient, but the two originally were distinct. It seems likely that the Feast of Unleavened Bread was a pre-Israelite festival related to the agricultural year in Canaan. Passover, on the other hand, probably originated among seminomadic groups such as the Israelites, as a festival related to the movement of their flocks from winter to summer pasture. The feast certainly was a family ceremony during the early history of Israel. In later generations, Passover was one of the three major annual pilgrimage festivals, for which the people were to come to Jerusalem (Deut. 16:2-7). It is not difficult to imagine a priest reading the present text, in effect taking the role of Moses in communicating the instructions for the festival.

The word "passover" (Hebrew *pesach*) is explained in this passage by connecting it with a verb for "to skip" or "hop over," but the actual etymology of the word is uncertain. Throughout the Old Testament it refers either to the festival described here or to the animal that is killed and eaten. Many passages use the word in both senses (e.g., II Chron. 35-1-19). The ceremony had both sacrificial and communal dimensions, in that the animal was ceremonially slaughtered but then consumed as a family meal.

No ceremony was more important in ancient Israel or early Judaism than Passover. To participate in the ritual was to remember and become a part of the story it celebrated. In that story, God promised to set the slaves free. What were they to do in anticipation of that freedom? They were to gather together and eat a particular meal. In doing so they acknowledged and celebrated both who they were and who their God was. Their God is the one who sets people free and makes them his own. The Passover celebration thus bound the people together and to their God.

Psalm 143:1-10

This selection from the Psalter is a psalm of lament written to be used in times of distress. The calamity, real or potential, threatening the worshiper is not clearly defined. References are made to an enemy (verse 3), enemies (verses 9 and 12), and adversaries (verse 12).

The psalm opens with a two-pronged appeal to the Deity (verses 1-2). In verse 1, the request is for a hearing and a response. Three expressions are used to state the totality of the request: hear my prayer, give ear, and answer. Three actions are requested: listening, considering, and responding. The appeal requests that the divine response be made on the basis of divine faithfulness and righteousness, that is, that God act on the basis of his nature and character. The second appeal (verse 2) asks that God not enter into judgment with the supplicant. The worshiper is thus asking that he/she not be subjected to divine scrutiny. A general reason for such a request is given: before God no living creature (not "no man living" as in RSV since the word "man" does not occur) is righteous. Such a statement is interesting for several reasons: (1) it makes a theological judgment about the totality of living creatures—none is righteous before God, none has fulfilled and lived up to the goal of creation; (2) the answer is evasive. The supplicant hides behind a generality rather than confront specifics directly. Other psalms allow the worshiper to confess total innocence in appealing to God (see Ps. 17:1-5). Perhaps this worshiper was aware of some sin or fault that was best left unsaid, merely to be covered over with the veneer of a generality.

The consequences of the person's predicament are noted in verses 3-4. "My foe hounded me;/he crushed me to the ground;/he made me dwell in darkness/like those long dead"

123

(NJPSV). Alienation, defeat, despair, and loneliness permeate the description. Many people in our congregations feel this way and preaching on such a text could help them identify their situations and articulate their real feelings. In verse 4, the supplicant describes the personal price and trauma that have resulted from the despair: "My spirit failed within me;/my mind was numbed with horror" (NJPSV). In modern psychological terms, one would speak of personal depression and despondency that saps motivation, energy, and orientation.

The psalm has the worshiper reach back to the past, to the memories of better times, that lie on the other side of the present trouble (verse 5). Certainly the ancients realized the value of perspectives on life drawn from outside the confines of one's present state of anarchy and anxiety. Better times and better days cast light on present shadows that can change the configurations of the present. The NJPSV translates this verse: "Then I thought of the days of old;/I rehearsed all Your deeds,/recounted the work of Your hands."

On the basis of the past, the worshiper now reaches out for help in the present (verse 6). Although the psalm uses God-talk, "I stretch out my hands to thee;/my soul thirsts for thee like a parched land," such language no doubt embodies the person's desire to get things together, life organized and centered, in order to proceed with living normally.

Verses 7-10 string together a series of confessional statements, specific requests, and expressions of fear. The expressions of fear are "my spirit can endure no more," NJPSV ("my spirit fails," RSV) and I shall "be like those who go down to the Pit" (the fear of life becoming only a living death). The confessional statements are: "in thee, I put my trust," "to thee I lift up my soul," "I have fled to thee for refuge," and "thou art my God." This mixture of fear and faith is probably characteristic of much of human existence. The requests are "make haste to answer me," "hide not thy face from me," "let me hear in the morning of thy steadfast love" (worshipers probably spent the night in the temple to await a favorable word from God mediated through dreams, other experiences, or a word from the priests), "teach me the way I should go," "deliver me . . . from my enemies," "teach me to do thy will," and "let thy good spirit lead me on a level path."

The requests may be said to fall into four categories: (1) a plea for the alleviation of the trouble: (2) a desire for personal contact and relationship with the Deity, (3) personal empowerment to face life, and (4) knowledge of how life ought to be lived so as to do God's will.

Romans 8:31-39

Today's text is directly linked with the preceding passage treated in last week's lesson. The theme of human weakness has been a recurrent concern of chapter 8. It is expected that God's children will suffer (8:17-18), that God's creation will undergo cosmic strain as it moves toward the fulfillment of the divine purpose. Even with God present among us through the Spirit, we inevitably experience the inexplicable and unutterable (8:26-27). Confounded by life, we wonder about God's purpose and if it will finally be achieved. We ask whether the evil we experience merely masks the good that God intends to achieve or whether it negates it altogether.

In response, Paul has assured us that the Spirit present within us can render our speechless groans in ways that God can hear. He also sketches the purposes of God broadly as extending over history from primordial foreknowledge to eschatological glorification.

But there is more, and today's text supplies it. We should read these words "with all this in mind" (verse 31, NEB), that is, in light of what has been said earlier in the chapter.

To say that "God is for us" (verse 31) is to recall the mighty acts of God (verses 29-30). For God to call, justify, and glorify us is to have "God on our side" (JB, NEB). God with us constitutes a majority, and thus "who is against us?" Such confidence is reminiscent of the psalmist who said, "With the Lord on my side I do not fear. What can man do to me?" (Ps. 118:6).

Yet another step is taken in today's text, however. Still

more can be said, and Paul now says it: "Since God did not spare his own Son, but gave him up to benefit us all, we may be certain, after such a gift, that he will not refuse anything he can give" (verse 32, JB). The gift of Christ becomes the clue to God's solidarity with us. If we find ourselves speechless, wondering whether God can be present in the midst of evil, indeed within the evil we experience, we have only to reflect on the Christ-event.

The language of "not sparing his own Son" recalls the sacrifice of Isaac (Gen. 22:1-4). God praises Abraham, "You . . . have not withheld your son, your only Son" (Gen. 22:16). In this case, Abraham's absolute fidelity was proved. So in the giving of Christ was God's integrity upheld. Abraham's act becomes a paradigm of divine fidelity (Heb. 11:17). Also an unexcelled instance of divine love (cf. John 3:16, 18; Rom. 8:3; Gal. 4:4; I John 4:9).

The work of God in Christ becomes a clue to the work of God within us: "Will he not also give us all things with him?" (verse 32). It may be important here to underscore *with him.* This may point to our complete solidarity with Christ as those who are "in Christ." If Christ is to be thought of essentially as gift, as that bestowed by God as generous Giver, by identifying with Christ, indeed by entering Christ, we fully participate in God's generous love. We may be unable to see evidence of this love in our own circumstances, but we can at least see it vividly in the Christ-event. In that moment, all the ambiguities of death and life converged, yet through them divine love became manifest.

To be sure, when we side with God and take our place among God's elect, we will have our detractors. We may even hear the detractor's cry in our own protests as we bring charges against God. We may charge God with being absent, unintelligible, or even negligent. What to do when such voices of protest are raised?

At this point, our text becomes problematic. Depending on how we punctuate verses 33-34, the text yields different answers. The different options may be determined by careful comparison among the RSV, NEB, JB, and NIV. The preacher will also want to consult commentaries in this regard. But the gist of Paul's line of argumentation seems to be this: any

126

charges leveled against God's elect by detractors who wish to condemn come to grief on the Christ-event.

The Christ who died, was raised and exalted, illustrates how God vindicates the divine purpose. Christ now serves as intercessor in our behalf (verse 34; Heb. 7:25; 9:24). What cannot be denied is that the Christ who died was a Christ who loved (verse 35; II Cor. 5:14). What's more, the Christ-event was both instance and extension of God's own love. We can only speak of "the love of God *in* Christ Jesus our Lord" (verse 39, italics added; Rom. 5:5). It was thus not God's love sketched in broad, general terms but God's love embodied in a single human figure, a definable, visible human event. It was located *in Christ* and thus locatable within time and history.

To be in Christ is to be located within the sphere of divine love. The result: "Nothing therefore can come between us and the love of Christ" (verse 35, JB). Two kinds of realities threaten this relationship: distresses "down here" and those "up there." First we have sketched those "everyday" menaces: being "troubled or worried, or being persecuted, or lacking food or clothes, or being threatened or even attacked" (verse 35, JB). These are "life's tribulations" (Rom. 2:9; 5:3; II Cor. 11:26-27; 12:10) that even the psalmist knew as daily realities (Ps. 44:22; cf. I Cor. 4:9; 15:30-31).

Beyond these are those forces that are larger than life, bigger than any one of us: death, life, spirits, superhuman powers, the world as it is, the world as it shall be, forces in the universe, heights, depths (verse 38, NEB). These are the forces that stretch time to its limits, that push the boundaries of space to their outer edge, that hover above us even as they conspire within us, that oppress and dominate. Yet these too come to grief in the Christ-event, for that is where they were vanquished by the "love of God made visible in Christ Jesus our Lord" (JB).

What emerges from this text is a sense of power and triumph as it is focused in the Christ-event. It should be noted that Paul nowhere denies the existence of these earthly and heavenly menaces that threaten our relationship with Christ; but he does deny that they are ultimately catastrophic.

Matthew 14:13-21

Jesus feeding the five thousand is one of the relatively few stories recorded by all four Evangelists (Mark 6:30-44; Luke 9:10-17; John 6:1-14). In general Matthew follows Mark's story. The feeding occurs at a lonely place which Jesus and the disciples reached by boat but which the crowds reached on foot. The miracle is an act of compassion on the people who are away from home and without food, and the hour is late. The disciples favor dismissing the crowds, but later cooperate with Jesus in the feeding. From five loaves and two fish everyone eats to satisfaction and there are twelve baskets of leftovers.

However, in some important details Matthew alters Mark's story. In Mark (6:30-31), the disciples have just returned from a mission and Jesus invites them to withdraw and rest. Matthew tells of Jesus sending the Twelve on a mission but never reports their return. Since in Matthew Jesus has just received the news of the death of John the Baptist (14:1-12), we are left to assume that Jesus withdrew to a lonely place in response to that news. But why? To escape a similar fate? To grieve John's death? To reflect on what John's death portends for his own future? Matthew gives us no clue. The disciples are not mentioned until verse 15; Jesus alone is in Matthew's eye both when he enters the boat and when he arrives at the lonely place. Matthew also abbreviates the conversation between Jesus and the Twelve. They volunteer the information about five loaves and two fish and do not appear at all as being dull to the point of insolence as in Mark ("Shall we go and buy two hundred denarii worth of bread, and give it to them to eat?" Mark 6:37b). Mark's harsh view of the Twelve is generally softened by Matthew.

But none of these details tells us what to make of the story. In its background lies the multiplication of loaves by Elisha (II Kings 4:42-44), but that information still leaves us with the question, How did the church and how does the church understand Jesus feeding the multitude? Primarily in two ways.

First, the story is for Matthew as well as Mark and Luke (but not John) a compassion story. Jesus had withdrawn to a lonely place, but when met by a huge crowd he had compassion and ministered to their needs. While holding the miracle to be unique to Jesus, the church has accepted the compassion as obligatory for all Jesus' followers. And there has been no scene more generative of compassion than that of hungry men, women, and children. Long-range programs as well as emergency relief have occupied followers of Jesus (not sufficiently or consistently, to be sure) for twenty centuries. In fact, Jesus said the question, What did you do in the face of human hunger? would be on the final exam (Matt. 25:35).

Second, the feeding of the multitude was and is understood as a eucharistic story. This is its primary meaning for the Fourth Gospel, but it is evident in the Synoptics as well. Eucharistic language is used: he blessed, broke, and gave (verse 19). But just as significantly, notice how this story ends. One does not, as in other miracles, read of amazed crowds; no one is asking, Who is this? No one believes because of this and there is no comment about the spread of Jesus' fame throughout the region. Why? Because the miracle was paltry compared to others? No. More likely it is because the story, by the time the Gospels were written, had become an inside story, a church story, an account of Jesus feeding his followers. In other words, it was recited when the church gathered at the Lord's Table.

Proper 14

Sunday Between August 7 and 13 Inclusive

Exodus 14:19-31; Psalm 106:4-12; Romans 9:1-5; Matthew 14:22-33

The Hebrew crossing of the Red Sea to escape from Egyptian oppression and to begin their trek toward the Promised Land is the theme of the Old Testament lesson. Psalm 106 uses the departure from Egypt as its point of departure in presenting the time from the Exodus through the settlement as a scenario of disobedience and rebellion. The Epistle reading introduces a lengthy section in Romans, chapters 9–11, in which Paul expresses his thoughts about the failure of Jews to respond favorably to the proclamation of the Christian faith. The Gospel lesson also concerns faith and endurance, presenting Peter as an enthusiast without staying power sufficient for the situation.

Exodus 14:19-31

This passage concludes the account of Israel's deliverance at the sea. The report of the episode began in Exodus 13:17 and is followed by the songs of Moses and Miriam in Exodus 15:1-21. It is an extremely important story in Old Testament tradition, but it is not—as some commentators have thought—the central point of the Exodus itself. Israel has already been released from Egypt (Exod. 12:29-51). Both in terms of the structure of the book of Exodus and the motifs of the passage, the account of the rescue at the sea is part of the wilderness traditions.

The importance of the events reported here is seen in the rich and complex history of tradition that they evoked. The narrative account itself is the combination of at least two of the Pentateuchal sources, and then there are the songs of

Moses and Miriam that reflect further responses. Although the sources are combined into a complete story, and there is no scholarly consensus on all the detailed source division, recognition of their existence here enables one to hear the different religious and theological concerns in the passage.

There is first of all a basic disagreement in the account concerning how the rescue was effected. Did the sea divide to allow Israel to cross, or did a strong east wind blow back the waters so that the Egyptian chariots became clogged in the mud? There are further repetitions, duplicates, and differences in style and perspective that lead to the conclusion that there is a more or less complete account from the Priestly Writer and another from the older sources J and E. They differ not only on the details of events but on their purpose and meaning as well.

According to the Priestly Writer (found mainly in 14:1-3, 8-10a, 15-18, 21a, 22-23, 26-27a, 28-29), the Lord hardened the heart of Pharaoh so that he pursued the Israelites, because he had a purpose in mind from the outset: "I will get glory over Pharaoh and all his host; and the Egyptians shall know that I am the Lord" (verse 4).

The deliverance appears to have taken place in the daytime. Upon instructions from God, Moses stretched out his hand, the sea divided and the people of Israel crossed on dry land with the Egyptians in pursuit (verses 16, 22-23). Then Moses lowered his hand and the waters returned, killing the Egyptians (verses 26, 28-29). The divine intervention is dramatic, and the purpose is revelation: that the Egyptians know the Lord is God.

According to the older sources the people flee, but when they see the Egyptians approach they become fearful and complain to Moses (verses 10-12), who commands them to be still and see the deliverance that the Lord will perform for them (verses 13-14). In this tradition, there is no report of an Israelite crossing of the sea. The angel of God keeps the camps apart, with the pillar of cloud which had led the Israelites moving between them and the Egyptians (verses 19-20). The event seems to have happened at night. The decisive events transpire when Yahweh "drove the sea back by a strong east wind" (verse 21b). Then Yahweh "looked down on the Egyptian army through the pillar of fire and cloud, and he threw them into a panic" (verse 24, NEB). The Egyptian chariots became clogged in the mud, and when the sea returned to its usual position they seemed to run into it (verse 27*b*). This imagery is very similar to the traditions of the holy war, when Yahweh fights for Israel against her enemies. The account concludes with a summary and a theological interpretation: "Thus the Lord saved Israel that day from the hand of the Egyptians . . . . And Israel saw the great work which the Lord did against the Egyptians, and the people feared the Lord; and they believed in the Lord and in his servant Moses" (verses 30-31).

While preaching is hardly the place to display the source critical analysis of a biblical passage, recognition that diverse documents have been combined here calls attention to some of the different ways that this story can be recalled and interpreted.

1. One may stress the deliverance at the sea as unqualified good news, deliverance from trouble. That would be consistent with the JE source, which also makes it clear that the people of Israel by no means earned this deliverance through good works, but to the contrary they only complained. Then in that tradition, the results of the divine initiative is the faith of the people, not only in God but in his designated representative.

2. In the younger source P, the divine intention is to let the wider world, represented by the Egyptian pharaoh, know that the Lord is God. It is not surprising, therefore, that the saving event takes place in broad daylight, and that it is an unmistakably miraculous intervention.

3. Finally, these diverse sources and traditions have been combined into the complete story before us now. The final editors probably knew the different theological emphases, but saw no contradiction between them. They are complementary. Even the different pictures of the event itself agree about the agency. God acts dramatically to divide the sea, or God acts through the strong east wind and then throws the enemy into a panic. Whether directly and through Moses or through so-called natural phenomena, it is the God of Israel who acts to save.

Psalm 106:4-12

On the basis of the opening stanza of this psalm (verses 1-3), it would have to be classified as a thanksgiving psalm. The plural verb forms in the opening verses would suggest that it was composed for use in communal worship.

Portions of the psalm are formulated as direct speech to the Deity (verses 4-7 and 47), that is, they take the form of a prayer. The remainder of the psalm speaks about the Deity in the third person. Two other issues should be noted.

1. Verses 4-5 appear to reflect an individual rather than a communal concern for the psalm. Note the references "remember me" and "help me." (The pronoun "I" which appears three times in the RSV of verse 5 does not appear in Hebrew; the verbal forms are infinitives—"to see," "to rejoice," and "to glory.") Some manuscripts of the Hebrew and some copies of the ancient versions (Greek and Syriac) read plural forms—"remember us" and "help us." The general rule in textual criticism, however, assumes that the more difficult reading is probably more original. In this case, that would mean the singular first person readings ("remember me," "help me"). Perhaps the king or the high priest was the speaker of these verses.

2. What type of psalm is this? The opening lines would suggest thanksgiving but the content of the psalm focuses on the sins of the people in their early history. The enumeration of the sins of the fathers suggests something like preaching or at least confession from a distance. Perhaps we should think of what might be called a doxology of judgment. God is praised (and even thanked) through the means of confessing the sins of the past. A text that perhaps illuminates this idea is found in Joshua 7. In this chapter, Achan took some goods, captured in battle, which had been declared holy and thus dedicated to God. Anything dedicated to God could not be used by the ordinary people. In verse 19, Joshua tells Achan after his crime has been discovered: "Give glory to [Yahweh] the God of Israel, and render praise to him; and tell me now what you have done; do not hide it from me." Here acknowledgment of sin is viewed as the means for giving glory to God and praising him.

The first twelve verses of this psalm contain the following components: a call to the community to offer praise and thanks to God (verses 1-2), a pronouncement of blessing upon those who are just and righteous (verse 3), an appeal by an individual to share in the redemption of the people (verses 4-5), a confession that the people of the present have sinned like the fathers of the past (verse 6), and the first part of a lengthy description of the rebellion and sins of the generation long dead (verses 7-12).

In this psalm practically nothing good is said about the generation that came out of Egypt (verse 12 is the exception). (Note how differently the period is presented in Psalm 105; see Proper 12.) Later Israel spoke of the time of the Exodus generation in two completely different ways. One tendency was to explain it as the ideal good old days (see Hos. 9:10; 11:1; Jer. 2:1-3). Deuteronomy 8:1-4 describes the time as ideal, when even the clothes and shoes of the people did not wear out for forty years! (The later rabbis concluded that the clothes of the children grew as the children grew!) The most common tendency was to describe the period in negative terms, as a time of rebellion and griping which began as soon as the people were in the wilderness (see Exod. 15:22-26).

In Psalm 106, the rebellion and infidelity began while the people were still in Egypt. According to verse 7*a*, when the people were still in Egypt, they "did not consider thy wonderful works; they did not remember the abundance of thy steadfast love" (see Ezek. 23:1-3 for a similar view). The last part of verse 7 says, translating the Hebrew literally, "they rebelled at the sea, at the Red Sea." Since the text mentions the sea twice, later rabbinic interpreters said that Israel must have sinned twice before they crossed the sea.

Verses 8-11 emphasize that Yahweh saved the people but for the sake of his own name and reputation (verse 8). Verse 12 affirms that the Hebrews believed and sang his praise.

Preaching on this text could be explored along several lines. Solidarity with the sins of our fathers/mothers might be developed out of verse 6. Confession of sin as a doxology of judgment and a means to praise God could build on the entire thrust of the psalm. Another theme is the intertwining of disobedience and deliverance.

Romans 9:1-5

Today's text introduces the long, self-contained section of the Epistle (chapters 9–11), in which Paul wrestles with the question of how the inclusion of the Gentiles within the people of God affects the destiny of Israel. The fact was that the gospel had been received more warmly by Gentiles than Jews; indeed, it had met outright rejection by many Jews. Not only the message about Jesus, but Jesus himself had been resisted and rejected by Israel.

This created a problem for Paul. If God had been revealed in a new way in Christ, and if salvation was now more broadly defined to include both Jews and Gentiles, how did Israel's rejection fit into God's overall purpose? Surely God did not intend for the gospel to exclude Israel! Yet as a whole they were not responding favorably, at least not to Paul's preaching. By contrast, Gentiles were accepting the Good News. Does this mean that God has now tilted toward the Gentiles and turned away from the Jews? If so, what do we make of the many promises God made to Israel, such as the promise to form an *everlasting* covenant (Gen. 17:7-8)?

In short, the question was, What is the role of the Jews in salvation history? If they are no longer in a privileged position as *the* people of God, and if Gentiles have now come to be included among God's elect, what are the respective roles of Jews and Gentiles in God's overall scheme?

In this section, Paul struggles with this dilemma created by Israel's rejection of the gospel. His answer has several parts: God's integrity remains in tact. The divine promise was never intended to extend to Jews only, but was always meant to include everyone whom God chose, including Gentiles (9:6-13, 24). Even when the promise was directed to Jews, not all Jews responded (9:27-29), which shows that all along the promise came not through birth but through faith. Historically God had called for people to be obedient, and Israel was no exception; the same call now comes anew through Christ: respond to God in faith (10:1-13). But Israel has yet again failed to hear God's call (10:1-14).

Yet God is not willing to give up on Israel. There have always been pockets of fidelity among the people of God. A

135

few have always been loyal to the divine promise (11:3-4). So also now, the Gentiles serve as God's faithful remnant who will serve to call back disobedient Israel (11:11-16). This does not mean that the Gentiles can be arrogant toward disobedient Jews. Even if they are fresh branches that have been grafted onto the tree to bring it new life, the fact remains that the trunk is Jewish (11:17-24). Gentiles may witness to Jews but they are bound to do so in humility and faith.

So God's unfolding plan is this: the acceptance of the gospel by the Gentiles will work to bring about the conversion of Israel. Once the Gentiles demonstrate their responsiveness to the gospel, the Jews will be responsive in their turn. As it turns out, the conversion of the Gentiles represents yet another extension of God's mercy to the Jews (11:30-32).

The words of today's text introduce an emotion-filled discussion of Israel's role in salvation history. At the outset, Paul asserts his own integrity, which suggests that the issues he is about to discuss are highly controversial and of deep import to him (cf. Gal. 1:20; II Cor. 11:31; I Tim. 2:7). These are also matters of conscience for him (cf. Rom. 2:15), and they have caused him considerable pain and anguish (cf. II Cor. 11:28-29). So important are the issues that he is willing to place himself under divine curse on behalf of his fellow Jews (cf. I Cor. 12:3; 16:22; Gal. 1:8-9). Even more, he is willing to sever his connection with Christ for the sake of his kinsmen. Here we see yet another form of being willing to lay down one's life for one's brethren (I John 3:16).

Earlier, Paul had asked, "What advantage has the Jew?" (3:1). We now have an elaboration of his answer, "Much in every way," as he enumerates the eightfold blessing of being Jewish (verses 4-5): (1) Jews bear the distinguished name *Israelites* after their forebear Jacob (Gen. 32:28; 35:10; cf. II Cor. 11:22); (2) their relationship with God is one of *sonship* (Deut. 14:1; Hos. 11:1); (3) they basked in the dazzling presence of God, the divine *glory*, which provided protection in the wilderness (Exod. 16:10) and instruction through the Law (Exod. 34:29-35; II Cor. 3:7); (4) they were partners with God in several *covenants* (Gen. 17:3-8; Jer. 31:31-34; Sir. 44:12, 18); (5) they are the distinct heirs of the *giving of the law* (Exod.

19-20); (6) their *worship* is in the temple, with its impressive liturgy (cf. I Kings 6); (7) they are the recipients of God's *promises* (4:13; 9:8-9; 15:8); and (8) they have a rich ancestry of *patriarchs* (Exod. 13:5).

The capstone of these blessings is that Christ was of Jewish lineage: "of their race, according to the flesh, is the Christ" (verse 5). It had already become part of early Christian confession that Christ had descended from David according to the flesh (Rom. 1:3), and this was established through genealogies (Matt. 1; Luke 3:23-38). Even those who refused to accept Jesus as Messiah could hardly deny that he was of Jewish origin.

One important exegetical question here is whether Paul actually asserts that Christ was God. It depends on how one punctuates verse 5. RSV and NEB are less assertive, perhaps because Paul is elsewhere reluctant to apply the name "God" to Christ (cf. I Cor. 8:6; 15:27, 28; Phil. 2:6-11; also Eph. 1:20-23; Col. 1:15-20) and because such prayers of blessing are normally addressed to God (Rom. 1:25; II Cor. 11:31; Ps. 41:13). JB, however, is more explicit: "Christ who is above all, God for ever blessed" (also NIV).

Obviously, today's text will have to be read in light of the entirety of chapters 9–11. But as brief as these verses are, they serve as a salutary reminder that talk about exclusion from God and being deprived of access to divine promises are always occasions of emotion and pain. They also show us someone who is struggling with the richness of his religious heritage, on the one hand, and the light of new revelation, on the other. Perhaps this in itself is a parable of the religious life: the new transforming, perhaps even surpassing, the old, but never able to live apart from it.

Matthew 14:22-33

The story of Jesus walking on the water is joined in Matthew, Mark (6:45-52), and John (6:16-21) to the feeding of the multitude. Perhaps the two stories were united earlier in the tradition and may echo Israel's experience of the sea and the wilderness feedings. The part about Simon Peter (verses 28-31) is a Matthean addition, but even so, 14:22-33 is a distinct unit and can be treated as such in sermon and lesson. The lection begins with the disciples entering a boat and ends before they land at Gennesaret.

Jesus walking on the water may have served in some Christian circles as evidence of Jesus' cosmic power subduing the forces of nature. In biblical literature, the sea is often represented as the abode of demonic forces hostile to God. In the Apocalypse, the final reign of God will mean that the sea no longer exists (21:1). Matthew's picture of Christ standing on violent waves amid raging winds, saying to the fearful "I am" (verses 25-27) certainly affirms the lordship of Christ over the created world.

However, as it stands in Matthew the story functions differently. It is a kind of epiphany, an appearance of Christ not unlike a resurrection appearance. On a dark night of fear and helplessness, Christ comes to his disciples. Until reassured, they think they see a ghost. Special attention to Peter recalls resurrection narratives (Luke 24:34; John 21; I Cor. 15:5). In John 21 Peter jumps into the water, but does not walk on it. Whatever may be the relationship, literary or historical, between this story and others, we must look to the story itself to hear what Matthew is saying.

Matthew has made two major changes in the story as received from Mark 6:45-52: the insertion of Peter's attempt to walk to Jesus and the radical alteration of the ending. Before looking at those elements, it is important to keep in mind that this is a story to and for the church. The scene, set between a crowd (14:12-21) and a crowd (14:34-36), involves only Jesus and the Twelve. For the disciples alone to be the beneficiaries of a miracle is very unusual in the Gospels and provides a rare glimpse inside the church of that time. The fact that many find it easy to preach on this text is due to Matthew's having already made this event a sermon. The church in the world is as the church in a storm: the disciples are in a boat without Jesus; a threatening storm arises; Jesus comes, bringing first fear and then assurance; the disciples, in the person of Peter, now feel strong enough to handle the storm as Jesus did and the venture almost succeeds; Jesus again rescues them from the storm which ceases when he enters the boat; the disciples now worship Jesus as Son of God.

Notice, then, how Matthew's vignette about Simon Peter functions. This small story is inserted between the description of the disciples as fearful (verses 26-27) and as confessing and worshiping (verse 33). Simon Peter, the voice and heart of the group, is thus between fear and faith. He walks and he sinks; he trusts and he fears. His response enables Matthew to move the story along in three phases: "It is I," announces Jesus (verse 27); "Lord, if it is you," responds Peter (verse 28); "Truly you are," says the entire group (verse 33).

And finally, Matthew's altered ending allows him to join this story to his larger narrative in which the disciples respond to Christ's lordship with fear, doubt, and worship (28:16-18). Mark's insistence that the disciples never understood, here (6:52) and elsewhere, is modified by Matthew to a portrait of persons "of little faith" (8:26; 14:31; 16:8; 17:20). Jesus' followers have faith, but not enough, and so Jesus nourishes that little faith to the point of confession and praise. The continuing presence of Christ in the believing community is experienced as judgment, to be sure, but also as patience and grace.

Proper 15

Sunday Between August 14 and 20 Inclusive

*Exodus 16:2-15; Psalm 78:1-3, 10-20; Romans 11:13-16, 29-32;
Matthew 15:21-28*

In the final form of Israel's early history, now embodied in
the Pentateuch, the theme of disobedience and murmuring
in the wilderness plays a significant role. This week's Old
Testament lesson provides one of the first examples of this
motif. The psalm also develops this theme and chides its
hearers about lack of faith. In the Epistle lesson, Paul
continues to wrestle with the question of the role of Israel in
the plan of God in light of the growth and development of the
church. The narrative in the Gospel reading also has Jesus
speaking about his mission to the house of Israel and the
relationship of Gentiles to that mission.

Exodus 16:2-15

According to all levels of Old Tradition, between the
Exodus from Egypt and the settlement of the land of Canaan,
Israel wandered in the wilderness. As indicated in the
discussion of last week's text, Exodus 14:19-31, the deliverance of Israel at the sea took place when they were out of
Egypt and were in the wilderness. The scene that is played
out in chapter 16 is one that will recur over and over along the
way from Egypt to Sinai and from Sinai to the edge of the
Promised Land: The people of Israel complain because of
some real or imagined need, Moses remonstrates with them
and intercedes with the Lord, and the Lord responds
graciously, but not always without anger. The most
persistent themes concerning the wilderness wandering thus
are expressed: The dramatic contrast between the people's
persistent complaints and the Lord's gracious care and
preservation.

While the basic profile of the story as a whole is clear enough, Jewish and Christian commentators from the earliest times have recognized a large number of difficulties in the chapter. The rabbis in particular noticed that Moses gives in verse 8 divine instructions that he did not receive until verses 11-12, and that the sabbath is observed but the commandment was not given until later at Sinai, and that there is an allusion in verse 34 to the tent of the meeting that was not built until later. There are gaps, repetitions, and different descriptions of the manna. Only some of these difficulties are resolved by recognition of different sources. Most of the chapter comes from P but some (mainly verses 4-5, 27-31) came from the Yahwist. The latter stresses the gift of the manna as a test and the former emphasizes that the purpose was to demonstrate it was the Lord who brought the people out of Egypt.

It would be difficult indeed for the modern preacher to develop a line of thought concerning the story of the manna and quails that has not already appeared in the history of the interpretation of this tradition, either elsewhere in the Old Testament, in the New Testament (see especially John 6; I Cor. 10:1-13; II Cor. 8:15; Rev. 2:17), or in the history of the church and synagogue. The manna story has been used as the basis for moralistic homilies, it has been spiritualized, and there have been attempts even in the early Christian centuries to find a rational explanation for the miracle. Among the possibilities for homiletical reflection are the following:

1. Consider the murmuring or complaining of the people. The specific issue in Exodus 16 is food. Was the complaint legitimate or not, or—better—does the narrator of the story consider it a legitimate complaint? By his choice of words ("murmured," or "grumbled," NJPSV) and by the way he phrases the complaint our reporter disapproves of a whining people: "Would that we had died by the hand of the Lord in the land of Egypt, when we sat by the fleshpots and ate bread to the full" (verse 3). That is the dominant view in the tradition, that Israel's complaints were unfair. (There is elsewhere an alternative tradition that seems to think of the time in the wilderness as the period of Israel's full obedience

to and dependence upon the Lord. Cf. Hos. 2:14; 11:1; 13:4 ff.; Jer. 2:1 ff.) While on the surface the complaint concerns food, it is actually far more serious. In effect, the Israelites are objecting to their election, to the fact that Yahweh brought them out of slavery into freedom! Small wonder that preachers have used the Israelites in the wilderness as bad examples.

The Old Testament view about complaining to God, however, is not so unambiguous. One may not see God and live, but one could certainly complain in the strongest possible terms and not only survive but hope for relief. Such complaints are seen not only in the Book of Job but also in more than fifty Psalms of individual or corporate lament. There the individual or the community petitioned God for help in time of trouble, confessing either sin or innocence (cf. Pss. 6; 17; 22). The context for such prayers was worship, from which no human emotion or feeling was prohibited.

2. Here the gift is a test. When the Lord responds to the complaint with a promise to "rain bread from heaven," he says it is so "that I may thus test them, to see whether they will follow My instructions or not" (verse 4, NJPSV). What is the point, and what is the penalty for failure to pass? The instructions conceal a promise: "gather a day's portion every day." The test is whether they will do just as they are told, no more and no less. Some of the people, however, fail the test, for they do not trust the promise. Contrary to the further instructions (verse 19), they tried to save some of the manna. What happens when one fails to trust in the promise of daily bread? How is punishment handed out to those who do not pass the test? Not without a sense of humor the narrator reports that the hoarded manna "bred worms and became foul" (verse 20).

3. Then there is the giving of the manna itself. At one level the chapter is a popular etymology of the name of the wilderness food, a play on the sound of the question, "What is it?" (Hebrew *man hu*). But above all, the manna, like all good things to eat, is a gift. Deuteronomy views the gift as didactic, God's means of teaching the people one of the most fundamental points about life: "And he humbled you and let you hunger and fed you with manna . . . that he might make

you know that man does not live by bread alone, but that man lives by everything that proceeds out of the mouth of the Lord" (Deut. 8:3). Here "everything that proceeds out of the mouth of the Lord" has a double meaning. On the one hand, it is spiritual, calling attention to the divine law and teachings. On the other hand, it alludes to the creative power of the word of God, by which all good things are brought into being. Thus the manna is a test and it is a lesson, but above all it is God's graceful response to an ungrateful and even rebellious people.

Psalm 78:1-3, 10-20

Psalm 78 is one of the few psalms concerned with the history of Israel and Judah. Other examples are Psalms 105 and 106 (used in Propers 12 and 14). The intentions of Psalm 78 are (1) to show that the people's—especially the northern tribes'—history was one of disobedience and lack of faith (verse 9-66) and (2) to claim that God had forsaken the Northern Kingdom and chosen the (southern) tribe of Judah, the city of Jerusalem (Zion), and the family of David (verses 67-72). As with Psalms 105 and 106, this psalm illustrates how the people's historical traditions could be used for particular purposes in the people's later history.

The opening of the psalm is rather unique in that it begins with someone calling the people to listen to the recital of a historical presentation. (Ps. 49 is somewhat similar but there it is an autobiographical rather than a national history that is the concern.) The sense of verses 1-3 is better represented in the NJPSV than in the RSV:

> Give ear, my people, to my teaching,
>   turn your ear to what I say.
> I will expound a theme,
>   hold forth lessons of the past,
>   things that we have heard and known,
>   that our fathers have told us.

Who the "I" is who speaks is unknown. Was it the king, an officiating priest, some prophet preaching in a temple service? We cannot know. At any rate, the psalm shifts to the first person plural in verse 4 and first person address does not occur again in the psalm.

Some features of Israelite faith are evident in these opening verses: (1) the people constantly drew upon their past in order to understand the present; (2) the past was frequently understood and interpreted in terms of the interests of the present (just as today we are reexamining history in light of the civil rights and feminist movements); and (3) a very judgmental and condemnatory attitude was taken toward the past. Much of the history in the Old Testament debunks Israel's past and the people's life and practices. Such an attitude creates the ability of a culture to look at itself critically in the present without such an examination being considered "unpatriotic." Such an attitude not only allows but also engenders changes.

Verses 4-9, which are skipped in this reading, describe the giving of the law and testimony as a depository of the will of God to be transmitted to every new generation with the hope that that generation would have a steadfast heart and a spirit faithful to God (verse 8). Note that in this text, a primary role of the older generation is the transmission of the law and lessons from the past to the next and new generation. The fathers must teach their children. The NJPSV catches the tone of the text:

> He established a decree in Jacob,
>   ordained a Teaching in Israel,
>   charging our fathers
>   to make them known to their children,
>   that a future generation might know
>   —children yet to be born—
>   and in turn tell their children
>   that they might put their confidence in God,
>   and not forget God's great deeds,
>   but observe His commandments.

Such an attitude produces a culture that is past-oriented and ideally one that is neither overly fascinated by the fads of the present nor unrealistically wooed by promises of the future.

Verses 10-11 tick off the disobedience of the past—they did not keep God's covenant, they refused to walk according to his law, they forgot the things he had done and the miracles that he had shown them. The text then expounds on these miracles, marvels, or wonders in verses 12-16—the plagues (verse 12), the crossing of the sea (verse 13), divine guidance by day and night (verse 4), and the giving of water in the desert (verses 15-16). (In later rabbinic tradition, the rock that gave water to the Hebrews in the wilderness followed them throughout the forty years of wandering. Paul was familiar with this tradition and quotes it in I Cor. 10:1-5, indentifying Christ with the Rock.)

In spite of divine care, human complaint only increased, eventually demanding food in the wilderness (verses 17-20). Here the lection ends interfacing with the reading from Exodus.

Romans 11:13-16, 29-32

For Paul, even Israel's rejection of the gospel could be construed as a redemptive act! In refusing the gospel, the Jews might have "stumbled," but they had not fallen permanently (11:11). Their resistance was only a temporary stage in God's overall plan. It had provided the occasion for turning to the Gentiles, thus "through their trespass salvation has come to the Gentiles" (11:11). Stage one, then, was Israel's rejection, to be followed by stage two, the Gentiles' acceptance. Stage three would be Israel's acceptance.

Since it was Paul's unique vocation to serve as an "apostle to the Gentiles" (verse 13; Rom. 1:5; 15:16; Gal. 2:7), he could see his missionary work as the crucial middle stage in God's overall strategy for bringing about salvation for all people. Accordingly, he could "magnify [his] ministry" among the Gentiles, and in doing so accelerate God's purpose in the world.

He is quite pointed in conceding that his purpose in preaching to the Gentiles was to evoke the jealousy of the Jews (verse 14). The logic here seems to be that the Gentiles' acceptance of the gospel would testify to their reception of

God's love. Seeing God's love redirected toward the Gentiles, the Jews would sense that they were out of favor with God and become jealous. Like a jilted lover, they would then return to God to regain full favor.

The line of argument may appear to us trivial, but Paul is informed here by scriptural precedent. Divine jealousy is a prominent Old Testament theme. Just as Israel could stir Yahweh to jealousy by their flirtations with other gods, so could Yahweh provoke Israel to jealousy by accomplishing the divine will through other nations (Deut. 32:21; cf. 10:19). For Paul to conceive of his mission work to the Gentiles as provoking jealousy among the Gentiles, and thus prompting them to return to God, was merely to interpret his own work in light of God's past dealings with Israel.

It is in this sense that the rejection of Israel would mean the reconciliation of the world (verse 15; cf. II Cor. 5:19; Col. 1:19-20; Rom. 4:8). Their refusal would only be penultimate. It would allow opportunity for the Gentiles to respond to the gospel, and this in turn would trigger the Jews to respond in kind. In this way, God's reconciling work would reach its goal. Thus their rejection is but a middle stage toward God's ultimate reconciliation, and their final acceptance would be "life from the dead" (verse 15). We might push the metaphor even further, as does JB: "Nothing less than a resurrection from the dead!" For them finally to accept the gospel would be tantamount to the dead coming to life again.

And why should Paul hold out for such a redemptive role on the part of disobedient Israel? Because "the gifts and the call of God are irrevocable" (verse 29). It was a matter of inviolable principle for Paul that God's integrity remained in tact. The immutability of God's promise had become something of an axiom in Old Testament thought (Num. 23:19; I Sam. 15:29; Isa. 31:2; 54:10; Ps. 110:4). This confidence in God's truthfulness and fidelity had also become an ingrained feature of Christian faith (Rom. 15:8; I Cor. 1:9; 10:13; I Thess. 5:24). Once invited into the membership of God's elect, no one could be disinvited, at least not permanently. No matter how disobedient Israel might have been, it was inconceivable that God would turn away in an act of final, irrevocable abandonment.

Rather, God sought ways of working the divine will even in the midst of human mismanagement. Just as disobedient Gentiles had become recipients of God's mercy, so now would disobedient Jews become recipients of God's mercy. As Paul had shown earlier, all humanity—both Jews and Gentiles—is under the grip of sin (Rom. 1:18-3:21). Thus "God has imprisoned [everyone] in their own disobedience" (verse 32, JB), but not with a view to being vindictive. Rather, the universality of sin has become an occasion for the universality of divine grace: "that [God] may have mercy upon all" (verse 32; cf. 5:9; 15:9; I Tim. 2:4; Ezek. 18:23).

One obvious homiletical possibility presented by today's text is the unequivocal faith in God's integrity (verse 29). The God who gives and the God who calls may be trusted to retract neither the gift nor the call. Our own refusal to receive or to listen may become profound disobedience, but even this cannot thwart the divine purpose. Indeed, in an odd sort of way, our disobedience may even extend the work of God.

Matthew 15:21-28

Obviously Matthew 15:21-28 and Mark 7:24-30 are telling the same story, but the differences are so marked that some have conjectured two traditions about Jesus' visit to the region of Tyre and Sidon. The preacher would do well to read the two accounts together as a part of preparation, not only to assure that Mark's record not bleed unintentionally into Matthew, but also by so doing, to fix Matthew's story more clearly in mind.

In the district of Tyre and Sidon, Jesus is met by a Canaanite woman. The use of this ancient term is strange. Perhaps it was used to serve as a contrast to Israel in verse 24. It is a dramatic way of portraying her as an outsider. But even more strange is her address to Jesus: "O Lord, Son of David" (verse 22). She is not simply calling him an Israelite of David's family; she is using a title, in some quarters a messianic title. Considering that the people in Jesus' own country have not so perceived him, and even his disciples are yet to speak of him messianically (16:13-20), this title on the lips of a Canaanite living in another country is most unusual. But perhaps that is Matthew's point; in other words, Matthew may be saying that first from a Gentile, a foreign woman, came the confession of faith. While the story is historically difficult, it may thus be theologically understandable.

Even so, there is a painful harshness in this event that will not go away. To the woman's plea, "Have mercy on me," Jesus is at first silent (verse 23). Then the disciples say, "Send her away," she is a nuisance to us (verse 23). When Jesus does speak, he tells her that his ministry is "only to the lost sheep of the house of Israel" (verse 24). The woman repeats her plea, falling on her knees before Jesus. Again, Jesus puts up an obstacle, saying it is not fair to give the children's bread to the dogs (verse 26). Her final response is to say, in effect, then treat me as a dog and let me have the crumbs that fall from the table. At this display of tenacious trust Jesus commends her faith and heals her daughter (verse 28).

Commentators on this text make various attempts to relieve the story of its embarrassment. Jesus was testing her faith, say some; Jesus was struggling in his mind with the idea of a Gentile mission, say others; Jesus was bringing her to an appropriate humility, say yet others. All of these together do not smooth out the surprisingly harsh tones of this encounter between Jesus and the Canaanite woman.

That Matthew understood Jesus' mission during his lifetime to be confined to Israel is quite clear. Only three times in this Gospel does Jesus minister to outsiders: here, in Capernaum (the centurion's servant, 8:5-13), and in Gadara (8:28-34). After the resurrection, Christ commissioned his followers to preach to all nations (28:18-20). However, there were some in the early church who believed that the post-Easter church should continue to confine itself to Israel. Luke reports in Acts that even Peter, prior to the Joppa vision, believed Gentiles to be unclean (10:1–11:18). The first conference of the church, says Luke, was to debate the issue of admitting Gentiles who did not first become Jews (Acts 16). Paul's position was, to the Jew first, and then to the Gentile (Rom. 1:16; 2:9-10).

Matthew 15:21-28 registers this painful issue, forms of which still plague the church. Jesus healed the woman's daughter, but the blessing was hard won, the victory of a tenacious claim on the compassion of Christ.

Proper 16

Sunday Between August 21 and 27 Inclusive

Exodus 17:1-7; Psalm 95; Romans 11:33-36; Matthew 16:13-20

In the continuous reading from Exodus, this week's lesson reports the story of Moses striking the rock to supply water for the murmuring, faultfinding Hebrews. Psalm 95 describes God as "the rock of our salvation" and picks up on the hardening of the hearts at Meribah and Massah, places named in the Old Testament reading. In the Epistle reading, Paul ends his discussion of Israel and the inclusion of Gentiles in the purposes of God with a doxology of praise. In the Gospel reading, Matthew reports his version of the episode at Caesarea Philippi in which he includes Jesus' comments on Peter as the rock upon which he will establish the church.

Exodus 17:1-7

Like last week's Old Testament lesson, this reading presents an episode from the account of Israel's wandering in the wilderness. This story of water from the rock follows immediately after the account of the manna and is followed by the report of a war between Israel and Amalek (Exod. 17:8-16). The stories are linked on the chain of the wilderness itinerary that lists the stopping places along the way (17:1; cf. 16:1; 17:8). Although this itinerary has the appearance of precision, it is impossible to reconstruct an actual route of the travels from Egypt to Canaan. (Note that there is a parallel to Exod. 17:1-7 in Exod. 15:22-25.)

Exodus 17:1-7 presents the two major motifs of the wilderness tradition in sharp contrast. On the one hand there was the almost continual grumbling and complaining of the

149

people. They complained out of fear because the Egyptians pursued them to the edge of the sea (Exod. 14:10-12). They complained because they were hungry (Exod. 16:2-3). Then, after feasting on the manna for years, they complained that their diet was boring (Num. 11:4-9). Here they complain for lack of water (17:2-3). On the other hand, the time in the wilderness was remembered as a time of God's gracious and miraculous care for the people. He provided manna, quails, and water.

Although there are duplicates and tensions that show the presence of different documents or traditions—compare verses 2 and 3—the story that follows the itinerary in verse 1 comes mainly from the Yahwist and presents a plot that can be followed easily. Finding themselves at a place without water, the people found fault with Moses and uttered the by-now familiar complaint: Why did you bring us out of Egypt in the first place? Moses in turn complains to Yahweh, in words that are at once accusation and petition (verse 4). The Lord answers Moses' prayer by instructing him to strike the rock with his rod, promising that water will flow for the people to drink (verses 5-6a). Moses does as he is told and, presumably, the water appeared (verse 6b). The story concludes (verse 7) with the naming of the place in memory not of the miracle of the water but of the contentious people: Massah ("trial" or "proof") and Meribah ("contention" or "argument").

Particular points that require brief comment are the references to Moses' rod, to Horeb, and to Yahweh's standing on the rock. The writer reminds us that Moses' rod is the one he used to strike the Nile (verse 5), recalling the miraculous plagues against Egypt. The power for the miraculous action is not in the rod itself but in the word of the Lord. It, like Moses, is an instrument of the divine power. The reference to Horeb (verse 6) is out of place, for the people are not yet at the sacred mountain. The allusion is one of those tensions that show a complex oral tradition behind the story. The reference to Yahweh's standing on the rock (verse 6) is difficult to understand, but likely simply indicates the presence of the Lord as Moses carries out the instructions.

Were the people's complaints legitimate or not? The story

of the manna in Exodus 16 (see the commentary for last week's Old Testament lesson) had made it clear that the complaints were unnecessary grumbling. The passage before us today is ambivalent on that point. On the one hand, the Israelites found themselves at a place without water (verse 1), not unusual in the desert. Small wonder, then, that they should complain because of thirst. Yahweh grants the request and provides water, thus acknowledging the need. On the other hand, the complaint is seen to go far beyond a prayer for water. As in most other cases, the people blame Moses for their problems and call their very election and salvation into question (verses 2-3). Moreover, their contentiousness is emphasized in the names of the place of the miracle (verse 7). The complaint, finally, amounts to a denial of the presence of the Lord among them (verse 7). Most Old Testament use of this tradition (Pss. 78:15-16, 20; 95:8-9) reprimands the people for their complaints, uses them as bad examples, and recalls that Yahweh punished the people of that generation by not letting them enter the Promised Land.

The contrast between Israel's complaints and God's response is dramatic. The Lord neither reprimands nor threatens those who complain so bitterly. With Moses as his agent, he acts to meet the need. God will not allow the unfaith of his chosen ones to frustrate the fulfillment of the promise to make Abraham's descendants a great nation in their own land. Thus the story is a parable of God's patient grace. Grace comes here through miraculous means, but its form is as simple as it is essential—life-sustaining water.

Psalm 95

This psalm gives numerous indications of having been used in some worship service. References are made to singing, to coming into God's presence, to worshiping and bowing down, and to kneeling. The following is an outline of the psalm's content: a communal call to praise God (verses 1-2), the reasons for praising God (verses 3-5), a call to worship the Deity (verse 6), the reasons for worship (verse 7*a*), a human call to hear and hearken to God (verse 7*b*), and a divine speech in which God addresses the audience (verses 8-11).

In the opening verses, the people are called upon to sing, make a joyful noise, and offer praise. The term translated thanksgiving in the RSV (verse 2) can also mean praise; generally only the context helps distinguish the meaning. To praise another is a means of showing thanksgiving. The psalm thus opens with a very upbeat attitude.

The motivation for praising God is the fact that he is a great God and reigns as a great king over all other gods. Like Psalm 82, this text presupposes the existence of other deities but simply assigns them a subordinate place to Yahweh the God of Israel. (See Deut 32:8-9 where Yahweh seems to be one of the deities subordinate to the Most High and is assigned Israel [Jacob] as his allotted country on earth.) The greatness of Israel's God is manifested in his rule over all of creation. Two couplets are used to indicate his universal dominion; both describe two extremes to indicate totality. The depths of the earth are in his hand and the heights of the mountains as well. He controls things from bottom to top, from the lowest to the highest (verse 4). The sea and the dry land belong to him because he made them both (verse 5).

The call to worship (verse 6) is postulated again on the basis of creation. One might say there is an obligation to worship because of the divine source of our origination. Verse 7a offers a more present oriented and existential rationale for worship. Worshipers are described as "the people of his pasture, and the sheep of his hand." When describing the shepherd-sheep imagery as the divine-human relationship, the ancient rabbis noted that the sheep are completely dependent on the shepherd, that for their own good they should obey the shepherd, and that all the products of the sheep (wool and offspring) belong to the shepherd.

In verse 7b, some worship leader calls upon the congregation to hearken to Yahweh's voice (like sheep responding to the calls of the shepherd). This is then followed by an oracle or speech of the Deity, perhaps spoken in worship by a priest or prophet as representative of the Deity. The speech is a warning not to repeat the behavior of the past, not to act as the Hebrews had at Meribah and Massah in the wilderness. For that generation, Yahweh had determined that they should never enter the Promised Land, or the rest/resting place of God. God's rest was the land he had chosen, the place that was uniquely to be related to him. Even Moses, because of sin, was only allowed to view "the land of rest" from across the Jordan (Deut. 34:1-8). Perhaps hardness of heart and rebellion frequently keeps us from the restful places of life even if the rest is no more than a good conscience and a sense of peace with life.

Romans 11:33-36

Today's text forms the conclusion to Paul's extended treatment of the role of Jews and Gentiles within salvation history (chapters 9–11). And what a stunning conclusion it is! Theological discourse gives way to doxology. Paul has just finished speaking of the God who brings to fulfillment the divine purpose: "the gifts and call of God are irrevocable" (11:29). Even more remarkable, God is able to work miracles of mercy in the midst of human disobedience (11:30-32). What we see in human history appears not to be God's work; what we see as God's work appears not to have happened in human history. We ask then, Where has God been at work? How? Ours are questions of genuine puzzlement. They arise from our perceptions of a God dimly lit, perhaps even hidden. If God's tracks are so faint, what then can we confess? to whom?

The mystery was once hidden but is now revealed: God intends both Gentiles and Jews to be part of the people of God (11:25; 16:25-27; Eph. 3:1-6). The community of God's people is now genuinely universal—and inclusive. To Israel the promise first came, then to the Gentiles. Even Israel's recalcitrance will be overcome, and eventually there will be solidarity among God's people. This is Paul's hope (11:25-26). Thus even though God's chosen have not always conformed to God's expectations, God's promise is still not thwarted. Human disobedience does not close off the pipeline of God's mercy. Even when we disobey, and disobey radically, God continues to show mercy toward us in love. The disobedience of some does not prevent God's having mercy upon all (11:32).

It is this capacity of God to achieve the divine purpose even in the midst of, and even in spite of, human disobedience; this ability of God to act mercifully even when we refuse to cooperate prompts the final, and triumphant, outburst of praise. We have heard more muted doxologies earlier in the letter (1:25; 9:5; cf. 8:38-39), but none this extensive, nor this bold.

It unfolds in tightly constructed form. We may divide this "hymn to God's mercy and wisdom" (JB) into four parts.

1. In verse 33 we have two exultant *acclamations*. The first acknowledges God's threefold depth in lavishly positive terms—riches, wisdom, and knowledge. Elsewhere Paul conceives of God in terms of unfathomable depth (I Cor. 2:10). For most of us "riches" denotes monetary wealth, but the metaphor here is broader—sheer abundance. Most often, Paul speaks of the "riches of God's glory," which suggests abundance and generosity as dazzling as the primordial light of creation (Rom. 9:23; Eph. 1:18; 3:16; Phil. 4:19; Col. 1:27; also Rom. 10:12). Doubtless the primary referent here is God's mercy (11:30-32).

Equally profound in its depth is the wisdom of God—God's purposeful knowing within human history (I Cor. 1:21). To be sure, it has been, and still continues to be, obscure (I Cor. 2:7), but through the revelation of Christ it has become incarnate in a way not previously known (Eph. 3:10; Col. 2:3).

Closely allied, is the knowledge of God—cognitive to be sure, but also God's intimate interaction within human history. For God to know us is to elect us. Also suggested is thorough, intimate knowledge of us—the Creator of the creatures, the Parent of the children (cf. Ps. 139:1-6).

The second acclamation sketches the depths of God in terms equally profound, though negatively stated—unsearchable judgments, inscrutable ways. These are sentiments strong in the Wisdom tradition (Wisd. of Sol. 17:1; Job 5:9; 9:10). Just as the workings of God's mind are hard to describe, perhaps even unsearchable and unfathomable, so are God's ways, or paths, difficult to detect. God may stride across the ocean, or march across the sea, yet leave no footprints for us to see (Ps. 77:19).

As profound as the depth of this mystery is, we should not conclude that God is unknowable (cf. Rom. 1:20). It is precisely the point of chapters 9–11 that God's will is now being revealed as the truly inclusive character of the people of God is being seen by the inclusion of the Gentiles within salvation history.

2. In verses 34-35 we have *three rhetorical questions,* the first two drawn from Isaiah 40:13, the third from Job 41:11 (cf. Job 35:7; also Apocalypse of Bar. 14:8 ff.). The structure of these three questions is directly related to the threefold affirmation in verse 33*a.* In fact, the three questions take up each affirmation in reverse order. So profoundly deep is God's knowledge, "Who could ever know the mind of the Lord?" So vast is God's wisdom, "Who could ever be his counselor?" (cf. Job 15:8; Jer. 23:18). So abundant are God's riches, "Who could ever give him anything or lend him anything?" (JB).

In a sense, all three questions make the same point—the absolute autonomy of God. We are directed toward the God whose work can be done without the collaboration of humans, often in spite of human obstructiveness. It is the God whom we cannot place in the dock, upon whose goodness we cannot presume (I Cor. 1:18-25). To discern the will and way of this God is a gift, a matter of special perception made possible for those with "the mind of Christ" (I Cor. 2:16).

3. In verse 36*a,* we have a *confessional formula* in three parts: "for from him and through him and to him are all things." It provides the basis of the previous claims: we are dealing with the God who is "Source, Guide, and Goal of all that is" (NEB). In this form, we have early Christian confessional language. In other forms, God is confessed as the Creator, the source of all things (I Cor. 8:6), whereas Christ is confessed as the Agent who assists in the original creative act and sustains the ongoing created order (I Cor. 8:6; Col. 1:16-17). But in Hebrews 2:10 God can be thought of as the one "for whom and by whom all things exist"—both purpose and agent of all that is.

The formula is remarkably similar to the Stoic formulation in Marcus Aurelius, *Meditations* 4:23, "O Nature, from thee are all things, in thee are all things, to thee all things return."

Yet Paul's confession is decidedly not pantheistic (not "in thee" but "through thee").

4. Finally, in verse 36b, we have the doxology: "To him be glory for ever. Amen." The God who is acclaimed as profoundly deep, acknowledged as Ultimate Mystery, and confessed as Cause, Means, and Purpose of all is the One worthy of eternal praise (cf. IV. Macc. 18:24; Gal. 1:5; Eph. 3:21; Phil. 4:20; I Tim. 1:17; II Tim. 4:18; Heb. 13:21; I Pet. 4:11; II Pet. 3:18; Jude 25; Rev. 1:6; 4:11).

The homilist must proceed with caution in dealing with today's text. Read one way, it seems to present us with a God who is neither known nor knowable. Yet coming at the end of chapters 9–11, it can best be read as a hymn praising the God whose will is becoming more clearly visible as the people of God acquires its destined shape. It is, after all, the God whose purpose is manifest in the otherwise inexplicable tangle of human history that prompts this outburst of praise and confession. It is precisely because God has begun to achieve the divine purpose without our help, and in spite of our resistance, that we can respond in praise.

Matthew 16:13-20

In all three Synoptics, the events recorded in the readings for today (Mark 8:27-30; Luke 9:18-21) and next Sunday are crucial in the ministry of Jesus and in the disciples' understanding of who he was and what he was doing. In verses 13-16, Matthew follows Mark rather closely. Verses 17-19 are a Matthean elaboration and interpretation, relieving many readers of an uneasiness created by Mark's strange silence. In Mark the confession of Peter is briefer; there is no indication of what Jesus being the Christ really means, and Jesus neither affirms nor rejects Peter's confession. At verse 20 Matthew rejoins Mark.

Although Luke seems uninterested in locating this event, both Mark and Matthew place it at Caesarea Philippi, twenty miles north of the sea of Galilee on the slopes of Mt. Hermon. Formerly known as Paneas, an ancient Greek worship center, the area was now a part of the tetrarchy of Philip, one of Herod's sons. Philip named the place for Tiberias, and it became known as Philip's Caesarea to distinguish it from the Caesarea on the Mediterranean which Herod had built, or rather rebuilt, to honor Caesar Augustus. The population was mostly Gentile.

A few interpreters of Matthew have taken the position that much should be made of the contrast between "Son of man" (who do people say the *Son of man* is?) and "I" (Who do you say *I* am?). This is to say, Jesus seems to be distinguishing between the eschatological figure who was to come and himself. This has been, however, a minority view since the identification of Jesus with the Son of man is clear and frequent in the Gospels. The more obvious contrast is between the public view of Jesus and that of the disciples.

Matthew's version of Peter's confession combines the title "Son of God," used earlier at 14:33, and "Messiah," used for the first time here. This elaboration of the confession beyond that of both Mark and Luke probably reflects the Christology of Matthew's church. We are not made privy to the full investment of meanings in this use of the two titles applied to Jesus. Two matters, however, are quite clear: one, Jesus approves of the confession (verse 17); and two, at least part of what it means for Jesus to be Christ and Son of God involves Jerusalem, suffering, death, and resurrection (verses 21-28, the reading for next Sunday).

That Simon Peter was able to identify Jesus as Messiah and Son of God is not an indication that Peter was more perceptive or intelligent than others. His insight came by revelation (verse 17). That true understanding of Jesus' identity was and is a matter of divine revelation Matthew has already said (11:25-27) and in that view he is joined by Luke (10:21-22), John (6:45-46 among many such statements), and Paul (I Cor. 1:26-29; 12:3). This revelation and hence this confession may be what is meant by the rock on which Christ builds his church (verse 18). However, the preacher will want to review the commentaries on verse 18 to recall the claims for Simon Peter as the foundation of the church. Much of the debate hinges on the interpretation of the two words, *petros* and *petra* used in Jesus' response to Simon. In either case, we have Jesus' promise of a church, which will be his church, and which shall not be overcome even by death itself. Only here and at 18:17 in the whole of the Gospels does Jesus refer to "church." Of course, in Matthew's own day the church as a distinct community had been formed by and for those who confessed Jesus as Christ. But the fact that here alone Jesus speaks of building his church has long generated debate as to whether Jesus as a preacher of the kingdom of God had in mind during his earthly ministry the formation of a separate community as a "church." Discussions of what Jesus had in mind have always fallen short of conclusiveness.

What is abundantly clear, however, is the New Testament's affirmation that the continuity between Jesus and the church was provided by the apostles. They were chosen by Jesus and given authority during his lifetime (Matt. 10:1 and parallels), an authority to be exercised in the church after Jesus' departure. The granting of authority to Simon Peter is obviously symbolic for all the apostles (verse 19), for elsewhere in Matthew (18:18) and John (20:23) this bestowal of power is on them all. Even those least appreciative of authority can imagine into what sentimental and errant paths the church would have wandered had not responsible persons preserved and passed on to the church what Jesus said and what Jesus did. The apostolic tradition gives the church the memory out of which it lives.

Proper 17

Sunday Between August 28 and September 3
Inclusive

Exodus 19:1-9; Psalm 114; Romans 12:1-13; Matthew 16:21-28

In the Old Testament reading, the Hebrews who left Egypt arrive at Sinai and with Moses mediating, they agree to hear the words of God and obey them. The psalm is a hymn that celebrates the departure from Egypt and the arrival in the land of promise. In the Epistle lesson, Paul appeals to his readers to practice a particular style and way of life that is commensurate with the will and grace of God and that manifests the life of the Spirit in the Christian community. In the Gospel reading, Jesus teaches that following him involves the shaping of life according to the pattern of his ministry and thus suffering and being willing to die on a cross.

Exodus 19:1-9

The Old Testament readings for today and next Sunday are part of the account of the theophany on Mount Sinai. Exodus 19 begins the lengthy report of the establishment of the covenant and the revelation of the law by reporting the appearance of Yahweh and his initial instructions to the people through Moses. The Sinai pericope is the longest single unit in the Pentateuch, beginning at Exodus 19:1, including the remainder of the book of Exodus, the entire book of Leviticus, and concluding only in Numbers 10:10, which is followed by the report of the departure from the sacred mountain.

It is easy for the contemporary reader to pass quickly over the first two verses of the chapter, the notes concerning the chronology and the itinerary, if not to ignore them entirely.

These matters were, however, of great significance, especially to the Priestly Writer, and for theological and liturgical rather than historical reasons. Precise dates are important for ritual calendars. Moreover, the writer was eager to show an unbroken genealogy and chronology from creation to Sinai and beyond. He saw history organized according to a divine scheme of covenants that gave both structure and meaning to the past. There were covenants with Noah, Abraham, and the other patriarchs, but at Sinai he understands that God has reached the goal of all the others. For the Priestly Writer, and for earlier sources and traditions as well, what happened at Sinai was of central importance to all future history for there the law was revealed to a particular people.

Following the introductory report that the people arrived at Sinai, the passage is organized in terms of the travels of Moses up and down the mountain and the speeches of the parties. Moses went up "to God" on the mountain (verse 3) and God told him what to say to the people (verses 4-6). Moses went down, convened the elders, and reported the words of God to the people (verse 7). The people responded, and Moses, presumably after going up the mountain, reported the words of the people to God (verse 8). Then the Lord spoke again to Moses, who reported again to the people (verse 9).

This pattern of ascent and descent, speech and report, continues through the chapter. What this pattern makes clear is the role of Moses as the mediator between God and people, between people and God. His role as spokesman for God is parallel to that of a prophet. As speaker for the people he is more like a priest, especially when one realizes that he is mediating a service of commitment, the establishment of the covenant.

The theological content of the passage is carried in the speeches, both of God and of the people. A great deal is conveyed in God's first speech (verses 4-6). God identifies himself in terms of his deeds, reminding the people of his mighty acts in Egypt and his preservation in the wilderness (cf. Josh. 24:7; Deut. 32:11; 7:6; 14:2). Then he states first the conditions and then the effects of the covenant about to be established. The conditions are obedience to the stipulations of the covenant; "covenant" in verse 5 is a virtual synonym to law. The effects are to make Israel God's people. It is tempting to take verse 6*a* as part of the conditions, but syntactically they are part of the effects, the promise of the covenant. The "if" clause or protasis is "if you will obey my voice and keep my covenant." The apodosis or conclusion includes both "you shall be my own possession among all peoples . . . and you shall be to me a kingdom of priests and a holy nation."

The Lord's second speech (verse 9) announces a theophany, God's appearance "in a thick cloud," and states the purpose of the encounter. This actually begins the theme that will become central in the remainder of the chapter. The purpose of the encounter is quite different from that indicated in the first speech. No longer is there reference to the establishment of the covenant, the election of a particular people, but the purpose is revelation and belief: This form of appearance is in order for the people to hear God when he speaks to Moses in order to confirm the authority of Moses.

Only once do the people speak, and very briefly: "All that the Lord has spoken we will do" (verse 8). That such a response is part of a cultic ceremony of covenant renewal is shown by the pattern of events and speeches here as well as by the use of similar language in Joshua 24:16-18, 21. Yahweh has pledged himself to the people in deed and word, and now the people corporately accept the conditions of obedience and solemnly pledge themselves to the Lord.

This passage is rich in possibilities for exploration in the context of Christian worship.

1. Making and renewing covenants. Notice that God takes the initiative; thus the first word of biblical covenants is grace. Then obedience to the divine will is expected. Furthermore, biblical covenants are corporate, between God and the people of God.

2. The meaning of election. God makes a covenant with a particular people in history. Having already chosen and delivered Israel, God invites them to affirm and confirm their election through the covenant. Notice that election is put into a worldwide context: "for all the world is mine" (verse 5), says the Lord.

3. The identity of the people of God. Covenant and election above all serve to make it clear to these people who they are: they are God's. More specifically, through obedience they will be a "kingdom of priests and a holy nation" (verse 6; cf. Exod. 15:17 ff.; Deut. 33:2-5; I Pet. 2:9). Their kingship and their holiness in all of life are defined by the rule of the sacred God.

4. The role of mediator. In this passage Moses, the only individual human being mentioned, says not a word of his own, but is the conduit of revelation and response. That, of course, does not define his full responsibilities as a leader of the people of God, but it is an essential dimension of any ministry, whether lay—"kingdom of priests"—or ordained.

Psalm 114

In Jewish worship, Psalms 113–118 came to be associated closely with the festival of Passover. This collection of six psalms came to be called the "Egyptian Hallel," because they were seen as praise for the redemption from Egypt. How early this use of these psalms developed cannot be determined but it was certainly already a custom at the time of Jesus.

The lambs designated for Passover were slaughtered and dressed in the temple in the afternoon to be cooked for the Passover dinner eaten in the evening. (Additional lambs were often cooked if the size of the Passover party required it. But at least one lamb, from which all observers ate a portion, had to be so designated and slaughtered and cleaned in the temple.) The people with their lambs were admitted to the temple in three different shifts. As the lambs were slaughtered on each of the shifts, the Levites sang Psalms 113–118 in the main courtyard of the temple. These psalms were again sung as part of the Passover meal. Psalms 113–114 were sung at the beginning of the meal and Psalms 115–118 at the conclusion.

Psalm 114 was clearly written for the celebration of Passover. Some of these psalms were originally composed for other celebrations and secondarily adopted for Passover usage.

The psalm opens with general summarizing statements about the Exodus from Egypt and the occupation of the land of Canaan (verses 1-2). Egypt is described as a people of strange language. Egyptian belongs to a completely different language family (Hamitic) from Hebrew (Semitic) and was written, of course, in a strange non-alphabetic hieroglyphic form. In verse 1, Israel and house of Jacob refer to the larger inclusive Hebrew people (both "Israel" and Judah). In verse 2, Israel and Judah denote the Northern and Southern Kingdoms after the death of Solomon. That Judah is claimed to be his (God's) sanctuary suggests that Judah is considered more special than Israel which is spoken of as his (God's) dominion. It also suggests that this psalm originated in Judah. The reference to sanctuary is no doubt an allusion to Jerusalem and the temple.

In verses 3-6, four entities are noted—the sea, the Jordan River, the mountains, and the hills. The references to the (Red) sea and the Jordan hark back to the stories of the crossing of the sea in the Exodus from Egypt (see Exod. 14) and the crossing of the Jordan to move into the Promised Land (see Josh. 3, especially verses 14-17). In both cases the water parted, fled, or turned back to allow the Hebrews to cross. Interestingly, but certainly appropriate for the setting of this psalm in the Passover observance, the Passover preceded the Exodus from Egypt (see Exod. 12) and was the first celebration of the Hebrews in the land of Canaan (see Josh. 5:10-12). The Passover was thus celebrated as the last taste of Egypt and as the first taste of the Promised Land. The Passover recalls not only the scars of Egypt but also the first fruits of the land of promise.

The mountains and hills that skipped like rams and lambs (verses 4 and 6) are not mentioned in the Exodus and Joshua stories. That they are mentioned as skipping around suggests that the language is metaphorical. The same might be said for the action of the sea and the Jordan River although the final editors of the Hexateuch took both crossings as miraculous but actual events. Verses 5-6 are a taunt in form so formulated to heighten the action described. The one responsible for such actions does not get mentioned until verse 7 which refers to the presence of Yahweh.

The psalm concludes (verses 7-8) with a call to the earth to "dance" (probably a better translation than the RSV's "tremble"). Whether one should read "earth" (= the world) or "land" (= the Promised Land) remains unknown, although the latter seems more likely. The land is called on to break out in celebration at the presence of God who worked wonders in the wilderness.

Romans 12:1-13

This passage partially overlaps the epistolary lesson (Rom. 12:9-16*b*) for Visitation (May 31) in all three years. The reader may wish to consult our remarks in *After Pentecost*, Years B and C.

Today's text is an appeal, a piece of moral exhortation: "I appeal to you therefore . . ." (verse 1). Nor is it a mere afterthought, a cushiony way to end an otherwise difficult theological argument. The use of "therefore" links it directly with all that precedes it in chapters 1–11. It is not added to, but *derives from* what precedes.

We should understand the function of this passage, and the remainder of the letter, in light of what has been said earlier. The "Gospel according to Paul" was not without its detractors. The interlocutor, Paul's imaginary dialogue partner throughout the argument, has consistently raised objections, and these have set the agenda for the unfolding argument (cf. esp. 3:1-9; also 3:27-31; 4:1, 9; 6:1-2, 15; 7:7, 13; 9:14, 30; 11:1, 11). What becomes clear is that these questions are real not imagined. We are hearing the heated debates caused by Paul's gospel within the synagogues, churches, and streets.

One of the most serious objections to Paul's theology of justification by grace through faith was that it lacked an adequate ethical base. To insist that we are justified by faith and not by works of law, Paul's detractors argued, resulted in moral relativism. Take away law, and you remove all ethical boundaries. No rules, no ethics. Moreover, you create an open license to sin. Indeed, Paul's gospel would seem to encourage sin. If sin becomes an occasion for God to display grace, the more sin, the more grace. Ergo: sin more! (6:1-2).

To draw such conclusions, Paul countered, was sheer sophistry. It misunderstood the nature of baptismal participation in the death and resurrection of Christ (6:3-11). It also failed to recognize the moral transformation that occurs when one becomes united with Christ (6:12-23). Far from impelling one toward a life of sin, Paul's gospel found its motivating center in death *to sin* (6:10). If the cross meant anything, it signified the triumph of righteousness over sin in the person of Christ. In Christ disobedience gave way to obedience, and it did so not because Christ was impelled to keep a law, or the law, but because he was bound to God in faith. Christ, then, becomes the central paradigm illustrating the compelling ethical power of grace.

What form would such a life take among believers? Today's text begins to sketch the profile for us. (A similar move is made in Gal. 5–6.) Far from leaving us afloat, drifting in the sea of moral chaos, Paul's gospel calls for a clearly etched life-style.

Today's text may be treated in three parts: (1) the appeal (verses 1-2); (2) the nature of life together in community (verses 3-8); and (3) specific instructions (verses 9-13).

1. *The appeal* (verses 1-2). At the heart of Paul's appeal is a single guiding metaphor: "living sacrifice" (verse 1). Paul not only uses cultic metaphors to interpret the work and death of Christ (3:25; cf. Eph. 5:2; I John 2:2) but also his own apostolic ministry (15:16; Phil. 2:17). Here, of course, believers are envisioned as sacrificial offerings made to God, not dead, however, but "living . . . holy . . . and acceptable" (cf. I Pet. 2:5). This is to be done "in a way that is worthy of thinking beings" (verse 1, JB), or perhaps "in a spiritual way." Among Christians there is no official cultus with sacrificial offerings. Instead, there is the ultimate sacrifice of Christ himself and our "living bodies as a holy sacrifice" (JB). What this implies, of course, is that our lives are continually being offered up before God not as sacrifices to placate an angry God but as thank-offerings in response to a gracious God.

Along with this sacrificial metaphor is the twofold injunction that provides the rubric for the various exhortations that follow: not being conformed to this world but being transformed by the renewal of your mind (verse 2). Ethical transformation inevitably involves putting away certain forms of behavior and exchanging them for newer, more appropriate forms of behavior. Hence the standard scheme of "putting off—putting on" (cf. 6:13, 19; Col. 3:5-17).

The "pattern of this present world" (verse 2, NEB) no longer provides the mold into which behavior is cast as it once did. For one thing, it is now seen to represent an old order that is passing away, that has been rendered obsolete by the Christ-event (Gal. 1:4; I Cor. 7:31; II Cor. 5:17). Here we have a clear call to non-conformity: "Do not model yourselves on the behavior of the world around you" (verse 2, JB; cf. I Pet. 1:14).

What makes such non-conformity possible, however, is an inner transformation that encompasses the whole person: "let your minds be remade and your whole nature thus transformed" (verse 2, NEB). The process is one of essential renewal: a new nature (Col. 3:10), a new creation (II Cor. 5:17), a new spirit (Eph. 4:23). The renewing agent is the Holy Spirit (Titus 3:5). Though the process begins now, it culminates in the Eschaton (Phil. 3:21; I Cor. 15:43, 49, 53; Rom. 8:29; II Cor. 3:18; I John 3:2).

2. *Life together in community* (verses 3-8). What is striking about the instructions that follow is the way they define individual Christian behavior in the light of corporate responsibility. There is first the call for proper self-understanding, a warning not to overvalue our real importance (verse 3; cf. I Cor. 4:6). We should instead develop a "sober estimate based on the measure of faith that God has dealt to each of [us]" (verse 3, NEB). Fundamental is the recognition that whatever we have is a divinely apportioned gift (cf. I Cor. 12:11; also Matt. 25:15; Eph. 4:7; II Cor. 10:13). This in itself will curb our tendency to take credit for what is essentially God's work or gift.

To underscore the proper relationship between the one and the many, Paul introduces the metaphor of the body (cf. I Cor. 12:12-13, 27; also I Cor. 6:15; 10:17). It has the effect of reminding us of the plurality of gifts and functions among us, and of the diversity as well. We may be plural and uniform, or plural and diverse. For Paul, the latter is the divine intention.

Especially strong here is the emphasis on being "members one of another" (verse 5). It's the difference between being a group and being a community, between being related and being a family. What is called for is active concern for, and involvement with, one another.

Consequently, the list of gifts in verses 6-8 is remarkable, because each gift is outward directed. Prophecy denotes utterances intended to edify others not the self (I Cor. 14:3). Similarly, are teaching and exhortation (I Cor. 14:3; Phil. 2:1; Heb. 13:22; I Tim. 4:13). Serving obviously presupposes "others" as its object, thus eliminating behavior that is self-serving (Mark 10:45). Making contributions and doing acts of mercy also point away from the self, but the motive is crucial in each case: freely and cheerfully. Even being a leader, which calls for exerting oneself, should be an act done for the corporate good rather than for self-aggrandizement (verse 8; I Thess. 5:12; I Tim. 5:12; Heb. 13:17; esp. Mark 10:42-45).

In a word, the profile of behavior sketched here is a responsible sense of community, one that translates into a form of living together that embodies the "second great commandment" (13:9).

3. *Specific instructions* (verses 9-13). In a sense, we have here a miscellany of moral exhortations. Yet they largely continue the emphasis on social responsibility: having love that is undiluted (verse 9a; cf. II Cor. 6:6; I Cor. 13:6); brotherly affection (verse 10; cf. I Thess. 4:9; Heb. 13:1; I Pet. 1:22; 2:17; II Pet. 1:7); showing honor to one another (verse 10b; 13:7; I Pet. 2:17; II Pet. 1:7); active care for the needs of the saints (verse 13; Acts 6:3; 28:10; Phil. 4:14); showing hospitality (verse 13; I Tim. 3:2; 5:10; Titus 1:8; Heb. 13:2; I Pet. 4:9).

Even the other activities that are commended, such as constant prayer (verse 12), are perhaps best understood as being done toward the common good (Col. 4:2; I Tim. 2:1). So practiced, the Christian virtues become less privatistic pieties and more corporate responsibilities.

One way of appropriating this well-known Christian text is for the preacher to articulate the corporate responsibility called for here. Indeed, presenting ourselves as living sacrifices may all too easily become an act of *personal* sacrifice without due regard to the active care for one another that this requires. To be sure, Christian ethics takes concrete shape in the profile of individual service, but Paul's remarks here follow directly on an extended exposition about the joining of two *peoples*—Jews and Gentiles—into a single family of God. On no showing can that be done merely on an individual basis.

Matthew 16:21-28

"You are the Christ, the Son of the living God" (16:16). Whatever else may be involved in this identification of Jesus, at least it included the suffering, death, and resurrection of Jesus. We know this because Jesus approved of and accepted this confession (verse 17) and on the basis of it began to teach his disciples about his coming passion in Jerusalem. That Jesus "strictly charged the disciples to tell no one that he was the Christ" (verse 20) implies that Jesus did not regard the public, with its view of him as the forerunner of the Christ (verse 14, their view of Jesus is the same as our view of John the Baptist; that is, the one to prepare the Messiah's way), as ready to receive the announcement, "The Messiah has come and it is Jesus of Nazareth." The public would certainly not be ready for a suffering and dying Messiah; but then, as our reading reveals, neither were the Twelve.

Our lection consists of two parts: first, what his messiah-ship meant for Jesus (verses 21-23) and second, what it meant for those who were his disciples (verses 24-28). "From that time" (verse 21) is Matthew's addition to Mark's account (8:31–9:1), indicating a clear turning point in Jesus' ministry. He now begins to prepare his disciples for his passion, which, says Matthew alone, will take place in Jerusalem (verse 21). Jesus' suffering will be at the hands of the supreme council of the Jews, the Sanhedrin (composed of elders, chief priests, and scribes). That Jesus *must* go is not a reference to the Greek notion of fate or destiny but to the will of God. As to the suffering, death, and resurrection on the third day, no further details are supplied. This is the first prediction of the Passion.

Not unexpectedly, Simon strongly resists Jesus' words,

finding them a contradiction to his being the Messiah, the Son of God. Mark says Peter rebuked Jesus but gives no content to the rebuke. Matthew tells us that Peter remonstrated to the effect, "This shall never happen to you" (verse 22). Luke omits this exchange between Jesus and Peter (9:22-27). Although not as sharply stated as in Mark, Matthew still preserves what amounted to a shouting match (verses 22-23). We are not dealing with a disagreement; Simon Peter is the voice of the tempter seeking to turn Jesus from the will of God, and Jesus feels the presence of Satan just as strongly as in the wilderness (4:1-11).

Verses 24-28 are addressed to the disciples, not to the crowds as in Mark (8:34). Verses 24-25 were anticipated at 10:38-39 and the references to the cross, which did not appear in Jesus' prediction of his death (verse 21), not only anticipate Jesus' death but also reflect upon the past fact of it. The two sayings about the value of one's life in verse 26 are rather loosely joined to verse 25 and probably existed originally in other contexts. They seem to have been clustered about the common phrase "his life" and not about common subject matter.

The passage concludes on an eschatological note, promising the coming of the Son of man in judgment upon every person. We have come to expect the element of judgment as the conclusion to Matthew's record of Jesus' teaching on discipleship. Already in 13:36-43 and 47-50 we are told that judgment will be carried out by the Son of man and his angels. This emphasis will reappear dramatically at 25:31-46. And while Matthew will, in chapters 24-25, speak often of "the delay," here in our text the anticipation of the end within a short time has been preserved (verse 28). Since Matthew carries both perspectives, a delayed coming of the Son of man and a coming very soon, perhaps it is best to remind ourselves that Christian behavior does not flow from the belief that the end is near but from the belief that God is near. All else is secondary.

Proper 18

Sunday Between September 4 and 10 Inclusive

Exodus 19:16-24; Psalm 115:1-11; Romans 13:1-10; Matthew 18:15-20

The Old Testament reading describes the awesome appearance of God on Mount Sinai and the dialogue between Moses and the Deity over the incapacity of the people to come into the direct presence of the divine. The psalm praises the greatness of Israel's God and caricatures the use of images in the worship of other religions. In the Epistle, Paul discusses the role of authority and force in the government of the world and advises his readers to fulfill the demands of the law through love. In the Gospel, Jesus discusses how broken relationships in human affairs may be handled.

Exodus 19:16-24

For general comments on Exodus 19 see the discussion of last week's Old Testament lesson, Exodus 19:1-9. The chapter as a whole begins the report of the events at Sinai and introduces the establishment of the covenant with the giving of the law. The verses between last week's reading and the one for today contain the instructions for the appearance of God announced in verse 9. The Lord instructs Moses to "consecrate [the people]" (verse 10) for he will come down "in the sight of all the people" (verse 11). The mountain itself is sacred because of the presence of the Lord, so "bounds" are to be set so the people cannot touch it (verses 12-13). Anyone who violates the limits of sanctity are to suffer the death penalty.

Exodus 19:16-24 then is the report of the theophany of the Lord on Mount Sinai. The air of mystery is heavy and the mood is somber, for the event is awesome. Human senses are

170

stretched almost to the breaking point as the appearance of God is accompanied by dramatic transformations in nature. On the one hand, these phenomena sound like a mighty thunderstorm: There was the sound of thunder and the sight of lightning (verse 16). On the other hand, they remind one of a volcano: The mountain smoked and the earth quaked (verse 18). Probably these two images derive from different literary sources, but neither source analysis nor attempts to find rational explanations for the phenomena should be allowed to blur the imagery or dull the impression of frightful power. When God reveals himself directly to human beings, the event is dramatic and fearful.

In addition to the natural phenomena there are the appearances of a cultic drama. Distinctions between Moses, the priests, and the people are obvious. Moses alone speaks directly to God, the priests seem to come closer, and the people are kept at a distance. All of this is related to the sense of separation between sacred and profane, the care taken to maintain distinctions that protect the holiness of God and the people from the divine presence. Likewise the sounding of the trumpet and the almost processional movement of the priests and people suggest liturgical activity.

Although chapter 19 is preparation for the communication of the Decalogue in chapter 20 and the other laws that follow, the transition is quite rough. Exodus 19:25 has Moses speaking but the contents of the speech are not given. Rather, Exodus 20:1 begins with God speaking quite directly. Such rough transitions as this indicate that the section as a whole is the result of a long history of growth and composition. The events begun in chapter 19 eventually are concluded with the making of the covenant in chapter 24.

While there are numerous secondary issues, such as the role of the priests and the place of Aaron, a single theme dominates this passage. It is the attempt to account for the most fundamental of all human religious experiences, the encounter with the Holy. In antiquity, such encounters were related to holy places, locations where God was known to be or where his presence came. In later Israelite understanding, the sense of the sacredness of Mount Sinai also applied to Mount Zion. Deeply ingrained in this account is the sense that while people may be nearer the divine presence at certain times and places—because God chooses for that to be so—human beings must maintain their distance. There is thus the awareness, as in all genuine religious experience, of the radical difference between God and humanity. That radical difference is the basis for the careful procedures to maintain the separation between the people and the place of revelation. Consequently, for all the visual phenomena, no one—not even Moses—sees God here. Verse 9 had suggested that God would actually appear, but finally it turns out that God reveals himself through words, words such as those that follow in the Decalogue.

Psalm 115:1-11

Like the remainder of Psalms 113–118, Psalm 115 was utilized in Passover celebrations. One of the reasons for the psalm's employment in the celebration of the Exodus from Egypt is the parody on idols in verses 4-8. Egyptian religion was filled with a great diversity of gods and a wide variety of images and idols. Gods were sometimes represented in human form, at other times in animal fashion, or even a combination of the two. Thus the land of Egypt was not only the home of a "people of strange language" (Ps. 114:1) but also a land of multiple and diverse images of the gods.

Some factors in the psalm but not included in the reading are worthy of emphasis.

1. Note that in verses 12-13 and 15 the concern is with the divine blessing of humans while in verse 18, the interest is in the human blessing of the divine. The Deity's blessing of humans is related to their increase/offspring (see verse 14). The human blessing of God seems to be related to praise of the Deity (see "Praise the Lord" at the end of verse 18).

2. The assurance placed in the Deity is based on confidence in God as creator. In verse 15, God is depicted as the one who made heaven and earth rather than the God who brought his people out of Egypt. The appeal to creation as the theological basis and justification for divine activity is more common in the Psalms than appeal to God as redeemer from Egypt.

3. Verse 16b boldly declares that the earth has been given

over to human control. According to verse 16*a*, the heavenly world is under the jurisdiction of God. This affirmation of human control and responsibility for the world is even more frightingly expressed here than in Genesis 1:26 which speaks of humans being given dominion over the earth but not the earth itself. (For a different assessment of matters, see Ps. 24:1-2).

4. Verse 17 unashamedly declares that the dead do not praise God. Here we see a bold example of the ancient Israelite belief that meaningful life ended with death.

In the reading for today, the RSV presents verses 1-2 as addressed to the Deity. Other alternatives are possible and more likely. The address to God probably should be limited to verse 1 or else extended through verse 8. Either of the latter possibilities would mean that verses 2 and 3 should be read together, as in the NJPSV:

> Let the nations not say,
>   "Where, now, is their God?"
> when our God is in heaven
> and all that He wills He accomplishes.

At any rate, the psalm, in verse 1, requests that Yahweh not glorify Israel but himself since the issue at hand is the nature and activity of the divinity. With Israel and Judah so frequently defeated on the battlefield by the major near-eastern powers (Egypt, Assyria, and Babylonia) and with success or failure considered reflective of the power and will of the nation's god, then Israel and Judah must frequently have been chided about the nature and strength of their God.

The comparison drawn between Yahweh and the gods of the nations is twofold: (1) Yahweh is in the heavens (verse 3*a*) when the people's idols clearly are not since they (the idols) are the products of human hands and made of earthly metals (verse 4); and (2) what Yahweh wills to do he accomplishes whereas the idols of the nations have human features—mouths, eyes, ears, noses, hands, feet, and throats—but they cannot speak, see, hear, smell, feel, walk, or clear their throats. The psalm declares that the worshipers shall become like the idols they have made and serve: "Those who fashion them,/all who trust in them,/shall become like them" (verse 8, NJPSV). The parody on idols—whom the ancients often treated as if they were living by supplying them with food, clothing, and even toilet arrangements—was apparently a favorite among ancients Judeans (see Ps. 135:15-18; Isa. 44:9-10; and the Letter of Jeremiah in the apocrypha).

The reading closes out with an admonition for Israel (the laypersons) and the house of Aaron (the priests) and those who fear Yahweh (both groups together) to trust in God.

Romans 13:1-10

Today's text speaks of Christian responsibility in two areas: (1) our obligation to the state (verses 1-7), and (2) our obligation to love our neighbor (verses 8-10).

1. *The Christian and the state* (verses 1-7). The text is unusual in that it is one of the few times in the undisputed Pauline letters that Paul openly addresses the question of how Christians should relate to political powers (cf. I Cor. 6:1-9). Later in the Pauline tradition, this question is addressed in similar terms as Christians are urged not only to be "submissive to rulers and authorities" (Titus 3:1) but prayerful in their behalf (I Tim. 2:1-2).

Paul's remarks here are strikingly parallel in tone and content to I Peter 2:13-17, which calls for subjection to imperial officials both national and regional and for discretion in the exercise of freedom. It is recognized that freedom can be used as a "pretext for evil" (verse 16), suggesting that the urge to be free, or the impulse to speak freely, may be sabotaged by less than pure motives. Freedom movements may, in other words, become occasions for the most sinister forms of oppression, manipulation, and subversion. Along with the command to "fear God" is the charge to "honor the emperor" (verse 17).

Paul calls for similar subjection "to the governing authorities" (verse 1). It is a mandate with a hard edge—subjection, not simply giving honor. He has in mind a genuine sense of obligation: "one must be subject" (verse 5). There is no place here for a kind of Christian spirituality that is so superior to civic responsibilities and the political process as to be indifferent toward them. What is called for here is not Christian duty that transcends the political process, that soars in spiritual heights above mundane, earthly affairs, that focuses on the heavenly realm that *really* matters. Instead, Paul speaks of Christian duty that lives with its eyes open to political realities, that recognizes the divinely sanctioned value of government, and that acts accordingly. To be Christian in this fully engaged sense is to "pay taxes." It is hard to get more concrete than this!

This is a long way from a grudging view of the state as a necessary evil that pales in importance beside the infinitely more worthwhile kingdom of God. In mind here is Christian service that encompasses rather than denies civic duty, that embraces the social and political order as the world with which the church has to do.

Once we recognize that Paul calls here for serious subjection, for genuine obligation, and not mere political lip service, we can see why he does so, because the state is divinely ordained: " . . . all government comes from God, the civil authorities were appointed by God" (verse 1, JB). With this unqualified view, Paul stands squarely within the Jewish tradition, most especially the Jewish wisdom tradition, which saw the power of kings and princes as deriving from God. "By me [wisdom] kings reign,/and rulers decree what is just" (Prov. 8:15-16*a*). "Listen . . . O kings, . . . learn, O judges . . . your dominion was given you from the Lord, and your sovereignty from the Most High" (Wisd. of Sol. 6:1-11, esp. verses 1-3). Similar sentiments are expressed by the Johannine Jesus before Pilate, "You would have no power over me unless it had been given you from above" (John 19:11*a*).

Nor is he merely articulating general political theory. The ruler—any ruler, local, regional, national, or international—is "God's servant for your good" (verse 4). As difficult as it is for members of God's elect to admit that pagan rulers can be deemed "God's servants," instruments in divine service, we are so reminded nevertheless. Even Nebuchadnezzar, king of Babylon, is so designated (Jer. 27:6), to say nothing of Cyrus' being referred to as "God's anointed" (Isa. 45:1-3).

Thus when we resist the authorities, we resist those whom

God has appointed (verse 2). Obviously, a rather high view of rulers is presupposed here. They are envisioned as benevolent, as no threat to those bent on good conduct (verse 3). They do their work, including bearing the sword, for our good (verse 4).

In this text, Paul nowhere entertains the possibility of malevolent rulers, and in this respect his remarks are rather limited. In sharp contrast stands the Johannine apocalypse where rulers, indeed Roman rulers, are portrayed in the most sinister terms, with the savage images of wild beasts, who are in out-and-out opposition to the forces of good (Rev. 13:1-18, esp. 1-10; also 18:9-10). Rather than calling for docile submission to such beasts, Revelation longs for their overthrow.

To be sure, the situation has changed. By the time Revelation is written, the state has turned against the church. Even though we are not yet into the period where there is universal opposition to the church by the state, there are those local pockets where the church is being threatened with extinction, and the response that is called for is resistance.

Clearly, in Romans 13:1-7, we are hearing the biblical witness, but in light of the entire spectrum of the canonical voice, it is only one part of that witness.

Even so, this particular text calls for us to recognize authorities as "ministers of God" (verse 6). It also enjoins civic duty, in particular, the payment of taxes. In this respect, it is in keeping with the testimony of Jesus as reflected in the Synoptic tradition (Mark 12:13-17 and parallels).

2. *The obligation to love our neighbor* (verses 8-10). It may strike us as odd to speak of love as obligation, but this is the tone of these remarks: "Avoid getting into debt, except the debt of mutual love" (verse 8a, JB). The sentiments are in keeping with the commandment form we know from the Gospel tradition (Matt. 22:34-40; Mark 12:28-31; Luke 10:25-28). There is an oughtness to love: "If God so loved us, we also ought to love one another" (I John 4:11).

But we misconstrue love if we try to remove any sense of ought from it. Certainly love carries with it obligation, even though it is not knee-jerk obligation. To say that love does not obligate us renders it anemic. In fact, love in the biblical sense obligates in a compelling sense. It locks us into active concern for others.

We are even reminded that love encompasses the law: if we love our neighbor we have fulfilled the law (verse 8). The various commandments of the Decalogue dealing with mutual relationships with each other may be seen most properly as explicit formulations of the more fundamental obligation to love (verse 9; Exod. 20:13-17; Deut. 5:17-21). This conforms to Jesus' insistence that the whole law can be reduced to the twofold love for God and neighbor (Mark 12:28-31 and parallels; cf. Lev. 19:18). It is in this sense that the "whole law is fulfilled in one word"—love (Gal. 5:14; cf. Col. 3:14; I Tim. 1:5). Thus "love is the one thing that cannot hurt your neighbor; that is why it is the answer to every one of the commandments" (verse 10, JB).

To preach from this text, the preacher will have to confront its widely dissimilar halves: positive obligation to the state, in highly unqualified form, along with positive obligation to love our neighbor. Yet there is a sense in which the two parts complement each other, especially if one sees the aim of the social and political order as mutual obligation among citizens who live "under God."

Matthew 18:15-20

We have today the first of two sessions on 18:1-35, the fourth major body of Jesus' teaching in Matthew (19:1 is the formal ending). The last place mentioned is Capernaum (17:24), but the location for these sayings is unimportant. In fact, chapter 18 is really a collection of diverse sayings, some of which are in Mark (9:33-50), some held in common with Luke (15:3-7; 17:3-4), and some in Matthew alone. The discourse falls in two parts: verses 1-14, the treatment of children (new disciples?) and verses 15-35, the relationship of church members to one another. Our readings today and next Sunday constitute the whole of part two.

In order to understand our text, it is necessary to realize that the setting is not the life of the historical Jesus but the life of the church which came into being after Easter. These sayings presuppose the existence of congregations that gather at times to handle disputes and offenses among members. Verses 15-20 contain instructions as to how to negotiate such matters. Such teachings to Jesus' disciples during his earthly ministry would have been useless and confusing. As the word of the risen and living Christ who is with his disciples whenever two or three are gathered (verse 20), our text speaks clearly to the very common problem of offenses among Christians.

Here as in the Sermon on the Mount the instructions are addressed to the victim: "If your brother sins against you" (verse 15). The offended are to take the initiative. There is no room in the teaching of Jesus or in the conduct of the Christian life for sitting around, licking wounds, and sighing, "Poor me." One cannot always avoid being a victim but one can avoid the victim mentality. Finding oneself offended by a member of the faith community, the principle operative in the action one takes is respect, both for the offender and for the entire church. The matter is therefore settled privately, if possible, and if not, in the presence of "one or two others" (verse 16). Such use of witnesses echoes Deuteronomy 19:15. If this second step fails, then the whole congregation is to gather to hear and to resolve the dispute (verse 17). "Church" as used here refers to a local congregation. Paul called upon congregations to discipline members (I Cor. 5–6; II Cor. 2:5-8), but the history of this procedure is not one of unambiguous success. It often is a case of pulling up the wheat with the tares. Matthew is assuming a small gathering of Christians pure in motive and objective in judgment. Not all congregations can be so described, and therefore render the process questionable. What is without question, however, is the realism of the text: disputes do arise among believers, and it is important that the problems be addressed directly, as privately as possible, but always with care and respect.

The conclusion of verse 17 is quite a problem for the reader. That discipline by excommunication, presumably temporary until reconciliation occurs, occurred and occurs is historical fact. However, the expression "as a Gentile and a tax collector" sounds more like something coming from a conservative Jewish Christian community than from Jesus. We know some Jewish Christians had difficulty with the embrace of Gentiles (Acts 10:14, 28; 11:8; Gal. 2:1-16). But we also know Jesus sent his disciples to all nations (Matt. 28:18-20) and during his earthly ministry defended his practice of accepting tax collectors (Matt. 9:10-13). In fact, one of the Twelve was a tax collector (Matt. 10:9). The whole of Jesus' ministry argues against Matthew's derogatory reference to Gentiles and tax collectors. The interpreter sometimes must use Jesus against statements in the name of Jesus. The entire matter of verses 15-20 is not a simple one, or easy to translate into new settings.

The binding and loosing referred to here (verses 18-19) has to do with discipline and reconciliation in the congregation. Even if the gathered community number only two or three, heaven is alert to the business being transacted and the living Christ is present. The promise of Christ's presence, even if only two or three are gathered, has long since been extracted from the judicial context of making disciplinary decisions and extended as a general blessing upon every Christian community, whatever its size. Such a wider claim on verse 20 is not out of order and certainly accords with the church's experience everywhere.

Proper 19

Sunday Between September 11 and 17 Inclusive

Exodus 20:1-20; Psalm 19:7-14; Romans 14:5-12; Matthew 18:21-35

The Old Testament reading for today consists of the Priestly version of the Decalogue and might be profitably read alongside the Deuteronomic version (cf. Deut. 5:6-21). The psalm reading, with its lyrical praise of the "law of the Lord" as more desirable than gold and sweeter than honey, is an appropriate response to the Old Testament reading. In the New Testament reading, the passage from Romans deals with themes treated in the second part of the Decalogue: humans getting along with one another. Specifically, the focus is on how the "weak" and "strong" can live together in community. In the Gospel reading, we hear Jesus teaching about forgiveness and presenting us with the well-known parable of the unforgiving servant. Thus one theme echoed in at least three of today's texts is that of responsibility toward and sensitivity to our fellow human beings.

Exodus 20:1-20

The main body of today's reading is the Decalogue, but the initial and concluding verses that provide the immediate narrative framework stress the importance of considering these laws in their context. On the broadest level, the communication of these laws is part of the story from creation, at least to the Israelite occupation of the land of Canaan. More specifically, the revelation of the law takes place at Sinai where the story reaches one of its high points and is part of a covenant ceremony reported in Exodus 19 and 24. Exodus 20:18-20 alludes to the theophany of chapter 19 and anticipates the conclusion of the ceremony in chapter 24.

It is hardly possible to exaggerate the importance of the immediate narrative setting as indicated in Exodus 20:1-2. The laws are understood as direct expressions of the will of God (verse 1), who introduces himself in a special way: "I am the Lord your God, who brought you out of the land of Egypt, out of the house of bondage" (verse 2). This means that the law is given in the context of and with the precondition of God's grace. The people to whom these commandments are given have already been saved, quite literally, redeemed from slavery and chosen by God to be his own. At least in this passage, there is no room for righteousness works, for grace and salvation precede the requirement of obedience.

Laws were collected and handed down in ancient Israel, as in most cultures, in collections. The Decalogue is followed in Exodus 21–23 by a longer collection, the Book of the Covenant (Exod. 24:7). That collections of ten laws were a traditional genre is seen in the existence of a parallel to Exodus 20 in Deuteronomy 5:6-21 and a so-called ritual decalogue in Exodus 34. "Decalogue," or "Ten Commandments" is even an Old Testament term (Exod. 34:28; Deut. 4:13; 10:4).

All ten laws in Exodus 20:3-17 are apodictic in form; that is, they are brief statements of general expectations in the form of direct address in the second person. This contrasts with many of the laws in Exodus 21–23 that are case laws, giving a legal condition and its consequence: "If a man steals an ox or a sheep, and kills it or sells it, he shall pay five oxen for an ox, and four sheep for a sheep" (Exod. 22:1). All but the fourth and fifth laws are prohibitions, that is formulated in the negative.

Since the form of the individual laws is so clear, one can easily distinguish between the laws themselves and their elaborations. As elsewhere in the Old Testament, especially Deuteronomy, the elaborations include both commentary and preaching. They explain the law and urge the hearers to obey. Thus, lest there should be any question about the meaning of the prohibition of graven images in the second commandment, the elaboration specifies that there are to be no images of anything in heaven, or earth, or in the sea (verse

181

5*b*), and that such are not to be worshiped at all (verse 6*a*). The remainder of the elaboration goes on to urge obedience in terms of threat (verse 5*b*) and promise (verse 6). The elaboration of the sabbath commandment explains its meaning—no one is to work, verses 9-10—and gives the reason for its sacredness in terms of the days of creation (verse 11). By contrast, Deuteronomy 5:12-15 explains the reason for the sabbath rest in terms of the history of the Exodus: You and all your servants are to rest, remembering that you were slaves in Egypt and the Lord brought you out.

In terms of contents the last five commandments (verses 13-17) clearly belong together as regulations of social relationships in community. Likewise the first three specify directly the relationship between the people and their God. The fourth commandment, the sabbath law, is related to the first three, and the fifth is more closely akin to the final five, although it directly concerns the family instead of the community as a whole.

A few comments concerning some of the individual laws may be helpful. There can be no doubt that the first commandment is the most important one. It is the expectation of exclusive devotion to Yahweh that makes all the other requirements possible. The command to have no other gods is not an expression of monotheism but rather assumes the possibility of worshiping other deities. Likewise the second commandment (verses 4 ff.) assumes a real problem in ancient Israel's culture, the creation and worship of idols. The meaning of the third commandment (verse 7) is not so self-evident. "In vain" probably refers to the abuse or misuse of the divine name. The translators of the NJPSV go further and read, "You shall not swear falsely by the name of the Lord your God." The fundamental concern is with the attempt to manipulate Yahweh by invoking his name for evil or selfish purposes, as in curses or even prayers. The prohibition against killing (verse 13), in the wider Old Testament context, is neither limited to murder nor absolute. Since ancient Israel understood that killing in wartime and capital punishment could be in accord with the will of Yahweh, it is killing that is not in the interest of the community that is prohibited. The prohibition of bearing false witness (verse 16) does not refer to lying in general but to perjury in particular.

What is the preacher to do with a rich and full text such as this? There can be no doubt about the importance of the entire list. John Calvin considered the text so significant that he had it read regularly in the Geneva liturgy. One could hardly hope to expound all Ten Commandments in a single sermon! Consider also the fact that in recent polls of the American public, while the majority affirm that the Bible is in some way the word of God, only a small percentage can name as many as four of the Ten Commandments.

Certainly a major issue concerns the place of the law in the Christian faith. One form of that question, as discussed in the sayings of Jesus and then debated by Paul, his contemporaries, and his successors, relates specifically to the Old Testament law. Did one have to become a Jew first to be obedient to all the laws of Judaism? That particular form of the question is no longer alive, but continues in another form, Since God saves by his grace, what is the place of works of the law? An answer is already indicated in the Old Testament Sinai pericope. Obedience is not what moves God to save but it is the grateful response to God's saving actions. God's gracious deeds evoke a response of obedience.

Above all, the law defines what it means to be a covenant people. Verse 2 states God's part of the covenant: "I am the Lord your God." Verses 3-17 define the other side, stating in summary fashion what it means to be a covenant people and how they will behave toward God and one another.

Psalm 19:7-14

This lection from Psalm 19 forms an appropriate parallel to the reading of the Decalogue since much of it is concerned with the law. This psalm is generally divided in two parts and sometimes even seen as the secondary combination of two separate psalms. Verses 1-6 declare that nature and creation, especially sky and sun, proclaim the glory of God and testify to his will. Verses 7-14 praise the law (Torah) of God which has been made known in commandment, precept, and ordinance. The character of the psalm is further complicated, however, since the "law" section, verses 7-14, can be further subdivided. In verses 7-10, the law is praised and God spoken about in the third person while verses 11-14 are a prayer addressed directly to God.

In spite of its complexity, the psalm can be seen as a unity. The nature portion, verses 1-6, declares that creation, without normal words, voice, or speech points to divine will and control and thus prompts expressions of praise. The law portion, verses 7-10, focuses on the written law formulated in words that elicit attitudes of praise. Verses 11-14 are a prayer that one might be aware of sins, faults, and errors in order to live a life that is without great transgressions. The final plea, in verse 14, requests that not only the words but also the unspoken meditations of the heart be acceptable to God. Thus the psalm moves from describing the unarticulatable expressions of nature, which proclaim God's work and fill the whole expansive realm of creation, down to the inarticulated meditations of the heart. Thus the thought of the psalm moves from the outer reaches of the natural world to the inner recesses of the human personality, the human heart.

If we focus more closely on the psalm reading for this lection, verses 7-14, we are primarily concerned with the praise and glory of the law and the worshiper's petition offered in light of the will of God manifest in nature and law. The antiphonal praise of the law, verses 7-10, knows the Torah as an object of praise and not as a burden or a yoke to be borne in grumbling servitude. Six synonymous terms are used to speak about the Torah: law, testimony, precepts, commandment, fear, ordinances. Perhaps these six terms were used to express the fullness and completeness of the known will of God. The adjectival descriptions of the Torah are extremely positive in their affirmations: perfect, sure, right, pure, clean, true, righteous. Four aspects or benefits from the Torah are noted. The Torah revives the soul: it is life-giving and sustaining. It makes wise the simple by providing them with understanding. It rejoices the heart making one glad to know the will and way of the Lord. It enlightens the eyes by providing a perspective within which to view the world and one's own life. Thus the law of God is a nobler and finer possession than gold and sweeter than honey. The law is to be more desired than the most precious of human treasures or the most reviving of foods.

This praise of the law and its life-giving qualities was characteristic of much Israelite and Jewish thought about Torah. Christians, viewing matters from the Pauline perspective on the law as found in Galatians, frequently have difficulty affirming the value and goodness of law. Yet the positive aspects of the written Torah should be emphasized since Torah provides persons with specific directions, allows us to locate ourselves with regard to the understood will of God, and thus provides a sense of security. The law provides not only a general map for human living but also specific directions along the highway of life.

With verse 11, the focus of the psalm moves from the world of creation and the praise of the law to the sentiments and concerns of the individual worshiper. The law which like the sun is perfect, sure, and faithful also like the sun at noontime touches all so that "nothing is hid" from its preview. In light of this judging and quickening aspect of the law, the worshiper recognizes that the law not only warns but also calls into question human adequacy and constancy. Thus the psalmist prays to be kept from hidden faults, that is, those things one might do without realizing they are faults (verse 12), as well as presumptuous sins, that is, grave sins of arrogance or pride (verse 13). If one can be kept from hidden faults and presumptuous sins, then surely one is blameless, since these represent the two extreme poles.

The praise of God's glory in creation and the meditation on the law, in this psalm, led naturally to critical self-examination and to a focus on the whole range of disobedience from secret, hidden sins to overt, callous acts of open transgression. In the concluding petition, verse 14, the psalmist requests full acceptance from the words of the mouth, the external articulated word, to the meditation of the heart, the internal unarticulated thought.

Romans 14:5-12

Religious communities are like all other social groups in at least one important respect: our members disagree. What's different is that we disagree on matters of ultimate importance. To disagree on wages and benefits is one thing; to disagree on our final reward is quite another. It's the difference between welfare here and welfare hereafter.

The situation in view in today's text has to do with differences in everyday religious practice—the right and proper way of being religious: whether to eat meat or just vegetables (verse 6; cf. 14:2); whether to drink or not to drink wine (14:21); whether to observe certain days as holy (thus, holidays) or whether to regard every day as holy (verses 5-6). This is the stuff over which religious persons—Jews, Muslims, Christians, and others—have disagreed for centuries. They are the sand in the crankshaft.

Paul's treatment here is non-specific and slightly distant. It is not clear whether the "day" is the sabbath day, some other (Jewish) feast day, or days in general. Elsewhere, observing certain days is linked with astral speculation, and his response to those who would impose day-keeping on all Christians is more exasperating (Col. 2:16; also Gal. 4:10). Maybe he knows the Roman situation less well, never having been there (Rom. 1:11). Maybe he is casting his theological net more widely, hoping his teaching will be more widely applicable. As to the question of what to eat, we are clearly dealing with some form of religious asceticism, not the question of eating meats offered to idols (I Cor. 8–10).

What is striking is that Paul does not take sides. He is far less interested in the particular merits of the argument on each side than he is with the impact of the argument on the life of the community. In fact, he is remarkably tolerant, that is, if the dispute over religious holidays has anything at all to do with astrological speculation, which he clearly regarded as inimical to Christian practice (Gal. 4:8-10).

Yet he sees it in terms familiar from other discussions (cf. I Cor. 8–10): how the weak (14:1-2) and strong (15:1) live together in community. We do not know precisely who the weak and strong are—Jewish Christians, Gentile Christians, neither, both? We do know that the weak are taking a narrow line, the strong a broader line. In this sense the weak are rigorous in their insistence on vegetarianism, while the strong are less rigorous in believing that one "may eat anything" (14:2). The weak are conservative in insisting that one day is better than another, while the strong are liberal in insisting that all days are alike (verse 5).

Thus one group insists on making sharp distinctions while the other group sees shades of gray. One sees unbreakable principles at stake; the other sees principles as more flexible guidelines. One argues that to concede this point means that the whole house of cards collapses; the other argues that if the house is that fragile perhaps it should collapse, or that maybe this one point is not the single axis on which the religious universe turns. Small circles versus larger circles. Narrow boundaries versus wider boundaries. Black and white versus gray. Obedience versus freedom.

And how does Paul respond? First, even the eyes of faith see things differently. The religious positions articulated here are polar opposites, mutually exclusive. He makes no effort to harmonize them or to impose uniformity. For Paul "faith does not make all persons and things equal" (Käsemann).

In fact, he allows that radically different theological positions can stem from the same motive: honoring the Lord and giving thanks to God (verse 6). It is not that one is operating with sinister motives, the other with pure motives. Both are genuinely attempting to live properly before the Lord. Good and pure religious convictions can manifest themselves in radically different ways.

One thing that is important is for every one to "be fully convinced in his own mind" (verse 5). One might have thought that Paul would call for loosening the bolts of religious conviction in this situation. Instead he insists on firmly held, clearly conceived, intellectual positions. In the heat of religious controversy put the mind in gear, not out. The way forward is not through loosely formulated positions that one can renegotiate on demand. Rather what is called for is genuine conviction that remains open to God's future. "What the apostle has in view is the renewed reason of 12:2 whose critical capacity leads through the call into a circumscribed sphere to firm conviction and resolute action on the basis of insight into one's own situation, and from the perspective remains open to new situations and the assessment of the brother" (Käsemann). Before we can talk fruitfully we must think clearly.

A second perspective is offered in verses 7-9, which is perhaps the central section of our text. It seems to provide a central, guiding principle that informs the whole discussion, both what precedes and what follows: "None of us lives to [ourself], and none of us dies to [ourself]" (verse 7). With this sharply formulated principle Paul says no to robust individualism. No one is an island. We are creatures of the whole not of the part. Religiousness is not reclusiveness. Our personal existence is no city of refuge to which we can flee.

And why not? Because we live and die to the Lord (verse 8). The universal dominion of the Lord precludes the universal dominion of the individual. The whole spectrum of human existence, from death to life, lies outstretched before the risen Christ who alone encompasses life in its fullest. He alone is the "Lord both of the dead and of the living" (verse 9). We cannot be both "in the Lord" and "in ourselves." To be "in the Lord" is to recognize a larger dominion than the world of the self. Even more, we must recognize that we stand in solidarity with a host of others, dead and living, past, present, and future, who confess the universal dominion of the Lord. Thus however vital our own personal relationship with the Lord, it is neither unique, solitary, nor exclusive.

A final perspective is offered in verses 10-12, one that derives from our acknowledgment of the universal dominion of the Lord: ultimate self-accountability before God relativizes our sense of others' accountability to us. Our ultimate reference point is God's future, when "we shall all stand before the judgment seat of God" (verse 10; cf. 2:16; II Cor. 5:10; Matt. 25:31-46; Acts 10:42; 17:31; II Tim. 4:1; I Pet. 4:5). We must finally bow before God in worshipful praise (verse 11; cf. Isa. 49:18; Jer. 27:24; Ezek. 5:11; Isa. 45:23; also Phil. 2:10-11). But with praise comes responsibility—and accountability (verse 10).

So sobering is the thought that each of us is ultimately accountable to a just God that our own inclination and ability to "pass judgment" diminishes. The more concerned we are with our responsibility before God the less concerned we become with our fellows' responsibility to us. For one thing, in the presence of God we become painfully aware of our own inadequacies. The light of God makes us so transparent that we find it difficult to place others under the beam of our own investigative light. To recognize that God passes judgment on us makes us less ready to pass judgment on others, much less to despise them (verse 10).

Taken seriously, Paul's advice will make Christian individuals less judgmental and Christian communities more livable. It will also change our agendas from passing "judgment on one another" (14:13) to pursuing "what makes for peace and mutual upbuilding" (14:19; I Cor. 14:26). It will not make us any less variegated in the theological positions we take or in the religious life-styles to which those positions lead us. But it will place our diversity under the scrutiny of the Lord of the living and the dead rather than under the watchful eye of those bent on making us in their own image and in their own likeness, that is, those who think that the boundaries of life and death are theirs to define—and to guard. It will, in a word, place our destiny in the hands of God, not in the hands of those who think they can do God's work better and quicker than even God can do it. It will save us from those who make God's future their present and God's agenda their own.

Matthew 18:21-35

We complete today Jesus' teachings on relationships within the Christian community, the fourth of five major teaching sections in Matthew. The preacher may find it helpful to review the introductory comments on the lection for last Sunday.

After the rather detailed procedure outlined in verses 15-20 for seeking reconciliation with an offending brother or sister, verses 21-22 are most refreshing. In the final analysis, that which creates and sustains the Christian community is forgiveness. Forgiveness is not, of course, carelessness or indifference to wrong. It is not permissiveness or the absence of any sense of ethical standards. On the contrary, there can be no forgiveness without standards and values being violated, without persons and relationships being hurt, without a loss so deeply felt that efforts at restoration are pursued. From a distance, forgiveness may look like condoning or permissiveness, but in reality forgiveness takes the violators, the violated, and the violation most seriously. To be forgiven is to be taken seriously. Forgiveness does not abrogate but fulfills righteousness.

And how often should one forgive? A rabbinic tradition said three times. Simon Peter, in a generous gesture suggested possibly seven times (verse 21). Jesus says forgiveness does not count the times. Who is keeping score? In saying seventy-seven times (ancient versions translated the expression "seventy times seven" which has continued in modern versions even though the word means "seventy-seven"), Jesus is simply dramatizing the point that forgiveness is unlimited. Very likely the number seventy-seven was intended as a reversal of Genesis 4:24 in which Lamech claimed revenge seventy-sevenfold.

Our lection closes with a parable intended to underscore the fact that the Christian community is a community of the forgiven and forgiving. To lay claim to the one without extending the other is to demonstrate an inability to live in and by the forgiveness of God. The preacher will not want to press the parable in detail to the point that forgiveness takes on an ugly face. For instance, the parable contains exaggerations. How could a slave owe anyone ten thousand talents (verse 24) when just one talent was the sum total for fifteen years of common labor? Some commentators suggest the slave in the story is a subservient prince or territorial governor who failed to pay taxes due the king. Maybe. Another detail not to be pressed is the statement about selling into slavery one who is already a slave (verse 25). Or again, being delivered to the jailers (literally, torturers) until all the debt is paid strains the reason (verse 34). It is much better to accept such elements as the furniture of the story, the force of which is to say, We have been forgiven much; let us not withhold forgiveness for the lesser offenses that creep into our fellowship.

The preacher will, of course, be disturbed by the Matthean comment following the parable (verse 35). We have grown accustomed to Matthew's manner of underscoring his point by making reference to a final judgment. But Matthew, in saying that God will likewise torture all who do not forgive from the heart, makes an appeal that falls short of effectiveness for most Christians. It is difficult to forgive "from the heart" with such a threat hanging overhead. But sometimes conditions in a congregation can so deteriorate that the preacher speaks louder than usual and appeals to God's final judgment more frequently than usual. Such may be Matthew's situation.

Proper 20

Sunday Between September 18 and 24
Inclusive

Exodus 32:1-14; Psalm 106:7-8, 19-23; Philippians 1:21-27; Matthew 20:1-16

In the Old Testament lesson today we have one of the most well-known instances of Israel's infidelity: the golden calf incident. Along with their breaking the covenant occurs Moses' intercession on behalf of the people. The reading from Psalm 106 rehearses the same incident albeit in the form of a prayer of confession rather than biblical narrative. In retrospect Israel realizes the stupidity of their exchanging the glory of God for the image of an ox and the enormity of their amnesic act: forgetting the great things God had done in Egypt. In the New Testament lesson, we have the first of four semicontinuous readings from Paul's Epistle to the Philippians, the well-known confession "for me to live is Christ." The Gospel reading continues the teaching of Jesus from Matthew with the parable of the laborers in the vineyard who receive the same wage for different amounts of work. We hear the workers' understandable protest of inequity and Jesus' censure of them for questioning the master's right to determine wages and for being oblivious to his generosity in making it possible for them to work in the first place.

Exodus 32:1-14

The frame of reference within which this passage must be understood is the covenant between Yahweh and Israel. Hardly had the people agreed to bind themselves in covenant before they violated one of its most fundamental stipulations. Murmuring and complaining about needs both real and imagined were one thing, but the rebellion reported in the story of the golden calf is quite another matter, rupturing the covenant relationship and threatening the life of the community. This account of the making and worshiping of the golden calf is the initial part of a coherent unit of material that includes Exodus 32–34 and leads finally to the renewal of the covenant.

Our assigned reading contains three distinct units of narrative, and in all of them dialogue between the main parties dominates. In the first unit, verses 1-6, the dialogue is between the people of Israel and Aaron. While Moses is on Mount Sinai receiving the revelation of the law, the people become impatient and resentful of their leader's absence, so they demand that Aaron "make us gods, who shall go before us" (verse 1). Without visible resistance, Aaron calls for all the gold earrings and fashions them into a golden calf, declaring it to be the "gods" (!) who brought Israel out of Egypt (verse 4). When the people worship the image, he builds an altar and proclaims a festival.

In the second unit (verses 7-10) the scene shifts to the mountain, and a dialogue between Yahweh and Moses begins with a lengthy divine speech. The Lord tells Moses to go down "for *your* people, whom *you* brought up out of the land of Egypt, have corrupted themselves" (verse 7, emphasis added). He then informs Moses of the people's actions and declares his intention to let his wrath "burn hot against them" and destroy them (verse 10).

The third unit (verses 11-14) consists primarily of Moses' response to the Lord. It is a prayer of intercession on behalf of the rebellious people. Moses pleads the case for forgiveness by pointing out that the Egyptians would consider Yahweh's intentions evil from the outset and reminds the Lord of the promise made to the ancestors to multiply their descendants and give them the land of Canaan. The passage concludes with the report that the Lord "repented of the evil which he thought to do" (verse 14).

If one read no further in chapter 32 than verse 14 the tensions in the story as a whole would not be obvious. When Moses leaves the mountain and returns to the people, he hears the sound of the festival and apparently is surprised to learn what Yahweh had already told him in verses 7-10. He initiates punishment, having the Levites kill three thousand men, and then tells the people that he will go up to the Lord and attempt to make atonement on their behalf. When he pleads for forgiveness the Lord assures Moses his angel will lead the people to the Promised Land, but he will punish the guilty parties. He does so by sending a plague. The themes of the sin and Moses' intercession continue into the next two chapters. These various perspectives on the events indicate that while there is a thematic unity, the section has been composed of more than one source or tradition. The basic story line comes from one of the older Pentateuchal sources, most likely the Yahwist. Verses 7-14 almost certainly are a later Deuteronomic addition to the story.

The story of the golden calf probably has been influenced by the memory of the events reported in I Kings 12:25-33. When Jeroboam rebelled after the death of Solomon and established the Northern Kingdom, he set up golden calves in Bethel and Dan, saying "Behold your gods, O Israel, who brought you up out of the land of Egypt" (verse 28; compare Exod 32:4). In the Deuteronomic tradition of the seventh century and following, if not earlier, one of the functions of the story of the golden calf in the wilderness was as polemic against a concrete problem, the corruption of worship in the Northern Kingdom.

Three important themes for theological and homiletical reflection emerge from this reading.

1. The first, the sin of the people, is the one that has received the most attention in the history of Christian interpretation of the text. Note, above all, that in Stephen's speech in Acts those sinful people are accepted as "our fathers" (Acts 7:38). Specifically, the making and worship of the golden calf violated the second commandment, but in that it violated the first one as well. What was the calf, or what did it represent? In Exodus 32:1 the people seem to ask for a replacement for Moses, but in verse 4 it clearly is identified with Yahweh. In the Canaanite culture surrounding Israel, the calf must be related to the bull that symbolizes the god Baal. Aaron as religious leader responds to a religious need with a religious solution: a cult object, an altar, and a festival. But especially according to the Deuteronomic tradition, less religious activity is better than more of

questionable form. Even if people should construct an image only to make their worship of Yahweh more concrete, there is the danger that they will confuse the symbol with the reality that is beyond all symbols. Thus our narrator holds the people up to ridicule for their actions.

And what of the role of Aaron in this affair? At best his character is weak, for he gives the people what they ask for. It is a wonder that he is not among those punished by death. Compare the report of his construction of the idol in verse 4 with his own explanation in verse 24: "I threw it [the gold] into the fire, and there came out this calf."

2. The second theme concerns the role of Moses as mediator. He stands between the people and God and communicates in both directions. His immediate response to the Lord's report of the people's sin and the threat of punishment is to intercede. Although there is no threat to him (verse 11*b*), he identifies with the people, the same ones who have grumbled about his leadership so many times. As he pleads and argues, he neither offers excuses for the people nor insists that they deserve forgiveness. Rather, he appeals to the faithfulness and mercy of God.

3. The third theme, the capacity and willingness of God to repent, is noted only briefly but it runs like a thread through the entire story. It is the foundation for the prayer of intercession and the factor that makes a renewal of the covenant possible. Even as the Lord is announcing his decision to destroy the people he is leaving room for change by indirectly inviting Moses to interfere (verse 10).

Psalm 106:7-8, 19-23

A portion of this psalm was used earlier in Proper 14. The selections for this reading have primarily to do with the incident of the golden calf produced in the wilderness and thus parallels the reading from Exodus.

Verses 7-8 place the original murmuring against Moses and God already in Egypt itself. Probably what is referred to here is the incident noted in Exodus 14:10-13. In the story of the flight from Egypt when the people faced the sea and were being pursued by the Egyptian army, they, out of fear, complained that it would have been better to find a grave in Egypt than in the wilderness. In making their complaint against Moses, the people refer to the fact that already in Egypt they had said to Moses, "Let us alone and let us serve the Egyptians" (Exod. 14:12). Ezekiel develops this tradition of rebellion in Egypt claiming that the people refused to give up the detestable things and idols of Egypt (Ezek. 20:8).

The latter rabbis suggested that when their fleeing ancestors went down into the sea, they complained: "Out of mud and mire [their brickmaking work] we come forth, and now we come back to mud and mire." Another way the rabbis had of explaining the rebellion of the sea was as follows. When the tribes got to the sea, none of them wanted to go first down into the waters. Eventually, Judah did and for this reason was rewarded with having the king (the Davidic family) come from its number.

The incident of the golden calf is the concern of verses 19-23. The psalm describes three wrong acts in the episode: (1) they made an image thus breaking the second commandment (see Exod. 20:4-6); (2) they worship an image of an ox in place of God; and (3) they forgot God and his great acts in Egypt (in the land of Ham) and the awesome (not "terrible") things he did at the Red Sea.

The psalm emphasizes the intecessory role of Moses who places himself between the people and God to turn away the divine wrath. This intercessory role of Moses shows up frequently in the murmuring in the wilderness episodes. For an example of Moses' standing in the breach, see Numbers 11:10-15. In a very late rabbinic text, it is even suggested that Moses died by the hands of his own people.

Philippians 1:21-27

Since this is the first of four semicontinuous readings from Paul's Epistle to the Philippians, some introductory words are in order.

We should first note that the letter reflects a long-standing relationship between Paul and the church at Philippi. He can look back to the time when this church began active financial support of his ministry, and their generosity has been repeated (4:14-16). This letter is prompted in part by yet another financial contribution (4:17-18), and thus takes the form of a letter of thanksgiving (1:3-11; 4:10). The mood is intimate between Paul the missionary and his supporting church, and the tone is deeply moving and personal.

The letter is written from prison (1:7, 13) and serves to allay the church's anxiety about Paul's welfare. There is an apologetic tone noticeable in the first chapter as Paul seeks to reassure the church that in spite of his imprisonment the gospel is making progress (cf. 1:12). He still has his detractors, but he can still report that "Christ is proclaimed" (1:18).

From his repeated mention of "joy" and "rejoicing" (1:4, 18-19; 2:2) we should not conclude that all is necessarily well within this relatively well-established church. Signs of internal tension surface early in the letter (2:1-4, 14), and by the end he is mentioning by name persons who should be encouraged to get along with each other (4:2). Opponents from the outside also pose a threat (1:28), and the tone becomes especially polemical in chapter 3, which may have originally existed as a separate letter to the church.

Paul's pastoral concern is evident throughout the letter. Exhortation is combined with direct instruction. Warnings stand alongside ethical imperatives.

Today's text opens with some of the most familiar words of Paul: "For to me to live is Christ, and to die is gain" (verse 21). How one construes this will dramatically affect one's understanding of the whole passage. One option is to read it as the classic expression of Paul's Christ mysticism, his complete identification with the risen Christ as it came to be expressed in the Pauline formula "in Christ" (cf. II Cor. 5:17). Reciprocally, of course, this could be understood as the living Christ present within Paul, and by extension to all Christians (Rom. 8:10; Gal. 2:20; Col. 1:27; II Cor. 13:5; cf. John 17:23). Thus Christ could be spoken of as the one "who is our life" (Col. 3:4).

But there's another way of reading it. The immediate context is a discussion of Paul's imprisonment and its impact on his apostolic work (1:12-14). His main concern is to reassure his supporting church that the gospel has not been

197

hindered by this. Rather Paul insists that "now as always" (1:20) Christ is being magnified in his body, that is, the message of Christ continues to be echoed through his word and person (cf. II Cor. 4:11-12). He is confident that this will be the case whether he lives or dies. Thus, for him to live means that Christ gets preached. Life in the flesh means "fruitful labor" for the sake of the gospel (verse 22). To remain alive would expedite their "progress and joy in he faith" (verse 25). Yet even if he dies the gospel "gains" as well. His death would become a sacrificial offering that helped make possible their triumph in the day of Christ (2:16-17). Either way, the cause of the gospel is served.

This interpretation in no way reduces the tension presented by the two options. Nor does it dull Paul's desire to "depart and be with Christ" (verse 23). Clearly, he would prefer to experience the fullness of the presence of Christ that is possible beyond death to the partiality and fragility of human existence this side of death. To be "away from the body and at home with the Lord" (II Cor. 5:8) is much to be preferred.

Yet duty calls. Apostolic responsibility to his churches presses upon him and he knows it (verse 24). His chief concern is the solidarity of his pastoral charge, regardless of whether he can be present physically or must be absent (verse 27). Above all, he wishes for their strength and unity of spirit (verse 27; cf. 2:2; also I Cor. 16:13; Gal. 5:1; Phil. 4:1; I Thess. 3:8; II Thess. 2:15) and for their continued partnership with him in the struggle for the gospel (cf. 4:3; Rom. 15:30).

The homiletical task will be to expound what it means to say, "to live is Christ, and to die is gain." At least one possibility, however, is to plump for the practical over the mystical. "Life is Christ" (verse 21, NEB) may mean that Christ is seen and heard through us as much as it means the merging of ourselves with Christ in mystical union.

Matthew 20:1-16

Last Sunday's Gospel lesson was a parable; so is today's and the lessons for the next three Sundays. If the preacher did special study of the nature and function of parables when our texts were from Matthew 13 (Propers 10–12), then it would be helpful to review that material. C. H. Dodd said parables are drawn from nature or common life, but their exact meanings are left in sufficient doubt so as to tease the mind into active thought. Some parables have a surprise turn at the end, which not only teases the mind into active thought but which also shocks or even offends some listeners. Such, for example, was the parable of the loving father (prodigal son), and such, certainly is the parable of the generous employer.

The parable of the generous employer, sometimes called the parable of the workers in the vineyard, is clearly drawn from common life. The elements in the story are quite normal. When grapes are at their prime, the vineyard owner needs extra workers to harvest them quickly. Unemployed men were available in the marketplace. A deal is struck with some workers who agree to the usual wage of one denarius for a full day's work, sunrise to sunset. Concern that the harvest might not be completed that day sends the owner back for more workers at nine, at noon, at three, and at five, one hour before the close of the day. The owner promises to pay what is fair, presumably an appropriate portion of a denarius. There is no hint that any of the later workers deliberately delayed their availability so as to presume upon the employer's goodness. In fact, the workers who began at five in the afternoon said they were unemployed because no one had offered them a job (verse 7).

So far all is normal. The surprise jolt comes in the payment at the end of the day. There is no evidence that payment was usually made beginning with the last. Matthew has preceded (19:30) and followed (20:16) this parable with the often-used saying of Jesus to the effect that the last will be first and the first last. This saying may have influenced the order of payment, but it certainly does not capture the heart of the story. The last first and the first last expresses a reversal of fortunes, but such is not the case here. The first receive the agreed upon wage. Very likely we can account for the order of payment so that all can witness the owner's generosity and hence heighten the drama. This is simply good storytelling. It is also good storytelling to tell of the payments to the last and the first. That contrast provides the issue; details about paying the nine, noon, and three o'clock workers would have dragged the story to a halt.

The grumbling on the part of the full-day workers was natural. The answer to the question, "Do you begrudge my generosity?" (literally, Is your eye evil because I am good?) is in all honesty, yes. No one has been denied, no one cheated, no one given less than agreed upon. The offense lies in the generosity to others. The offense of grace is not in the treatment we receive but in the observation that others are getting more than they deserve. Jonah was offended that God accepted the people of Nineveh. Forgiveness and generosity do not seem fair. God sends sun and rain on the just and unjust, the good and the bad (Matt. 5:45). That offends some of us. God is kind to the ungrateful and the selfish (Luke 6:35). That offends some of us. The generosity of God quite often cuts across our calculations of who deserves what. For all our talk of grace, the church still has trouble with it.

In the course of interpreting this parable, sometimes the first and last workers have been understood as Pharisees and sinners in Jesus' day. At other times commentators have seen in the first and last the Jews and the Gentiles. But always and everywhere the parable addresses those of us who have difficulty celebrating the gift someone else receives.

Proper 21

Sunday Between September 25 and October 1 Inclusive

Exodus 33:12-23; Psalm 99; Philippians 2:1-13; Matthew 21:28-32

The Old Testament reading for today records the conversation between Moses and Yahweh after the golden calf incident in which Moses asks for confirmation of Yahweh's leadership. It also reports the intriguing episode where Moses asks to see God's glory and is given divine protection in the crevice of a rock. Psalm 99 is an enthronement psalm celebrating Yahweh as ruler of the earth, yet one who responds to the calls of those who cry out for help and guidance. In the New Testament reading we have Paul's exhortation to unity with the Christ-hymn depicting the ultimate example of self-emptying and obedience to the divine will. The Gospel reading from Matthew shows Jesus teaching about doing the will of God. Here we have the parable of the two sons, one who said, "I will," but doesn't; the other who said, "I won't," but does.

Exodus 33:12-23

Today's reading is part of the longer composition in Exodus 32–34, the account of Israel's violation of the covenant by building and worshiping a golden calf, God's forgiveness, and the renewal of the covenant. Viewed in that context, Exodus 33:12-23 serves two main purposes. First, it continues the theme of Moses' intercession with Yahweh on behalf of the people. Second, just as the theophany on the mountain in Exodus 19 set the stage for the revelation of the law and the conclusion of the covenant in Exodus 20–24, so the appearance of the presence of God to Moses in this passage prepares the way for the laws and the covenant renewal in Exodus 34.

The passage consists entirely of reported dialogue between Moses and Yahweh. It contains two relatively distinct units, verses 12-17 and 18-23. (The paragraph division in the RSV is misleading.) In the first section Moses intercedes successfully on behalf of the people, and he asks for and is granted a special revelation of the presence of God.

What is it that Moses asks on behalf of the people? It is difficult to understand the point of the dialogue in the first unit in particular without reading the first three verses of the chapter. There the Lord, having forgiven the people for the episode with the golden calf, promises to send an angel before them to drive out the inhabitants of the land. However, he says that he himself will not "go up among you, lest I consume you in the way, for you are a stiff-necked people" (verse 3). Having successfully pleaded with the Lord to forgive the people and not kill them and to remember the promise of descendants and the land, Moses wants more! He will not let the Lord go until there is a full restoration of the covenant relationship. The election of Israel, he insists and the Lord agrees, entails the presence of God with the chosen people (verses 14-16). (Notice that there is some disorder in the report, for in verses 15-16 Moses continues to ask for what was granted in verse 14.)

If there is a moral to verses 12-17 it is a familiar one: "Ask and it shall be given you." That is particularly the case when one asks on behalf of another. God seems here only to be waiting for the request. Thus the role of mediator is recommended to the readers.

The second unit, verses 18-23, is one of the most familiar passages in the Old Testament. The sequence of request and response is simple enough. Moses asks to be shown the Lord's "glory," and the Lord gives a three-part response: (1) he will make all his "goodness" pass before Moses and make known his name, Yahweh (verse 19; cf. Exod. 3:13-15); (2) but Moses will not be allowed to see Yahweh's face, lest he die (verse 20); notice, however, that Exodus 33:11 reports that the Lord "used to speak to Moses face to face, as a man speaks to his friend"; and (3) Yahweh instructs Moses to stand on a rock and when his glory passes by, Yahweh will put Moses in a cleft of the rock, cover him with his "hand,"

and take away his hand so that Moses can see Yahweh's "back" (verses 21-23).

It is the vocabulary of this passage and its meaning that have occupied the attention of interpreters for centuries. Usually in the Bible, human beings encounter God through his voice, but here the experience is visual as well. The mystery and the danger of the scene combined with the striking anthropomorphic language in reference to God produce an encounter that is both intimate and distant. God has a "face" and a "hand" and a "back." But it is God's "glory" that Moses had asked to see, the side of God that is revealed to and experienced by human beings. Interpreting his powerful inaugural vision, Ezekiel stressed God's transcendence: "Such was the appearance of the likeness of the glory of the Lord" (Ezek. 1:28).

Human language reaches its limits when it attempts to describe God, or even to capture the experience of the encounter with the One who is both radically other and immediately present. Anthropomorphic language is fitting because God is encountered as personal, but it must not be taken literally as descriptive, and it must be balanced with the language of otherness. Even Moses, who communicated more directly with God than any other Old Testament figure, could only catch a fleeting glimpse of the Lord's "back."

Psalm 99

One of the so-called Enthronement Psalms, this reading like the others in its class (Pss. 93, 96–98) begins with the expression "Yahweh reigns" or "Yahweh is king" or, perhaps better translated, "Yahweh has become king."

Several features in the structure of this psalm are noteworthy. Three times Yahweh is affirmed as holy (verses 3, 5, 9; note Isa. 6:3). In the first two, the expression is "Holy is he" while in the last occurrence the form is "Holy is Yahweh our God." This affirmation tends to divide the psalm into three units (verses 1-3, 4-5, 6-9).

In addition, verses 5 and 9 have the quality of a refrain. In both, the first four words in Hebrew are the same: "Extol the Lord our God; [and] worship" or "exalt Yahweh our God and bow down." This refrain would subdivide the psalm in two units (verses 1-5 and 6-9).

Another way of looking at the psalm structurally is in terms of the addressee. The Deity is spoken to in verses 3-4 and 8 whereas the rest of the psalm speaks to a human audience.

From the perspective of its content, the psalm may be divided into the topics, "Yahweh's universal kingship" (verses 1-5) and "Yahweh and his people" (verses 6-9).

In the opening verses (1-2), we have three parallel assertions made about the Deity: (1) he has become king or reigns as king, (2) Yahweh sits enthroned upon the cherubim, and (3) Yahweh is great in Zion. The emphasis here is on Yahweh as the ruler of the universe who sits enthroned in the city of Jerusalem on Mt. Zion where the temple was located. The expression "enthroned upon the cherubim" draws upon the old imagery of the ark as being decorated with cherubim (see I Sam. 4:4; II Sam. 6:2; and Exod. 25:10-23, especially verses 18-20). Two large cherubim with outstretched wings were placed in the Holy of Holies of the Jerusalem temple (see I Kings 6:23-28; 8:6-8). Cherubim, in the Middle Ages, came to be considered innocent, round-faced babes. In the ancient world they were celestial-type flying figures, probably composite in character, with animal bodies, human faces, and bird wings (see Gen. 3:24; Ezek. 41:18-20). In mythology, the cherubim provided transportation for the deities. In the temple, it was assumed that God "sat enthroned" over the cherubim with the ark as his footstool.

To return to the psalm, the three assertions about the Deity are the bases for two exhortations and an affirmation. All three emphasize the universal dominion of Israel's God. The peoples of the world are called upon to tremble and the earth to quake. In verse 2*b*, the psalm affirms that Yahweh is exalted over all peoples.

This psalm, like the other psalms of enthronement, was used in the great fall festival, the Feast of Tabernacles (or booths; Succoth). This feast, held following the time of the autumn equinox in late September or early October, celebrated the creation of the world and God as king and ruler over the universe. It marked the end of the old agricultural year and the beginning of the new (see Exod. 23:16b; Deut. 16:13-15; Zech. 14:16-19).

Verses 3-4 ask God to let or declare that all peoples praise God's great and awesome name. (The Hebrew allows either translation; compare RSV with NJPSV.) Yet at the same time, God is declared to be one who loves justice and establishes equity in Jacob (= Israel). The three terms used in verse four—justice, equity, and righteousness—emphasize the establishment of just and equitable orders in society. Yahweh is not only the ruler and monarch reigning over nature but also the author and custodian of justice in society. Yahweh's holiness is reflected in this area as much as in the world of nature. If the minister wished to analyze what Yahweh's holiness required in human life, an ideal way to handle this would be to examine Leviticus 19 where holiness is the theme of the chapter. Special note should be made that it is within the context of the proclamation of God's holiness that one finds laws on social justice and an emphasis on love of the stranger as well as the neighbor (Lev. 19:17-18, 33-34).

The rehearsal of Israelite history in verses 6-8 mentions three heroes, Moses and Aaron as priests and Samuel as prophet (though no reference is made here to him as a prophet). The emphasis here is on the role of the people as intercessors. (For descriptions of their intercessory functions see Exod. 14:15; 17:11-13; 32:11-14; 32:30-34; Num. 12:13; 14:13-25 for Moses; Num. 16:44-48 for Aaron; and I Sam. 7:8-11; 12:16-25 for Samuel.)

Verse 8 emphasizes the forgiving character of God but at the same time speaks of his role as avenger or punisher of wrongdoings. If the "them" in this verse is still Moses, Aaron, and Samuel then these three had wrongdoings attributed to them that were unforgiven or were at least avenged (Moses and Aaron in Num. 20:12; Aaron in Exod. 32; Samuel in I Sam. 8:1-3 where the disobedience of his sons demands changes in the people's mode of government and the requests for a king).

Worship and bowing down before the Deity are called for as the appropriate human response (verses 5, 9). "At his footstool" and "at his holy mountain" are synonyms meaning at the temple housing the ark in Jerusalem.

Philippians 2:1-13

So accustomed are we to hearing this profound christological text within the liturgical setting of Holy Week that it may take some doing to appropriate it into the Season After Pentecost as yet another epistolary reading from Philippians. The Christ-hymn (2:5-11) has, of course, justly earned a place as the New Testament reading for the Sixth Sunday of Lent which may be observed as Passion or Palm Sunday. Consequently, it is heard in this setting every year and has been treated in the *Lent, Holy Week, Easter* volumes for Years A, B, and C. Still another part of this passage (2:9-13), which focuses on the exalted name "Lord" that Jesus received by virtue of his resurrection and ascension, serves as the second option for the New Testament reading for Holy Name of Jesus, Solemnity of Mary, Mother of God in all three years. The reader may wish to consult our remarks in that connection in *Advent, Christmas, Epiphany* for Years A, B, and C.

Thus once again the church hears this classic Pauline text, but this time within the context of the whole Philippian epistle from which selections are read over a four-week period. Accordingly, we can look at the passage within its concrete setting.

It will be recalled from our remarks last week that this was no young, fledgling church. It had existed long enough to endear itself to Paul because of its continued support of his apostolic work. But with age had come the perennial congregational enemies: internal dissent and external threat. Today's text addresses the former concern as focal.

It has a twofold structure: (1) the appeal for unity and solidarity (verses 1-4), and (2) the basis for the appeal (verses 5-11).

1. *The Appeal* (verses 1-4). First there is a series of "ifs": "If then our common life in Christ yields anything to stir the heart, any loving consolation, any sharing of the Spirit, any warmth of affection or compassion" (verse 1, NEB). Could we but assume a capacity for mutual encouragement within the fellowship where Christ is present (cf. Rom. 12:8; I Cor. 14:3); or, the presence of a compelling power to love (I Cor.

206

13:4-7); or, a genuine sense of community in which the Spirit is the prime mover and actor (II Cor. 13:14); or, the presence of "tenderness and sympathy" (JB; II Cor. 6:12; 7:15; Philem. 7, 12, 20; Col. 3:12; I John 3:17) then we could become one. We should note the "if-then" structure. First the community must possess a certain character informed by the presence of Christ. Then comes the capacity to respond in faith to the demands of the gospel.

In this case, the demands are for unity and solidarity: being "united in your convictions and united in your love, with a common purpose and a common mind" (verse 2, JB). Elsewhere Paul conceives congregational harmony as a gift from God (Rom. 15:5; cf. 12:16), yet it can be commanded (4:7; I Cor. 1:10; II Cor. 13:11; I Pet. 3:8). It is this that makes the preacher "completely happy" (verse 2, JB), or perhaps less colloquially provides a true source of joy (cf. 1:4, 18; 2:17; 4:1, 10).

And how is this achieved, this community where there is "no competition . . . no conceit . . . " where everyone is "self-effacing" (verse 3, JB; cf. Gal. 5:26; I Pet. 5:5; Rom. 12:16). By adopting a single, fundamental perspective within our congregational life: by considering the other person better than ourself, by thinking of the interests of others before we think of our own (verses 3-4). This becomes something of a cardinal principle in Paul's theology of the congregation (I Cor. 10:24, 33; also I Cor. 13:5). Whether intentional or not, this paraenetic advice is the concretization of Jesus' teaching (Matt. 7:12; 22:34-40).

2. *The Basis for the Appeal* (verses 5-11). The form of the imperative is clear enough. Not only is it clear, it is also difficult. How then to translate imperative into indicative, apostolic theory into congregational practice? Paul's answer: christologically.

He proceeds to buttress his appeal with the magnificent two-part christological hymn with its "V-shaped Christology" that rehearses the descent of Christ from above (verses 6-8) and the ascent of Christ from below (verses 9-11). But how is this hymn intended to function? Does it present Christ as *exemplar* or *enabler*? If the former, the ethical move is one of imitation, conforming our lives to the example of Christ. If the latter, the ethical response is one of appropriation, being empowered by God's work in Christ.

Here, of course, we meet a crucial exegetical choice, and it depends on how we render verse 5. One option is clearly expressed by JB: "In your minds you must be the same as Christ Jesus," hence imitation. The other option is given by NEB: "Let your bearing towards one another arise out of your life in Christ Jesus," hence appropriation through empowerment. In the one case, we take our cue from Christ and conform our life accordingly. In the other case, we become what we already are, allowing our "bearing towards one another" to "arise out of [our] life in Christ Jesus" (verse 5, NEB). The critical differences is that the one accents our achievement, the other accents God's achievement. The one sees Christian behavior as our "conforming to" an external example, while the other sees Christian behavior as our "being transformed by" an act of God.

Analysis of the structure of the hymn itself, and the various claims that are made on behalf of Christ, receive treatment in our comments elsewhere on this passage. We would refer the interested reader there.

The preacher will find much here that addresses the hard realities of congregational life. We all know the fragility of church life and the delicacy required to maintain some sense of harmony. We also know the price of harmony and unity and the trade-offs that must occur for the common good. We also know the intransigence even of the converted soul and our resistance to thinking first of the interest of others. In a word, we know the sheer difficulty of translating this Pauline vision of unity, harmony, and solidarity into real-life form. Perhaps this is why he finally moves beyond the language of human imperative to transcendent, divine action.

Matthew 21:28-32

Between the reading for last Sunday and that for today Matthew records two events which provide the context and atmosphere for 21:28-32. The first is Jesus' entry into Jerusalem (21:1-11), as a result of which, says Matthew, "all the city was stirred." The second is the cleansing of the temple (21:12-13), the event that precipitated the crisis between Jesus and those who will plot his arrest and death (21:15-16, 45-46).

Our text, then, is to be read and understood in a context of controversy and tension. We are to understand, of course, that argument and debate were common in the discussions of Scripture and tradition among religious leaders of Judaism. In fact, at one time in the rabbinic tradition, teachers worked in pairs, one liberal and one conservative, arguing before the students the fine points of the law. Even today, Judaism tends to be more vigorous and open to polemic in its conversations with God and with itself than is Christianity. In the text before us, however, the reader of Matthew is aware that the debates between Jesus and the religious authorities will have far more serious consequences. Three times Jesus has predicted his death in Jerusalem (16:21; 17:22-23; 20:17-19).

The controversies in which our text is couched are recorded in 21:23–22:14. The opposition to Jesus consists of "the chief priests and the elders of the people" (verse 23). The substance of this entire section consists of Jesus' responses to the question put to him, "By what authority are you doing these things, and who gave you this authority?" (verse 23). While we may, out of faith in Jesus as Son of God, consider the question out of order, it was not. It was an appropriate question by those responsible for the faith, morals, and institutional life of Judaism. The "these things" of their question is best taken as referring not solely to the disruption of the temple but to the whole of Jesus' ministry in Jerusalem which had stirred the city and attracted to Jesus large favorable crowds (verses 14, 46).

Jesus' response to his opponents consists of two parts. First, he counters with a question about the authority of the ministry of John the Baptist (verses 24-27), a question his interrogators were unwilling to answer. Second, Jesus took the offensive, offering three parables (21:28-32; 33-43; 22:1-14). These three parables will occupy us today and the next two Sundays.

The first parable (verses 28-32) is found in Matthew alone. The parable proper ends at verse 31a with verses 31b-32 serving as commentary not only on the parable but on the real issue imbedded in verses 23-27. This is to say, Jesus' opponents had already demonstrated who and what they were in their response to John the Baptist. They had resisted and rejected John's proclamation of the kingdom and call for repentance; there is no reason to expect any different answer now that Jesus is the preacher. The issue is not Jesus' authority; the issue is how one responds to God's call to repentance and invitation into the kingdom. Before such urgent preaching, ecclesiastical debates over clerical roles and credentials are treated as so much smoke screen.

The parable says that responses to God are of two kinds: that of the person who has said no but who repents and whose life says yes; and that of the person who says yes but whose life says no. Jesus' opponents represent the latter; tax collectors and harlots, the former (verses 31*b*-32; see Luke 7:29-30). By admitting that those who say no but then repent are the ones who do the father's will, the chief priests and elders indict themselves (verse 31*a*). They know the necessity of repentance; they know God accepts the penitent. Their resistance to John and to Jesus is not due to lack of knowledge but to lack of trust. They did not believe the truth about themselves and the truth about God. Those who do believe, regardless of past behavior, enter the kingdom of God first.

Proper 22

Sunday Between October 2 and 8 Inclusive

Numbers 27:12-23; Psalm 81:1-10; Philippians 3:12-21; Matthew 21:33-43

After a succession of thirteen Old Testament readings from the book of Exodus, today we have one of the rare uses in the Common Lectionary of a text from the book of Numbers—the narrative account in which Joshua is ordained as the successor of Moses. The responsorial psalm is a didactic psalm used in the celebration of the Feast of Tabernacles. It opens in a festive mood and reminds the worshipers of God's deliverance even as it cautions against the worship of foreign gods. The New Testament reading comes from the polemical section of Philippians in which Paul stresses the unrealized dimension of the Christian calling, urges his readers to imitate him and keep their eye out for those who oppose the way of the cross. The Gospel reading presents us with the parable of the vineyard in which the tenants mistreat the servants of the householder, finally kill his son, and reap the consequences of their misguided actions.

Numbers 27:12-23

Today's reading concerns the continuity of leadership for the people of God. Like so much of the material concerning Moses, this passage consists primarily of the report of dialogue between the Lord and Moses. The exception is verses 22-23, which report that Moses did what the Lord told him to do. While the passage is a continuous account, it has two parts. The first (verses 12-14) is the Lord's speech to Moses about his death and the second (verses 15-23) concerns the commissioning of Joshua as Moses' successor. The first section comes from the Priestly document from the time of the Babylonian captivity or later, but doubtless rests on ancient tradition. The account of the installation of Joshua, which is repeated in Deuteronomy 32:48-52, probably depends upon Deuteronomic tradition.

In the present context, the Lord's reminder of Moses' death serves to introduce the need for a successor. In itself, however, the most interesting point is the fact that Moses is not to be allowed to lead the people into the Promised Land. The structure of sin and punishment comes into play as the theological interpretation of what must have been well known in Israel, namely, that Moses died and was buried in the plains of Moab before the occupation of the Promised Land. Our passage alludes to the incident reported in Numbers 20:1-13. In 27:14 Moses is accused of rebelling against the Lord and failing "to sanctify" him. Numbers 20:12 indicts Moses, along with Aaron, for failing to believe in the Lord. However, in neither case is the specific sin identified, nor does Moses protest or ask for forgiveness. He is shown to accept the punishment without challenge.

Knowing that he will die before the promise of the land has been fulfilled, Moses asks the Lord to appoint a successor. Moses gives what is in effect a job description: This man will be "over the congregation," "go out" and "come in before them," "lead them out and bring them in," and be to them like a shepherd to the sheep (verses 16-17). Most of the distinctive terminology of this description is that of military leadership, consistent with the main traditional functions of Moses' successor. In responding to Moses, Yahweh names Joshua and notes a single qualification for the position: "a man in whom is the spirit" (verse 18). Although it is not defined, this "spirit" certainly is a gift for leadership given by God.

In the books of Exodus through Second Kings the history of Israel is organized to some extent in terms of different kinds of leaders for the people of God. First, the leader during the foundational period of the Exodus and the making of the covenant was, of course, Moses, who has no peers. Second, the leader during the settlement of the Promised Land was Joshua, who is shown to parallel his predecessor in many ways. For example, as Moses led the people through the sea, Joshua led them across the Jordan and as Moses was the mediator of the original covenant, Joshua led the people in a renewal of the covenant at Shechem (Josh. 24). However, Numbers 27:20 indicates that Moses is to invest Joshua with "some" of his authority, and while Moses communicated directly with God, Joshua is to have the chief priest Eleazar seek God's will. The third period, that of the judges, is viewed generally as chaotic: "In those days there was no king in Israel; every man did what was right in his own eyes" (Judg. 21:25). The fourth and final era defined by leadership was that of the monarchy.

What the Lord commands and Moses performs in Numbers 27:17-23 is an ordination service. The leader is designated by Yahweh, and authority is conferred upon him by Moses. The ritual for the transfer of authority—to take effect at the death of Moses—is by the laying on of hands. The participation of others is important. First there is the chief priest, Eleazar, who has inherited the role from his father Aaron. Then "all the congregation" are present, acknowledging the authority of Joshua. Thus even when leadership in Israel seems such an individual matter between leaders and God, corporate participation is taken for granted.

So long as the people of God are in the world, they will need human leaders. Continuity of that leadership through history, consistent with the needs of particular times and places, is important. Any leader, and any form of leadership, has limits. Old Testament tradition remembers that there was no leader as important as Moses. Still, the time came for him to hand over the role to another. Moreover, Moses himself acknowledged that it was time for another to take his place and to lead the people in different ways.

Psalm 81:1-10

An association of this psalm with the reading from Numbers 27:12-23 can be seen in various ways. First of all, there is a reference to Meribah which also occurs in the Numbers text. The episode at Meribah is twice reported in the Old Testament. In Exodus 17:1-7, Moses is commanded to strike the rock and does so to provide water for the murmuring Hebrews. In Numbers 20:1-13, Moses is commanded to "tell" the rock to yield its water. When he strikes it twice (verse 11), either the striking or the numbers of strikes is taken as unbelief. Second, the psalm is a call to obedience which is appropriate in connection with the selection and ordination of Joshua as Moses' successor. Third, rebellion against Yahweh is a theme in both texts.

Psalm 81 was a widely used psalm in Judean worship. Seven psalms were selected for singing in the temple during the course of a week. These were Psalm 24 (Sunday), 48 (Monday), 82 (Tuesday), 94 (Wednesday), 81 (Thursday), 93 (Friday), and 92 (Saturday). Thus this psalm was utilized throughout the year. Its choice for such usage was probably based on the psalm's call for obedience.

Psalm 81 has frequently been interpreted as a prophetic liturgy utilized in worship to remind the people of the necessity to obey the law or even as part of the covenant renewal ceremony. In such an analysis, verses 1-3 call for the assembly to offer praise and worship to God; verses 4-5*b* provide the reasons for worship; and verses 5*c*-16 contain the prophetic sermon spoken as a direct address of the Deity to the people, as was common in prophetic speech.

Verse 3 connects the psalm's original usage with a festival or feast day. The new moon was the first day of the month in a lunar calendar. The full moon, or the fifteenth of the month, is here stipulated as the feast day. The soundings of the trumpets to mark the first day of the seventh month is commanded by Leviticus 23:23-25. This is the day that was and still is celebrated as Rosh Hashanah or New Year's day. (The term actually means "the head of the year.") The fifteenth of the month marked the beginning of the Feast of Tabernacles or Booths (Succoth) which lasted for seven days (Lev. 23:33-36).

One of the features associated with the Feast of Tabernacles, according to the legislation in Deuteronomy, was the reading of the book of Deuteronomy. According to Deuteronomy 31:10-13, Moses commanded, "At the end of every seven years, at the set time of the year of release, at the feast of booths, when all Israel comes to appear before [Yahweh] your God at the place which he will choose, you shall read

214

this law before all Israel in their hearing." Psalm 81 may be seen as part of the admonition to observe the law that formed a part of the great autumn feast.

The opening verses of this psalm call for various forms of praise: singing, shouting, and the playing of various music instruments. See II Samuel 6:12-19 for some of the celebration that went on at festival times. The rabbis noted that verse one refers to the God of Jacob, and they questioned why only Jacob or none of the other patriarchs are mentioned. The answer they arrived at was in terms of Balaam's statement in Numbers 23:21. "Why did Balaam choose to mention Jacob—not Abraham and not Isaac—only Jacob? Because Balaam saw that out of Abraham had come base metal—Ishmael and all the children of Keturah; and he also saw that out of Isaac there had come Esau and his princes. But Jacob was all holiness."

The motivation for celebrating the festival is given in verses 4-5, namely, God commanded it and established it as a statue, ordinance, and decree.

The divine oracle consists of two types of material: reviews of the past (verses 6-7, 10*a*, 11-12) and admonitions to obedience (verses 8-9, 10*b*, 13-16). The reviews of the past, on the one hand, stress the redemptive action of Yahweh emphasizing the deliverance from Egypt and the testing in the wilderness. On the other hand, the reviews highlight the people's unfaithfulness to which God responded by giving them over to their stubborn hearts and allowing them to follow their own counsels (verse 12: a good sermon topic!). The admonitions call upon Israel to hear, to listen, to have no other gods (see Exod. 20:3; Deut. 5:7), to be receptive to divine blessings; all with the promise that such responses will be rewarded abundantly.

Philippians 3:12-21

Today's New Testament reading overlaps with two epistolary lections used in Year C: the Second Sunday of Lent (Phil. 3:17–4:1) and the Fifth Sunday of Lent (Phil. 3:8-14). The reader may wish to consult our remarks in *Lent, Holy Week, Easter* for Year C.

As part of the semicontinuous reading of the Epistle to the Philippians, however, this text should be set within the overall context of chapter 3. With 3:1 there is a clear break in the letter literarily ("Finally, my brethren . . . "). With this comes a radical change in both mood and theme. Even though there are earlier references to detractors (1:15-17) and opponents (1:28), the caricature here (3:2, 4, 18-19) is especially harsh. The theological exposition of a "righteousness from God that depends on faith" (3:9), as opposed to self-achieved righteousness "based on law" (3:9), introduces a new theme into the letter that is strongly reminiscent of Romans and Galatians (though, cf. 1:11). The entire chapter (3:1–4:1) may even have existed as a separate letter, or a fragment of a Pauline Letter, that was sent to the Philippians on a separate occasion when Paul sought to address directly the threat of outside opponents. The mood, then, is thoroughly polemical, though the section ends on a note of affectionate reassurance (4:1).

Today's text consists of the last half of this major section and follows Paul's polemic against those who put their confidence "in the flesh" (3:4), his rehearsal of the pedigree in which he once placed so much stock (3:5-6), and the great exchange that took place "for the sake of Christ" (3:7). It was a trade between two conceptions of righteousness: between a righteousness measured by one's capacity to keep the law, hence a self-generated, self-measured righteousness, and a righteousness that comes from God as a gift to those with faith in Christ (3:8-9). It was a trade between righteousness construed as human achievement and righteousness experienced as divine gift, between righteousness that finds confidence in past performance and righteousness that finds confidence in future possibility (3:10-11).

Our text for today may be treated in two parts. The first part (verses 12-16) sketches the *critical perspective* of genuinely "mature" existence, while the second part (Verses 17-21) sketches the *critical choice* between two life-styles.

The Critical Perspective (verses 12-16). The dominant theme of these verses is "not yet," the perspective of unrealized existence. Paul eschews all claims to full attainment and realized perfection (verse 12). His experience of the fullness of Christ is still partial, even though Christ's "seizure" of him is complete and final (verse 12). What Christ has done, he has done completely and finally: Christ's work upon Paul is one of full comprehension, absolute knowing, complete ownership. Consequently, it is an "upward call of God in Christ Jesus" (verse 14); it comes from without, from beyond, as a result of what God has already done in Christ (cf. Heb. 3:1). To be sure, we are caught up in our pursuit of Christ just as the sprinter strains "forward to what lies ahead" (verse 13; cf. I Cor. 9:24). The thrust can only be forward toward future realization not backward toward past achievement (3:10-11). The one who plows with a backward glance is not fit for the kingdom of heaven (Luke 9:62).

This is the perspective of the genuinely "mature," the "perfect" (*teleioi*, verse 15). This is likely a slap against those self-professed "perfect" who know only the life of "already" and are uncomfortable before the "not yet" (cf. I Cor. 3:1-3; 14:20). There were those in the early church for whom resurrection had to be a present reality, fully experienced here and now, something to be clutched not attained (cf. II Tim. 2:18; cf. I Cor. 15:12). The genuinely mature recognize their own partiality (I Cor. 13:9-10). The way to "perfect" wisdom and knowledge is to admit to our own folly and ignorance (I Cor. 3:18). To know truly is to confess that God can still reveal more truth to us (verse 15). There does exist a higher Christian wisdom but it comes from God, not ourselves (I Cor. 2:6-16).

Yet maturity of this sort does not lapse into paralysis of the will: "Only let us hold true to what we have attained" (verse 16). Even though we may not have attained everything, we have at least experienced something of the fullness of Christ. Here we are called to live within our own partiality, recognizing the "not yet-ness" of our existence. As Paul insists elsewhere, "We have this treasure in earthen vessels" (II Cor. 4:7). Finally, we must see that God's transcendent power works amidst the fragility of human existence. Imperfection is the crucible within which the work of God is carried out.

The critical perspective offered here, then, is that "the righteousness from God that depends on faith" is a process not an achievement. It moves toward the fullness of God's future. It does not rely on the fullness of past human performance. To be "mature in Christ" is to recognize the partiality of our own existence. *The Critical Choice* (verses 17-21). This second section opens with the call to imitation, specifically for the imitation of Paul's own example. Before looking at this exhortation more closely, we should notice the structure. First, there is the exhortation: the call to imitation. Second, two types of examples are sketched, one negative—the way of enemies of the cross (verses 18-19)—the other positive—the way of citizens of heaven (verses 20-21). Third, the exhortation is restated in a different, even bolder form (4:1).

Paul's exhortation here conforms to a well-known form of exhortation used among Greek and Roman moralists, who often charged their readers (or hearers) to follow certain forms of behavior and then illustrated their appeal by providing concrete examples, both negatively and positively.

We are not surprised, then, to find Paul frequently urging his readers to follow his own example (I Cor. 4:16; 11:1; Phil. 4:9; Gal. 4:12). It was quite acceptable for a teacher to present himself as an example for his students to follow; or, for a parent to do the same for children. Moreover, we have instances where early Christians are said to have followed the example of others: of Paul himself (I Thess. 1:6); of other Christians, especially who suffered on behalf of the faith (I Thess. 2:14-15), but also those who earned their keep by physical labor (II Thess. 3:7-9); Christian leaders (Heb. 6:12; 13:7); of Christ (I Cor. 11:1; I Pet. 2:21; possibly Phil. 2:5-11); and of God (Eph. 5:1). Indeed, it was expected that Christians would be exemplary in their behavior in all respects (I Tim. 4:12; Titus 2:7).

It is not unexpected, then, when Paul urges his readers to look about themselves for examples of commendable behavior (verse 17).

First, the negative example is sketched—those who are "enemies of the cross of Christ" (verse 18). This would include those who are enemies of the cross ideologically, that is, those who find the essential message of the gospel repulsive, uncompelling, and intellectually inconceivable (cf.

I Cor. 1:18-25). They are further described as edging toward their own destruction (cf. II Cor. 11:15; II Pet. 2:1), as being self-indulgent (cf. Rom. 16:18; II Tim. 3:4), as glorying in what is shameful (cf. Hos. 4:7), as being mind-bent on earthly things (cf. Col. 3:2). It is an outlook alien to the cross, which stands for self-giving not self-gratification, response to the divine not clinging to the earthly, leaning into God's future not our own. It is a way to be avoided.

Second, the positive example—those who are citizens of a heavenly commonwealth (verses 20-21). The cast of the eye here is upward, toward the "heavenly places" where Christ dwells in exaltation (Eph. 2:6) and to which the Christian life is directed (Col. 3:1). Elsewhere, it is depicted as the heavenly Jerusalem, Mount Zion (Heb. 11:10; 12:22; 13:14; Gal. 4:26; Rev. 5:11; 21:2).

With this portrait, we return to a theme mentioned earlier (verse 14)—it is the future not the past that beckons (cf. I Cor. 1:7; I Tim. 6:14; II Tim. 1:10; Titus 2:11, 13; 3:6; II Pet. 1:11). And the hope that is sketched is one where genuine transformation will occur, where our "partial existence" is transformed into a resplendent form of existence (I Cor. 15:43, 49, 53; Rom. 8:29; 12:2; II Cor. 3:18; I John 3:2). It is a transformation accomplished through divine power (verse 21; cf. Eph. 1:19-22; I Cor. 15:27).

As we can see, it is difficult to separate verses 12-21 from the chapter as a whole. The critical perspective offered in verses 12-16 and the critical choice between competing outlooks and life-styles sketched in verses 17-21 flow directly from the earlier theological exposition. To be sure, these are sentiments expressed in the heat of debate, and their intention is polemical in their original setting, but they transcend that moment of conflict as they urge us to a life of faith that is compelling even if it is partial.

Matthew 21:33-43

Our text falls within the controversy section, 21:23–22:14. As we have already seen, the controversy is between Jesus and the chief priests and elders of the people (21:23). Jesus is quizzed about his authority and his credentials, and he responds with a question concerning their opinion of John's authority (verses 24-27). Following this counter, Jesus takes the offensive, pointing out that the real issue is not his authority but the response of his interrogators to his preaching and that of John which called for repentance and the bearing of fruit appropriate to the kingdom of God (3:7-10; 7:20-21; 7:24-27; 35:31-46). Jesus' indictment of his critics is presented in three parables (21:28-32, 33-43; 22:1-14). Our lection is the second of the three.

Matthew has placed the parable immediately after the parable in verses 28-32. Both are vineyard stories and concern obedience and so have natural kinship. However, both Mark (12:1) and Luke (20:9) separate this parable from preceding material. Matthew has not only given the story a thematic context, but added commentary. Verse 43 makes it clear that the subject is not a vineyard but the kingdom of God. The reader had known this from the outset, however, because the parable opens with direct use of the image of Israel as God's vineyard from Isaiah 5:1-7. In other words, the story of a vineyard is not really a story of a vineyard; the issue is God and the people of God. This is made even more clear by the insertion of a quotation from Psalm 118:22-23 (verse 42), which concerns not a vineyard but a building, and the rejected stone that God made the head of the corner. Why this insertion which evokes a different image? Because, the change of image notwithstanding, the quotation corroborates the parable's climax: the tenants cast out and kill the owner's son (verse 39). By this time, of course, it is clear to the reader that the story is about the rejection and killing of Jesus, preceded by the beating and killing of the prophets whom God had sent, calling for fruitfulness among God's people.

With these comments we have as much as called verses 33-40 an allegory and not a parable. A parable is a self-contained story, the meaning of which is found within its own actions and characterizations. An allegory has its meaning in events and actions outside itself to which it refers. Our text clearly is referring to the rejection of the prophets, the killing of Jesus, the punishment of the tenants (destruction of Jerusalem) and the transfer of the vineyard to the Gentiles. Since this involves developments dated years after Jesus' lifetime, apparently Matthew has taken a parable of Jesus, interpreted it in light of post-Easter developments and the shift from a Jewish to a Gentile mission, and given to his readers this story. Many scholars believe Luke (20:9-18) preserves a version closer to Jesus' own telling, and perhaps the Gospel of Thomas (Logion 65) is even closer to what Jesus said. Whatever the case may be, Matthew here clearly shows us what Scripture and preaching are all about: bringing the tradition forward to address a new condition facing the church.

But the question now is, Why did Matthew tell this? Is this an anti-synagogue polemic? Is this gross triumphalism, dancing over the grave of those who lost their tenancy in God's kingdom by fruitlessness and efforts at taking over the arena of God's rule? Is the reader to applaud (we now have the kingdom) or weep (others have lost the kingdom)?

There is no cheap shot here. There is, to be sure, some encouragement to those who have, at great price, followed a crucified Messiah. But beyond that is a warning; unless the new tenants (and Christians are tenants, not owners) bear fruit, the vineyard may again be transferred. The owner of the vineyard is still expecting righteous living, human caring, and courageous witnessing; these three being Matthew's understanding of "fruit." The preacher of this text is not to be a teller of stories about disobedient Jews but a listener to stories told to disobedient Christians.

221

Proper 23

Sunday Between October 9 and 15 Inclusive

Deuteronomy 34:1-12; Psalm 135:1-14; Philippians 4:1-9; Matthew 22:1-14

With last week's Old Testament lesson reporting the ordination of Joshua as Moses' successor, this week's selection from Deuteronomy provides a natural sequel. It is the account of the death of Moses, accompanied by a fitting obituary of him as Israel's peerless prophet, and the passing of the torah to Joshua. Psalm 135 is a hymn of praise composed of reminiscences from other psalms or biblical texts that rehearse the mighty acts of Yahweh. Especially central is the emphasis on the deliverance of Israel in the Exodus and Yahweh as the performer of signs and wonders against Pharaoh. The New Testament lesson is the last of four semicontinuous readings from the Epistle to the Philippians. It consists of concluding exhortations that lay special stress on rejoicing, the nearness of the Lord, and the reassuring nature of God's peace. In the Gospel reading we have Jesus' parable of the marriage feast in which the host's invitation is refused by the invited guests and is thus extended to a wider, more receptive audience. It concludes on a note of rejection as the man dressed in improper attire is turned away.

Deuteronomy 34:1-12

The events described in this passage, the death and burial of Moses, define the book of Deuteronomy as a whole. In its final form, the book is the report of the last words and actions of Moses. Most of it is then the last will and testament of the one who led Israel out of Egypt, through the wilderness to the border of the land promised to the ancestors. And what a testament it is: the law, the covenant, and a series of sermons on the law.

By no means did all this material attributed to Moses arise at the same time and in the same place. Some of the individual laws are indeed quite ancient, but it is difficult if not impossible to establish their provenance. The core of the book, chapters 12–26, is identified with the reform of King Josiah in 621 B.C., but some of the materials arose earlier in the oral tradition. The initial and concluding chapters of the book come from the latest strata, associated with the deuteronomistic historian(s) who composed the account of Israel's past from the time of Moses to the Babylonian Exile. Chapter 34 comes from the latest strata of the book, from the deuteronomistic historian who worked about 560 B.C. Verses 9-12 are perhaps an even later addition to the book. Thus our passage was composed centuries after the events it reports, by and for people who had experienced a long history of living with the heritage they believed Moses had left them.

Deuteronomy 34 is the immediate narrative continuation of Deuteronomy 32:48-52, in which Yahweh commands Moses to ascend Mount Nebo and survey the Promised Land. The blessing of Moses in Deuteronomy 33 has been inserted into the previously established story. Although a new era in the history of Israel begins with the death of Moses, there is no sharp break at the end; Joshua 1 continues directly where our passage ends.

The book of Deuteronomy mentions over and over again the point that was a subject of last week's Old Testament lesson (Num. 27:12-23; cf. Num. 20:1-13), that Moses was not to be allowed to enter the Promised Land (Deut. 1:37; 4:21; 3:27) and that he died in Moab "according to the word of the Lord" (Deut. 34:5). Given the author's presupposition that this fact was punishment for sin, it was considered an act of grace that Moses was allowed to see the land, an act not to be shared by the original wilderness generation of sinners (Deut. 1:34-39). In order to view the land, Moses ascends a mountain in the land of Moab in Transjordan, opposite Jericho; verse 1 contains two traditions about either the place or its name, Mount Nebo or Mount Pisgah. Recalling his promise to the ancestors (verse 4), Yahweh shows Moses the sweep of the land, generally to the north, the west, and then the south. Actually, there is no mountain in Moab from which one can see all the way to the Mediterranean, the "western sea" of verse 2. Some commentators have seen in this visual survey an allusion to a form of legal conveyance of the land (cf. Deut. 3:27; Gen 13:14 ff.).

In the initial and brief notice of Moses' death, the reporter gives a relatively modest epitath that describes him when he died: he was one hundred and twenty years old, and "his eye was not dim, nor his natural force abated" (verse 7). Both the literal and figurative meaning of the first phrase is relatively clear; his eyesight and "vision" were strong. The reference to undiminished "natural force" is unusual, and probably refers to sexual power, and is thus a figure of speech for vitality. To some extent this characterization conflicts with what Moses said on his one hundred and twentieth birthday, "I am no longer able to go out and come in" (Deut. 31:2).

It is a curious note that "he [that is, the Lord] buried him" (verse 6). This tradition must be based on the fact that there was no knowledge of the place where Moses was buried.

The final paragraph (verses 9-12) marks the transition from Moses to Joshua and makes a final comment upon the special relationship between Yahweh and Moses. Joshua successfully assumes the reigns of leadership because the gift of the spirit had been transferred to him by Moses (verse 9); that is, Joshua has authority indirectly through Moses. What had been identified only as "the spirit" in Numbers 27:18 (see the comment on last week's Old Testament lesson) is now called "the spirit of wisdom."

Moses is both identified with and distinguished from the usual prophetic role: "There has not arisen a prophet since in Israel like Moses" (verse 10). His functions were quite different from the classical prophets such as Amos, Hosea, Isaiah, Jeremiah, and the others, who announced the word of God concerning the immediate future. What such prophets shared with Moses was the fact that they were mediators of the divine word and will to their people. Thus Deuteronomy 18:15-22 can anticipate future prophets who will be like Moses. What was different was the mode of revelation to and through these figures. While ordinary (!) prophets would see visions and have auditions of the word of God, Moses was the only one "whom the Lord knew face to face" (verse 10; cf.

Deut. 33:11). Not only that, the mighty power of God was manifest through him in "all the great and terrible deeds which Moses wrought in the sight of all Israel" (verse 12).

In no sense, then, does our reporter recommend Moses as an example to be followed. Because of his special and direct relationship with God that is impossible. All this praise of Moses is rather to commend the words attributed to him as authoritative and to be followed. Thus even the report of the death of Moses serves for these writers a homiletical purpose, to urge faithfulness to the covenant that Moses established and obedience to the laws that he taught.

Psalm 135:1-14

Except for the confessional statement in verse 13, addressed to the Deity, this psalm has all the qualities of a hymn. The opening (verses 1-3) and closing units (verses 19-21) call upon various components among the people to praise and bless God—the priestly classes (the "servants of Yahweh" in verse 1 and "house of Aaron/Levi" in verses 19b and 20a) and laypersons (those standing in the temple in verse 2 and "house of Israel/you that fear Yahweh" in verses 19a and 20b). Verses 4-12 and 14 give the reasons for praise. Verse 13 tends to break the scheme but may be seen as the congregational response to the personal affirmation in verses 5-12.

The content and liturgical directions clearly indicate use in worship services. The distinction between the plural imperatives in verses 1-3 and 19-20 and the first person affirmation in verses 5 following could be explained on the basis of a congregation and either the king or high priest jointly participating in worship.

The immediately preceding collection of psalms (120–134) are pilgrim songs utilized as worshipers made their way to Jerusalem and the temple. Psalm 135 may have been placed in this context as sort of a response to this collection or as a psalm to be sung by the pilgrims within worship services of a particular festival.

After the initial, short reason for praise in verse 4 that affirms the people's election by Yahweh and their existence as a special possession (see Exod. 19:5; Deut. 7:6; Mal. 3:17), the psalm turns to two expanded reasons for praise.

The first stresses Yahweh as the lord of all (verses 5-7). (1) Yahweh is above all gods, (2) is able to do as he pleases, everywhere, and (3) controls the climate. The emphasis on clouds, rain, lightning, and winds could indicate that this psalm was used in the fall festival which anticipated the beginning of the rainy season (in October) and the plowing and sowing that followed.

The second expanded reason focuses on Yahweh as lord of history. Two strands of tradition are noted. Yahweh worked wonders and signs in Egypt (verses 8-9) and destroyed Israel's enemies in granting the nation the land as a heritage (verses 10-12).

Philippians 4:1-9

Part of today's epistolary lection (4:4-9) also serves as the New Testament lesson twice in Year C: the Third Sunday of Advent and Thanksgiving Day. The reader may wish to consult our remarks in *Advent, Christmas, Epiphany* and *After Pentecost* for Year C.

Today's text consists of "last words," final reminders from the apostle to his beloved readers. The tone of the passage is endearing and reassuring, yet it is filled with straight talk and clear directives. We are hearing Paul the father, pastor, and teacher give words of lasting advice. As is often the case in words of farewell, we have a miscellany of exhortations, and homiletical possibilities are as numerous as the advice is diverse. Any attempt to systematize is somewhat artificial. Hence we can treat the passage as it is divided into paragraphs in the RSV.

Standing Firm in the Lord (verse 1). This call for steadfastness and fidelity arises directly from the preceding remarks, and may in fact be taken with 3:12-21. The language is intimate. Paul is unabashed in his love and yearning for this church with whom he has had a long-standing relationship. They are his "joy and crown," to be counted among his fondest memories (1:4, 18; cf. I Thess. 2:19; 3:9). The tone here resonates with the effusive language of the opening thanksgiving (1:3-11).

His advice to his beloved brethren is simple and straightforward: "stand firm . . . in the Lord." It is advice he commonly gives his churches, often as a parting word. It may suggest being alert and courageous (I Cor. 16:13), faithful in the pursuit of Christian freedom (Gal. 5:1), steadfast in the face of suffering (I Thess. 3:8), responsible and obedient to the received tradition (II Thess. 2:15), and unified in purpose (Phil. 1:27). In this particular context, especially when taken with what precedes, it probably suggests being resistant to the advances of opponents who live as "enemies of the cross of Christ" (3:18-19).

Agreeing in the Lord (verses 2-3). Within the space of two verses we are introduced to four persons, three of them named, who belong to Paul's circle of co-workers. It is well known, of course, that he carried out his apostolic work assisted by a large number of such colleagues (cf. Rom. 16). What becomes clear, however, is that working together in the Lord has put a strain on the relationship between two of them, Euodia and Syntyche. We do not know any more than this, nor need we, for it is a situation we all know: two colleagues striving together soon find themselves disagreeing, pulling against each other, finally at odds. Their common task that once bound them together has given way to their separate agendas. They are no more two working as one, but two working as two.

Paul's response is, "Agree in the Lord" (verse 2). Find common ground again in your mutual participation in the One who transcends both of you. Such harmony is, after all, a gift from God (Rom. 15:5), yet it can be enjoined as a form of appropriate Christian behavior (Rom. 12:16; I Cor. 1:10; II Cor. 13:11; I Pet. 3:8).

There is a further element in the remedy: ask a third party, the "true yokefellow" (verse 2) to mediate, to bring about reconciliation (II Cor. 5:18-20). Remind them of the size of the endeavor and the number of others who are cooperating in the venture (Rom. 15:30).

Rejoicing in the Lord (verses 4-7). Once again, the exhortation is anchored "in the Lord." We first hear the

227

familiar call to rejoice (2:18; 3:1; cf. I Thess. 5:16). Then comes the call for "tolerance" (JB), "magnanimity" (NEB), "gentleness" (NIV), or "forbearance" (RSV). One test of the righteous person is whether he or she can be rattled by the insults and taunts of the ungodly (Wisd. of Sol. 2:19; cf. Titus 3:2).

Part and parcel of such rejoicing is being able to pray, which includes giving thanks as well as making petitions to the Lord (verse 6). To be "in the Lord," that is, to be Christian, is to pray. Prayer is the earmark of Christian existence (Acts 2:42; Rom. 12:12; I Thess. 5:17-18; Eph. 6:18; Col. 4:2; I Tim. 2:1). Here it is seen as the antidote to anxiety (Matt. 6:25-34; Luke 12:22-32; I Pet. 5:7; I Tim. 6:6, 8).

And what provides the basis of our confidence? Reassurance that "the Lord is at hand" (verse 5)—temporally (1:10; James 5:8-9; Heb. 10:37) and spatially (Ps. 145:18). The Lord's presence is experienced as peace, understood not merely as the absence of strife, but as the state of positive well-being and fullness—an eschatological gift that we begin to experience now (John 14:27; Col. 3:15).

The Contours of the Christian Mind (verse 8). The sentiments commended here are as Stoic as anything we find in Paul. They represent the finest aspirations of pagan thought. "Excellence" (*arete,* verse 8) is unusual here because it is Paul's single use of a term that abounds in Greek thought. What is called for here is to "think about these things" (verse 8). Seen one way, this appears to be rationality pure and simple, but taken with Paul's thought as a whole it suggests a way of thinking that goes hand-in-glove with moral transformation in Christ (Rom. 12:1-2; II Cor. 10:5).

Embodying the Tradition (verse 9). Once again, Paul calls on his readers to imitate him (cf. 3:17; cf. I Cor. 4:16; 11:1). But the notion is expanded here to include "learning and receiving" what is taught *as well as* emulating what they have heard and seen him do. Passing on the tradition must finally occur at both the intellectual and moral level, combining both message and messenger. The witness must finally come to life in the witnesses (II Tim. 2:2). Teaching and doing, word and deed, are interlocked in the genuine transmission of the faith (Acts 1:1).

As noted earlier, this text is a sampler. The advice is diverse, yet there are some common themes that the preacher may profitably explore. Among other things, one might explore what is possible "in the Lord" and the difference this stance makes as opposed to other stances not directly anchored in one's experience of Christ.

Matthew 22:1-14

The parable of the marriage feast (22:1-13; verse 14 is a typical Matthean proverb of the type used to conclude stories but which do not deal precisely with the messages of the stories) is the last of the three parables against Israel's leaders, set by Matthew in the context of Jesus' final days in Jerusalem.

This parable is strikingly similar to the one preceding it, the story of the wicked tenants (verses 33-43). The king parallels the vineyard owner, the guests refusing the invitation parallel the wicked tenants, and so on. In both, waves of servants are sent; in both, servants are mistreated and killed; in both, severe punishment is meted out; and in both, something is expected of the newly invited. Both stories conform to historical events: Israel's mistreatment of the prophets, Israel's rejection of early Christian missionaries, the destruction of Jerusalem, and the movement of the church toward a Gentile constituency. Today, as last Sunday, we are listening not to a parable but to an allegory. The meaning lies outside the story in those persons and events to which it refers. As is true of most allegories, the story loses its lifelike qualities in order to make evident its point; for example, troops execute guests and burn a city while a prepared meal is waiting. Those brought in off the street are described in moral terms: the bad and the good (verse 10). And the man thrown out is not simply rejected; he is cast into outer darkness, the place of weeping and the gnashing of teeth (verse 13). Matthew is not being subtle at all; the man lands not in the street but in hell. In other words, Matthew is not talking of a banquet and guests but of God, the kingdom, Jews, Gentiles, and the demands of the kingdom life.

Both Luke (14:16-24) and Thomas (Logion 64) tell simpler

and perhaps earlier versions of the banquet story. This is not to say that they preserve exactly Jesus' own telling of it. On the contrary, Luke's fingerprints are on his version as Matthew's are on his. For example, Luke is in character when he invites to the banquet "the poor and maimed and blind and lame" (14:21), just as Matthew is when he refers to those off the streets as the "bad and good." Those who argue that the parable originally ended at verse 10, verses 11-14 being Matthew's addition, miss the fact that the entire story, verses 1-14, is now Matthew's story. His concerns are evident in the telling from beginning to end, not only in the ending.

Whatever may have been the focus of the story when first told, in Matthew it is the final, the eschatological banquet. The story assumes the banquet occurs *after* the Jewish rejection, *after* the destruction of Jerusalem, *after* the Gentile ingathering. Here as in other parables (the weeds, 13:24-30; the ten maidens, 24:1-13; the talents, 25:14-30, and others), Matthew calls attention to the final judgment, no minor theme for this Evangelist.

And what is the basis of judgment? It is not simply whether one says yes or no to the invitation. The invitation is most gracious; all are invited, both bad and good. But just because all are invited does not mean there are no standards, no expectations of the guests. A wedding garment (kingdom talk for new life, righteous conduct) is expected. (The preacher will want to avoid dipping into Luke's guest list of the poor and crippled and then raising the issue of those who could not afford a wedding garment. Luke's guest list and Luke's concerns are not Matthew's.) Matthew knew how easily grace can melt into permissiveness; he knew that for those who presume upon grace, forgiveness does not fulfill righteousness but negates it. Matthew apparently is addressing a church that had lost the distinction between accepting all persons and condoning all behavior. Those who tend to wallow in grace, to sever sanctification from justification, may be startled by the king's question, "Friend, how did you get in here without a wedding garment?" (verse 12).

Proper 24

Sunday Between October 16 and 22 Inclusive

Ruth 1:1-19a; Psalm 146; I Thessalonians 1:1-10; Matthew 22:15-22

Today marks the beginning of two new sets of readings. The Old Testament lesson is the first of three semicontinuous readings from the Book of Ruth, while the New Testament lesson is the first of five semicontinuous readings from the Epistle of First Thessalonians. The passage from Ruth, which introduces the book, contains the well-known pledge of fidelity in which Ruth the Moabitess pledges to remain with Naomi the Jewess as she returns to the land of Judah. The passage from First Thessalonians is the introductory section of the epistle, which consists primarily of the opening prayer of thanksgiving.

Interestingly, these two readings share a common theme: the inclusion of Gentiles within the purpose of God. Just as Ruth pledges to follow the God of Naomi (Ruth 1:16), so do the Thessalonians turn from the worship of other gods to worship "a living and true God" (I Thess. 1:9). In the reading from Psalm 146, a hymn of praise to God, we find the same motif: Yahweh's help and protection extends to strangers and foreigners (Ps. 146:9). Even though this convergence of themes is fortuitous, it is a happy coincidence and provides one possibility for relating these three texts homiletically. The Gospel text is not so directly related since it gives us the Matthean version of Jesus' conversation with the Pharisees and Herodians in which he responds to their question concerning paying taxes to Caesar.

Ruth 1:1-19*a*

The readings from the Book of Ruth these three Sundays are chosen in part because of the location of the book in the

231

Christian canons, following the Book of Judges. The story can continue from Moses and Joshua into the era of the judges. The canonical tradition represented in the Greek versions of the Old Testament that shaped later Christian Bibles has the book in that place because its first verse sets the events, "In the days when the judges ruled." In the doubtless more ancient tradition of the Hebrew Bible, Ruth and four other short books or scrolls, "Megillot" (Song of Songs, Ecclesiastes, Lamentations, and Esther) are in the Writings, the third part of the canon. Each of those scrolls is read in its entirety in devout Jewish circles at its own annual festival. Ruth is the assigned reading for the Feast of Weeks, or Shavuoth.

The preacher who chooses to proclaim the texts from Ruth in Christian worship would do well to follow Jewish practice and read the book in its entirety, at least in preparation for preaching. While the individual scenes often are compelling and some individual lines are powerful, the book is a total composition that was meant to be read or heard in its entirety. The messages of the story are carried by the plot as a whole.

The Book of Ruth is a carefully crafted literary creation, the work of a skillful and sensitive author. It is best identified as a historical novella or short story; its setting, circumstances, characters, and plot are entirely plausible, and its author captures and holds the readers' attention by creating and eventually resolving tension at several levels. It shares features in common with several other Old Testament stories, including the books of Esther, Judith, Tobit, Jonah, and the story of Joseph in Genesis 37–50. Although there are differences—e.g., some of the others contain legendary features not found in Ruth—all these are deeply interested in the development of the human characters, and they intend to be both entertaining and edifying.

There is considerable disagreement among students of the book concerning its date of composition. Because of the similarity of perspective to that of some early works, such as the Yahwistic document of the Pentateuch and the court history of David (II Sam. 9-20; I Kings 1–2), some scholars date it as early as the tenth century B.C. Because of its similarity to later literature such as Esther and Tobit, as well as the fact that its heroine is a foreigner, others have seen it as a postexilic document written in opposition to Ezra and Nehemiah's prohibitions against keeping foreign wives (Ezra 10:1-5; Neh. 13:23-27). Whether it arose in such circumstances or not, the book certainly could have been used to advocate the same kind of appreciation of foreigners that the Book of Jonah also commends. It would be helpful to know when and where the book was written, but that is not possible. Finally, however, the important world is the one the story itself assumes and creates.

At every turn the book is the story of women making their way in a man's world, the patriarchal society as known in general throughout all ancient Israel's history, and in particular as it was in the time before the monarchy. Thus to say that it is a story of women is to say that it is about the socially and economically weak, if not oppressed. Its characters are ordinary people, some of whom have extraordinary qualities, such as wisdom, loyalty, devotion, and courage. Its main characters are scrupulous about following the law, due process and custom, but there are those who go beyond duty. In the end, it is a tale of the triumph of justice against strong odds. It has a happy ending, but the grace in the end is not cheap or won without great risk.

Our reading for today contains most of the first episode of the story, which runs through the end of chapter 1. The two distinct parts are verses 1-5 and 6-19a. Verses 1-5 provide the setting of the actual story that will unfold by giving the time, place, circumstances, and main characters. In a time of famine in Judah, Elimelech, his wife Naomi and their two sons left Bethlehem for Moab. Elimelech died, his two sons married Moabite wives, Orpah and Ruth, and ten years later both of these sons died. By the end of the introduction, which is the point of the real story's beginning, three widows stand before us. What took years to develop is told quickly, leading to a dangerous predicament. The narrator considers it unnecessary to tell the reader that widows in that world have no means of support. How they will survive is the question that leads the story on.

If the introduction compresses time, the next scene (verses 6-18) is occupied with a single moment in time, a conversation between Naomi and her two daughters-in-law as they set out to return to Judah. Naomi urges the others to return to their maternal homes with her blessing and prayer that they find husbands, but they both refuse to separate from her (verses 8-9). Naomi urges them a second time, pointing out that they have no hope for husbands through her, since she has no other sons to give them, and no prospects at her age (verses 11-13). This time Orpah bids Naomi farewell, "but Ruth clung to her" (verse 14). Once again Naomi insists that Ruth return to her own people, and Ruth, going beyond what law and custom require, declines in terms that Naomi cannot refuse.

Ruth's speech to her mother-in-law contains some of the best-known lines of the Bible, often applied to romantic circumstances: "Where you go I will go, and where you lodge I will lodge; your people shall be my people, and your God my God" (verse 16).

The young woman has thrown her lot in with the older one in total solidarity, even beyond death (verse 17). She has chosen separation from homeland and family and risked her life and future. Why does Ruth put herself in such jeopardy? The narrator gives no direct answer but shows us the feelings and motives of the characters by their words and actions. By the time the story is ended we will know that Ruth is a woman of courage, wisdom, and compassion. Now we only know that she has chosen to go with Naomi, who otherwise would be alone. Thus she becomes for us a model of one who goes beyond what law and custom require to stand with the one in need.

Where is the hand of God in these affairs? The narrator gives no direct answer, allowing the tragedies of the famine and the deaths of the three men to transpire without explanation. However, Naomi has her view, expressed in the language of complaint, "For it is exceedingly bitter to me for your sake that the hand of the Lord has gone forth against me" (verse 13; cf. also 1:21). Whether the author shares Naomi's interpretation or not, he or she—it is quite possible that the book arose among women storytellers—knows that

Naomi has every right to complain and that such complaints are not inconsistent with faith in God.

Psalm 146

The Old Testament lesson for today is the first of several from the Book of Ruth. This book is concerned, among other things, with the quest for redemption and salvation by persons at the periphery of society. One of the issues in Psalm 146 is the plight of the sojourner and the widow, certainly a basic concern of the story of Naomi and Ruth.

This psalm is the first in a small collection (Pss. 146–150) in which each of the psalms begin and end with a call to praise, with a hallelujah ("Praise Yahweh"). The psalm is structured around two opposite poles. The negative, cast as a warning, in verses 3-4, admonishes the audience not to trust human leadership, princes or a son of man, who cannot aid and whose efforts and plans are destined to sleep with him in the same tomb. (The NJPSV translates verse 3 as "Put not your trust in the great, in mortal man who cannot save.") The best laid plans, the highest hopes, the grandest designs die with their architects; they dissipate with their discoverer's demise. The one who trusts and hopes in such is doomed to disappointment since the son of man (*adam*) always returns to earth (*adamah*).

The opposite end of the spectrum is viewed in verses 5-9. Over against the human, the transitory, the disappointing, the inadequate stands the divine, the eternal, the satisfying, the sufficient.

Verse 5 declares "happy" anyone whose help and hope lie with the Deity. The term "happy" denotes a state of well-being and contentment but not necessarily a state of extravagance and luxury. Beginning in verse 6, a series of four characteristics of God are presented as supporting the contention that happy is the one whose help and hope is in God.

1. First of all, appeal is made to God as creator. As the one who made heaven, earth, and sea—that is, the totality of the universe—God is not bound by the structures and limitations of creaturehood. As creator, he is owner and ruler.

2. Second, appeal is made to the fidelity and constancy of the Creator "who keeps faith for ever." Unlike humans whose plans and programs die with them, God and his help endure forever. Unlike humans, God is not threatened by the possibility of non-being.

3. God is the one who is not only concerned for but also executes (guarantees) justice for the oppressed. In this affirmation and throughout verses 7-9, one finds a consistent emphasis of the Old Testament: God takes a special interest in and acts on behalf of the downtrodden, the powerless, and the despairing.

4. The satisfaction of physical needs is also the concern of God who "gives food to the hungry." As the maker of heaven and earth, God does not will that humans be oppressed or that they should suffer from hunger.

Following these four divine characteristics, the psalmist speaks of seven activities of God in which the Divine acts to alleviate human distress and to defend those without rights. Most of those noted as the object of God's care are persons without full authority and potential to assume responsibility for and to exercise rights for their own welfare: the prisoners (at the mercy of the legal system or perhaps in slavery); the blind (at the mercy of the seeing); those who are bowed down or with bent backs (in debt or oppressed by others thus carrying burdens not their own); the righteous (the innocent in the legal system who were at the mercy of the upholders of justice); the sojourners (foreign settlers or visitors, not members of the native culture and thus aliens); and the widow and fatherless (who were without the support of a male patriarch in a male-dominated culture). God is declared to be committed to the care of all these while at the same time God sees to it that the wicked come to their just reward—ruin.

The psalmist obviously presents the basic nature and character of God but does not claim that conditions and circumstances conform to this idealized divine will. In the list of attributes, God is primarily contrasted with human leaders (verses 3-4 over against 5-9). Verse 10 adds an eschatological note and points to the future as the time when the intervention of God on behalf of society's rejects and subjects will occur.

I Thessalonians 1:1-10

Over the next five Sundays (Propers 24–28), the New Testament lessons are drawn from Paul's first letter to the Thessalonians. A few words about this letter are in order. A brief narrative account of Paul's establishment of the church in Thessalonica is given in Acts 17:1-10. Several details of this account are worth noting since they are echoed in Paul's letter to the church. Even though Paul preached first to the Jews in the synagogue at Thessalonica (Acts 17:2), the positive response among Gentiles was especially noteworthy (Acts 17:4; cf. I Thess. 1:9-10; note Aristarchus in Acts 20:4; 27:2). The church was born amidst conflict as the young church met fierce opposition from Thessalonian Jews (Acts 17:5-9, 13; cf. I Thess. 1:6; 2:14-16; also Phil. 4:16). We should also note the prominent role of Silas, Paul's loyal co-worker (Acts 17:4; cf. I Thess. 1:1; II Thess. 1:1; also Acts 15:22-35; 15:40–18:5; II Cor. 1:19; I Pet. 5:12), as well as the less conspicuous role of Timothy (Acts 17:14-15; cf. I Thess. 1:1; II Thess. 1:1; also Acts 16:1; 18:5; 19:22; 20:4; Rom. 16:21; I Cor. 4:17; 16:10; Phil. 2:19-22; Heb. 13:23; I and II).

Paul wrote First Thessalonians only a few months after he had established the church (I Thess. 2:17-20), though he had remained in contact with them through Timothy his emissary (I Thess. 3:1-3). Now that he has received from Timothy a positive report about their faith (I Thess. 3:6-8), he is refreshed and able to continue his apostolic teaching through the medium of letter writing. Much of the letter recalls his time among them (I Thess. 2:1–3:13) and serves as an occasion for reflecting on the nature of his apostolic ministry. These reflections also become an occasion for thanksgiving (I Thess. 2:13; 3:9-10), and as it unfolds the letter takes the form of a pastoral prayer (I Thess. 3:10-13; 5:23-24).

Since the Thessalonians have been Christians for only a short time, they are still in need of exhortation in the life of faith (I Thess. 4:1-2; 5:12-22) and instruction concerning questions that puzzle them, most notably the fate of those who die before the Lord's coming (I Thess 4:13–5:11). The tone throughout the letter is that of moral exhortation, and hence it should be read as a paraenetic letter.

Today's text consists of two parts, the salutation (verse 1) and the opening prayer of thanksgiving (verses 2-10).

This opening prayer is reminiscent in both form and function of other Pauline thanksgivings which serve to introduce his letters (cf. Rom. 1:8-15; I Cor. 1:4-9; Phil. 1:3-11; II Thess. 1:3-4; Philem. 4-7). Like the others, it introduces some of the main concerns of the letter, and thus functions as a loosely conceived table of contents. In addition, it sets the mood of the letter.

This particular prayer is marked by reminiscence, as it recalls Paul's work in founding the church and the nature of its response to the gospel. It, like his other churches, is a source of constant concern to Paul, and hence is repeatedly in his prayers (verse 2; 2:13; cf. Rom. 1:9; also II Cor. 11:28). Several features are worth noting, though they overlap in certain respects.

1. The Thessalonians' exemplary commitment is summarized as Paul recalls their "work of faith and labor of love and steadfastness of hope" (verse 3). They have come to embody the familiar Christian triad of virtues (cf. 5:8; also I Cor. 13:7, 13; Rom. 5:1-5; 12:6-12; Gal. 5:5-6; Eph. 1:15-18; 4:2-4; Col. 1:4-5; I Tim. 6:11; Titus 2:2; Heb. 6:10-12; 10:22-24; I Pet. 1:3-9). The form of expression used here, however, makes it clear that these are by no means abstract virtues but aspects of living action: "how you have shown your faith in action, worked for love and persevered through hope" (verse 3, JB). Faith, love, and hope have come to living expression within the Thessalonian church.

2. They came into being as the result of divine election: "[God] has chosen you" (verse 4). This emphasis on divine initiative is recurrent (II Thess. 2:13-14). Behind these words we hear echoes of election as understood in Old Testament terms (Deut. 7:6-11; I Chron. 16:9-13; Jer. 33:19-26; Amos 3:2; Hos. 11:1-2), but the summons of God is now focused more specifically in Jesus Christ.

3. The gospel is seen more as divine power than persuasive word (verse 5). As noted earlier, the call of God is now heard through the gospel (II Thess. 2:14). The form of the message is inescapably human; it is articulated through human speech, even persuasive speech, but we are mistaken to

think that its power to convict arises from the preacher's way with words. Rather, the gospel should be construed as the Divine Voice resonating through the human voice, as the Word of God reverberating through the human word. The preached word of the messenger of God provides an occasion for the Spirit to act, and to do so in the power of God (verse 5; cf. I Cor. 2:4-5; Rom. 15:18-19; also Acts 1:8). So construed, the act of preaching is a moment of divine empowerment that leads to conviction.

4. The Thessalonians "received the word in much affliction" (verse 6). Their response to the gospel was met with stout resistance and became an occasion for suffering (Acts 17:5-9; I Thess. 2:14-16). Yet in this respect they were merely following in the path of Paul (I Thess. 2:1-2), becoming his imitators (cf. I Cor. 4:16; 11:1; Phil. 3:17; 4:9; II Thess. 3:7, 9; Gal. 4:12). More important, their suffering in behalf of the gospel made them imitators of the Lord (I Pet. 2:21-24).

5. Their faith and steadfastness became exemplary to other believers (verse 7). The gospel is preached not only by rehearsing the story of Christ, the kerygma, but also by rehearsing the story of the faith of others (Rom. 1:8; 16:19). This is illustrated through the emergence of the two-volume work of Luke-Arts, which links the words and deeds of Christ in the gospel with those of the church in Acts—clear testimony that the story of the church (and churches) has kerygmatic value along with the story of Christ. The steadfastness of the Thessalonians in the face of persecution had enabled the gospel to "speed on and triumph" (II Thess. 3:1).

6. Theirs had been a conversion from the worship of idols to the worship of the one God who is "living and true" (verses 9-10). In these concluding words of the opening prayer of thanksgiving, we have an embedded kerygmatic summary of missionary preaching to Gentiles. It consists of several elements: (1) the call to turn away from the worship of idols (Acts 14:15; I Cor. 12:2); (2) the acceptance of one God, confessed as "living and true" (cf. Heb. 9:14; John 17:3); (3) faith in Jesus as the One whom God raised from the dead (cf. Acts 3:15; 4:10; 5:30; 10:40; 13:30, 37; Rom. 1:4) and as the Son

of God expected to return and deliver from the coming wrath (I Thess. 5:9; Rom. 5:9; also Matt. 3:7).

This suggests that the conversion of Gentiles entailed repentance, or turning away from a false form of worship, and faith. We should observe, however, that faith for Gentiles had two prongs: belief in a monotheistic God and belief in a Christ who was raised from the dead and expected to return in the future to redeem his own from a coming judgment. As we know from the latter part of this epistle, Gentiles could find notions of resurrection and eschatology befuddling. Thus we find Paul continuing to expound the kerygma to them and explaining its full implications.

One homiletical possibility is to link this New Testament lesson with the Old Testament lesson, which unfolds the story of Ruth, the Moabitess, a foreigner, a non-Israelite, her adoption of the faith of Naomi (Ruth 1:7), and God's inclusion of her within the divine purpose (Ruth 4:17-22). This may serve as the occasion to address the theological problem of the particularity of divine election and the way it relates to the role of other peoples and other religions within the divine purpose.

Matthew 22:15-22

The lection for today is the first of four question-and-answer encounters between Jesus and Jewish leaders in Jerusalem during the closing days of Jesus' life. Of these four (22:15-22, 23-33, 34-40, 41-46), all but the second involves the Pharisees. These four confrontations are set by Matthew between the three parables against Israel (21:28–22:14) and Jesus' scathing word against scribes and Pharisees (23:1-36).

The form of our text is that of a "pronouncement story," a unit of material that consists of a pronouncement of Jesus cradled in a simple narrative relating the barest essentials as framework for the pronouncement. These stories probably circulated in a variety of contexts as the church looked to the authority of Jesus' words to address opponents and critics. Matthew 22:15-22 follows the basic outline of Mark 12:13-17: questioners come to Jesus with flattering lips and hostile intent; they pose the question of paying taxes to Rome; Jesus perceives their evil design; Jesus asks for a coin and poses a question; Jesus answers their question; they marvel and go away.

The interrogators of Jesus are Pharisees, the major party to survive the wars with Rome. Because the Pharisees were the principal representatives of Judaism in Matthew's day, because they were concerned with interpretation of Torah, and because they operated out of the synagogue, debates between them and Jesus had direct transfer value for Matthew's church in its debate with the synagogue. Their plan to entrap Jesus involved sending to Jesus a delegation of their own disciples accompanied by Herodians. This union of forces is strange, found only here (verse 16; Mark 12:13) and in Mark's record of an attempt to destroy Jesus (3:6). The Pharisees smarted under Roman taxes (here probably referring to the poll tax levied in A.D. 6 and sparking many Roman-Jewish clashes) and other such intrusions into Jewish life. Herodians, however, supported the Rome-endorsed Herod dynasty and, therefore, the tax. The delegation thus represents both yes and no on the tax issue; Jesus will surely displease someone in his answer.

"Is it lawful [permitted, proper] to pay taxes to Caesar, or not?" In verses 18, the word translated "malice" in the RSV can also be translated "evil" as in "deliver us from evil" (Matt. 6:13). And "put me to the test" can be translated "tempt me" as in the Lord's Prayer and Jesus' experience in the wilderness (Matt. 4:1-11). If one uses the words "evil" and "tempt" in understanding verse 18, then it is clear Jesus perceived the occasion as something more than a game of wits, a mental trap. If Jesus is being tempted, then the evil one is, through these questioners, seeking to lure Jesus into the political power struggle. The scene is reminiscent of the wilderness offer of the kingdoms of the world. In other words, Jesus understands that he is being confronted by evil, not just "a tough question."

On one level, therefore, one can cheerfully conclude that Jesus is of a keen mind and again outwits his opponents. On another level, one can see that evil is very real; it often approaches through flattery (verse 16); its agents may be religious leaders, and the issue most often is complex, demanding discernment. It is difficult to believe Matthew preserved this story to show how clever Jesus was. In Matthew's world, Caesar was still Caesar, the tax was still due, and Christians were still struggling with the place of Caesar if Jesus Christ is Lord.

Jesus' response to the question did not and does not solve the problem but simply defines the nature of the struggle. For Jesus, discerning what is God's and what is Caesar's was a test or temptation. For the early church, the task of interpreting Jesus' statement continued: how is the Christian to relate to political structures (Rom. 13:1-7; I Pet. 2:13-17; I Tim. 2:2; Titus 3:1; Rev. 13:1-18; 18:1-24)? For those who call Caesar "Lord" and for those who call Caesar "Satan" answers are simple. But if the church can at times support and at times must resist the state, then the answers are never simple nor are they final; the struggle resumes with every new situation.

From this wrestling Jesus was not exempt. In fact, in his decisions he was finally alone, with church and state conspiring against him. One can hardly imagine a heavier demand: called upon to obey God, not simply in the face of political wrath but without the support of the community of faith. But it still happens.

Proper 25

Sunday Between October 23 and 29 Inclusive

Ruth 2:1-13; Psalm 128; I Thessalonians 2:1-8; Matthew 22:34-46

The Old Testament lesson for today continues the story of Ruth, providing us with an account of her first encounter with Boaz. The reading from Psalm 128 promises to the God-fearing and obedient a blessing in the form of prosperity and productivity, both agricultural and domestic. In the New Testament lesson from First Thessalonians, Paul reflects on his missionary preaching among the Thessalonians, giving us a profile of exemplary ministerial service. In the Gospel lesson we have the Matthean account of Jesus' teaching concerning the two great commandments of loving God and neighbor and his biblical exposition concerning Christ as the Son of David.

Ruth 2:1-13

For general information concerning the Book of Ruth see the comments on last week's Old Testament reading.

Missing between last week's reading and the one for today is the brief account of the arrival of Naomi and Ruth in Bethlehem. They create a stir among the people, and when Naomi is recognized by the women, she responds with a play on her name that is at once an account of what has happened to her and a complaint to God: "Do not call me Naomi [Pleasant], call me Mara [Bitter], for the Almighty has dealt very bitterly with me" (1:20). The narrator also points out, significantly, that their arrival coincided with the beginning of the barley harvest (1:22).

We have already met two of the main human characters and now we are introduced to a third, Boaz. He is identified as a relative of Naomi's husband and "a man of wealth" (2:1), or better, "man of substance." His character and personality are developed further through his words and actions. Just as Ruth did more than law and custom required by her solidarity with Naomi, so Boaz is more generous to Ruth than necessary, offering her his protection and hospitality (verses 8-10). He recognizes and appreciates what Ruth has done and blesses her for it (verses 11-12). All these praiseworthy characteristics are made explicit in Ruth's words of thanks (verse 12).

The storyteller takes it for granted that the readers know the laws and customs concerning gleaning (verses 2, 3, 7, 8). According to Old Testament law, landowners were not to reap their fields to the border, or glean after harvest, or gather the fallen grapes, but leave them for "the poor and for the sojourner" (Lev. 19:9-10; cf. Lev. 23:32; Deut. 24:19-22). The practice was one of the ways the society provided for the poor and the homeless. Deuteronomy 24:20-21 specifically names the orphan and the widow.

Also assumed is knowledge of customs concerning the remarriage of widows to near relatives. Naomi had that in mind when she cautioned her daughters-in-law that she would have no more sons to become their husbands (1:12-13; cf. Gen. 38). This point will figure significantly in the story, explaining why it is important that Boaz is a relative of Naomi's husband. Verse 1 is thus a foreshadowing of events to come.

A great deal of this passage is taken up with dialogue among the three main characters. At every point they address one another with extreme politeness, emphasizing that they are above reproach. Ruth tells Naomi that she will go to the field of one "in whose sight I shall find favor" to glean among the grain (verse 2). When Ruth deferentially asks Boaz's permission to glean in his field behind the reapers (verse 7), he responds in the kindest and most generous way possible (verses 8-10). Moreover, the characters regularly address one another with words of blessing. The blessing that Boaz gives to Ruth is in effect a prayer that God appropriately reward her deed of kindness toward her mother-in-law.

How is the situation of the two widows—their poverty and insecurity—to be resolved? The plot develops slowly but surely, for human and divine actions are working hand-in-hand. Ruth goes out to glean for herself and her mother-in-law, assuming the status of the poor and the homeless. Significantly, "she happened to come to the part of the field belonging to Boaz" (verse 3). And there she worked hard, "without resting even for a moment" (verse 7). While we, knowing how the story will turn out, might be inclined to believe that Ruth planned things this way, and then did everything she could to make herself attractive to Boaz, for our narrator there are no hidden motives. It happened this way because of the character so seldom mentioned except in prayers and blessings: Yahweh. It was the means the Lord would take to fulfill the prayer of Boaz to reward her for her kindness.

Psalm 128

Martin Luther once described this psalm as a "marriage song." Its content is actually more a description of the contented life than a song concerned with marriage.

As part of the pilgrim songs (Pss. 120–134) sung as groups made their processional way to Jerusalem to observe the festivals, one can imagine that it was sung antiphonally—verses 1 and 5-6 by one group or the leader and verses 2-4 by another group. As the festivals celebrated the divine blessings of the year so this psalm gives expression to some of the images associated with human happiness.

Like the Beatitudes in Jesus' teachings, this psalm begins with a declaration about blessedness or happiness. The one who fears Yahweh and walks in his ways (the expressions are synonymous) is declared blessed. In verses 1-2, the blessed one is spoken of as "everyone" although in verses 3-4 the imagery is very male-oriented as was typical of the ancient world in general and the Old Testament in particular. When using this text in a service or sermon, the minister should be aware of the general male-cast of biblical materials and avoid reinforcing this cultural conditioning.

The beatitude states the general principle and verses 2-4

spell out what this means. Four factors are emphasized as expressive of blessedness.

1. The one whose hands had produced the fruit of labor would also eat it (verse 2*a*). For us, this seems so obvious—persons should possess and live off of what that labor has produced (Isa. 3:10). Life in the ancient world was far more precarious. Enemies passing through Palestine, pestilence and disease, and other calamity-produced situations frequently robbed one of life's products. Note also that the text assumes one must work to produce (see Gen. 3:19). In the Old Testament persons who failed to keep the law were promised that someone else would benefit from their labors (see Lev. 26:15-16; Deut. 28:30-35; Amos 5:11; Zeph. 1:13).

2. Life will be characterized by contentment and a sense of well-being (verse 2*b*). The psalm writer does not speak of any extravagant life-style or grandiose existence, no palaces or great wealth or widespread popularity. At peace with oneself and sufficiency for the needs of life are what is envisioned. (The discontented in life are those whose wants so exceed their needs that the two are unrelated. The misfortunates in life are those who dare not want what they need.) Something of this ideal life and existence can be seen in Micah 4:4. Verse 2*b* clearly refers to what modern psychologists would call the well-adjusted, self-satisfied individual.

3. The person's spouse would be like a fruitful vine in the house (verse 3*a*). The imagery of the text here and in verse 3*b* is drawn from the botanical work of Palestine. Three crops—wheat, olives, and grapes—comprised the basic crops of the land; from these came the basic staples of the Israelite diet—bread, oil, and wine.

4. Offspring as numerous and as vigorous as shoots around an olive tree graces the table of the blessed (verse 3*b*). Children provided not only a supply of labor for agricultural pursuits and a guard against one's enemies in life but also security in one's old age and descendants to carry on the family line.

The reference to the table in verse 3*b* is noteworthy since in Judaism the table became the center of family life (as it frequently has in many cultures). In the New Testament period and following, the meal in the Jewish home was treated like a sacrificial service in the temple in which the parents functioned as high priests.

The psalm closes out with a requested blessing upon the worshiper. As the pilgrims looked forward to arriving at Jerusalem so they looked forward to being blessed. "From Zion" indicates that the source of blessing was Yahweh. The hoped-for blessing is twofold.

1. The first, in verse 5bc, asks that the person be able to witness the prosperity of Jerusalem, that the capital city, the urban heart and soul of the state, will know peace and tranquility. The hope is that the prosperity will be enduring and lasting, "all the days of your life." The fate of Jerusalem, the life of the whole, is taken as intimately related to the life of the individual. As Jerusalem goes, so goes the people.

2. The second blessing is for a long life in which persons will live to see their grandchildren (verse 6). The hope of watching one's grandchildren grow into maturity expresses that desire to see the family's future safely secure.

This psalm could be preached to illustrate some of the ideals of life in ancient Israel—obedience to the will of God, productive labor, contentment with one's state of being, an ordered family with healthy offspring, long life, and a community at peace.

I Thessalonians 2:1-8

With the memory of his founding visit still fresh in the minds of his readers, Paul recalls the circumstances in which the Thessalonian church was born. By virtue of their existence as a "church of the Thessalonians in God" (1:1), they bore witness to the productivity of his first visit. It had not been in vain (verse 1).

They are asked to recall that the opposition he met at Thessalonica was typical rather than exceptional. Prior to coming to Thessalonica, Paul had preached the gospel in Philippi (Acts 16:11-40). There too he had met stiff resistance, even to the point of being beaten and jailed (Acts 16:20-24). It was in this respect that he "had already suffered and been shamefully treated at Philippi," and this had apparently become common knowledge. His reputation had preceded him.

The preaching of the "gospel of God" (verse 2; cf. Mark 1:14; Rom. 1:1; 15:16) had called for courage "in our God." On other occasions he had experienced a failure of nerve when he reflected on the odds against the gospel (cf. I Cor. 2:1-5; Acts 18:9-10). It was not a question of dipping into his inner, human resources and finding the strength to speak, but rather of relying on the power of God (I Cor. 2:5; II Cor. 4:16; 5:5-8). Such confidence and boldness became an earmark of apostolic witness (Acts 4:13, 29; 28:31), and it characterizes Paul's ministry (II Cor. 3:12; Phil. 1:20: Phile. 8; cf. I Tim. 3:13).

At this point, Paul begins to depict some of the features of his ministry among them. The tone is slightly apologetic as if he is defending himself against the charges of opponents. In other settings, Paul encountered opposition from those who accused him of behaving in ways unbecoming to an apostle (cf. esp. II Cor. 2:17–3:2; 4:2-3; 10:7-12). No such explicit reference to opponents occurs here, however.

In any case, we are assured of the purity of his motives: "our appeal does not spring from error or uncleanness, nor is it made with guile" (verse 3; cf. II Cor. 12:16). He further denies having gained entry among them through the use of flattering words, insisting that his aim was not human but divine approval (Gal. 1:10). He carried out his work before God as his witness (verse 5; cf. Rom. 1:9), as the One who "triest the heart and the mind" (Jer. 11:20).

Nor did he ever use his speeches as "a cover for trying to get money" (verse 5, JB). The wandering preacher, or itinerant philosopher, whose speeches were followed by requests for money, was commonplace in the Greco-Roman world, and Paul constantly had to distance himself from such charlatans. His consistent practice was to preach free of charge, working to support himself (I Cor. 9:12-18), and in this way he excluded himself from the "peddlers of God's word" (II Cor. 2:17; II Pet. 2:3).

He also chose gentleness over harshness as the form in which to couch his ministerial practice (verses 6-7). As an apostle of Christ, he might have made it his practice to pull rank and appeal to his authority as a common ministerial device. And sometimes he does lay express claim to apostolic authority and the power that comes with it (cf. I Cor. 4:19-21; II Cor. 10–13, esp. 10:8; 13:3-4, 10; Gal. 1:6-9). But more often than not, we see Paul placing limits on his apostolic authority, restraining himself in his use of power rather than unleashing harsh threats (Philem. 8).

The image used here to capture this mode of ministry is that of the wet nurse who cares for her children (verse 5; cf. I Cor. 3:2; Eph. 5:29). This same image was also used by Greco-Roman authors to depict the proper way of philosophical instruction—nurturing rather than intimidating. What is suggested here is a level of genuine commitment, a willingness to give of himself completely in the work of ministry (verse 8).

Today's text is first and foremost a statement about the nature of ministry. It provides us with a sort of catalog of characteristics of authentic ministry, both negatively and positively: not error, uncleanness, guile, flattery, greed, but courage, gentleness, affection, self-giving. It may well provide an appropriate occasion for the preacher to explore the dynamic between church and ministry.

Matthew 22:34-46

Today we conclude the question-and-answer encounters between Jesus and leaders of Judaism recorded in Matthew 22:15-46. Three units deal with questions posed by these leaders to Jesus (two by Pharisees, one by Sadducees) and one, the concluding unit (verses 41-46), consists of a question by Jesus to the Pharisees. Jesus and these leaders can argue because they have a common heritage and embrace common sacred texts. It is in interpreting that heritage and those texts that tension arises. At verse 46 a major section of Matthew closes. In chapter 23 the audience changes; Jesus now talks to the crowd and to his disciples about the religious leaders. In these closing chapters of Matthew Jesus moves from the leaders, to the crowds, to his disciples, to the cross.

The reader will notice immediately that this lection consists not of one unit but two (verses 34-40; 41-46). Each unit begins with the Pharisees coming together (verses 34, 41), but in the one the Pharisees ask the question; in the other it is Jesus who is the interrogator. Verse 46 concludes not only the unit begun at verse 41 but the entire section begun at 22:15. The decision facing the preacher is whether or not to embrace both units in one message. After all, the first part concerns Old Testament commandments, the second concerns Christology. Understandably, some lectionaries conclude the reading at verse 40. As a suggestion, why not focus on verses 34-40, using verses 41-46 as a christological affirmation to conclude the debates and conflict? It would be most appropriate to declare who the Christ is as a climax to a period of grueling interrogation.

Matthew 22:34-40 has parallels in Mark 12:28-34 and Luke 10:25-28. Luke agrees in some detail with Matthew but locates the story earlier as preface to the parable of the Good Samaritan. Mark has the question about the great (first) commandment come from a sincere scribe whom Jesus commends. The question itself is neither unusual nor new. Rabbis had long engaged in classifying commandments, sometimes according to weight (light or heavy). It was inevitable, both in the context of a classroom and in the common struggle to keep, if possible, the weightier laws, that the question arises, Which one is greatest, first?

Jesus' answer is not surprising. He joins the Shema of Deuteronomy 6:5 (Matthew uses the Septuagint but substitutes "mind" for "might." Mark and Luke have both "mind" and "might,") to Leviticus 19:18, the command to love one's neighbor. That Luke says it was the lawyer who cited the Old Testament texts (10:27) and that Mark says the scribe approved of Jesus' citation of these two texts should remind us that Jesus and the Pharisees had much in common. These two commandments had been joined by rabbis long before Jesus. Too often Christians want everything good to originate with Jesus, and much too often assume an "over against" posture in relation to all leaders of Judaism mentioned in the New Testament. The message of Jesus' response to the question is clear: love God totally, and the love of God is expressed in love of neighbor. This is vital, not simply as a discussion topic with the synagogue but for the church as well. As Matthew has repeatedly said, love toward all, without partiality, is a distinguishing mark of life in the kingdom (5:43-48; 7:12; 9:13; 12:1-8; 18:12-35; 25:31-46).

The second unit of our lection, verses 41-46, has parallels in Mark 12:35-37*a* and Luke 20:41-44, but with noticeable differences. Only in Matthew is Jesus' question confrontive, "What do *you* think?" Earlier the Pharisees had said to Jesus, "Tell us . . . what you think" (verse 17). Now the roles are reversed. That the Christ was son of David was supported by numerous texts (Is. 9:2-7; 11:1-9; Jer. 23:5-6; 33:14-18; Ezek. 34:23-24), and Matthew clearly accepts the view (1:1-17; 1:18-25; 9:27; 12:23; 15:22; 20:30-31; 21:9, 15). The answer of the Pharisees is not wrong, but it is incomplete. The Christ is also David's Lord. Psalm 110 is used to enlarge the Pharisees' view of the Messiah. This text, Psalm 110:1, was understood messianically by the early church, and is, in fact, the most used Old Testament citation in the New Testament to affirm the exaltation and enthronement of Christ. Just as the record of Jesus' baptism ends with heaven's affirmation (3:17), just as the Transfiguration ends with heaven's affirmation (17:5), so here, following a period of intense conflict, Matthew concludes with a triumphant note. After that, no one asked any more questions.

"Sit at my right hand, *till* . . ." (verse 44, emphasis added). The preacher would do well to pause over the word "till" (until). Christ is Lord; Christ is becoming Lord. The exaltation of Christ is our song, but it is also our assignment.

Proper 26

Sunday Between October 30 and November 5 Inclusive

Ruth 4:7-17; Psalm 127; I Thessalonians 2:9-13, 17-20; Matthew 23:1-12

The psalm for today provides a clear theme evident in all the readings: "Unless the Lord builds the house, those who build it labor in vain." Such was the conviction of Boaz (Ruth 4:7-17) who carried out his obligation to the widows of deceased kinsmen. Of the house he established on moral and legal grounds came Obed, Jesse, David, and the Christ. Such was the conviction and example of Paul (I Thess. 2:9-13, 17-20) as he sought to "parent" the house (family) of God in Thessalonica. And certainly such was the instruction of Jesus to his followers: not by privilege, place, and preference but by obedience, humility, and service the community of faith is established.

Ruth 4:7-17

For general information concerning the Book of Ruth see the comments on the Old Testament lesson for Proper 24 in this volume.

With this reading we come to the close of the story of Ruth, the final resolution of the tensions established at the outset: How will two widows survive in their patriarchal society? The reading for Proper 24 had included most of the first episode of the book and the lesson for Proper 25 presented most of the second episode. Between that text and today's lesson a great deal has happened. The relationship between Ruth, young and poor, and Boaz, an older man of substance, continued to develop. Notice that Boaz was attracted to Ruth entirely because of her character, epitomized in her devotion to her mother-in-law and her hard work in the fields. Naomi recognized the hand of Yahweh in these events, that he has led Ruth to Boaz as the means of caring for the widows (2:20-21), so she encouraged Ruth to do her part to ensure the success of the divine plan (2:22-23). The third episode (chapter 3) reports how Ruth did just that, meeting Boaz on the threshing floor and inviting him to exercise the right of the next of kin toward her. That scene contains the main climax of the story, when Boaz affirmed his intention to exercise the right of the next of kin (3:10-13).

Today's reading is part of the fourth episode of the story (4:1-12), set at the gate of Bethlehem where legal matters were to be resolved, and the report of the aftermath of the drama (4:13-22). The actions concern civil law and the rights and responsibilities of relatives to one another. Boaz goes to the city gate to accomplish what he promised Ruth the night before, but there is one possible impediment to the plans, a relative who is closer to the family of Ruth's father-in-law than he. Boaz calls this next of kin and convenes what is in effect a civil court, before ten elders of the city.

Two legal considerations stand behind the scene in the court, one involving the "redemption" of land and another concerning the perpetuation of the name of dead males by the next of kin. Boaz invites the unnamed next of kin to purchase the parcel of land that belonged to Elimelech. A parallel to this practice is noted in Jeremiah 32, in the story of the prophet's purchase of land that belonged to his relative. The purpose of this practice was to respect and protect the allocation of land according to families. If it had to be sold, a near relative should keep it in the family. Tension rises in the scene at the gate when the next of kin readily agrees to buy the land.

But at that point Boaz calls attention to the other legal concern, linking it to the redemption of the land: "The day you buy the field from the hand of Naomi, you are also buying Ruth the Moabitess, the widow of the dead, in order to restore the name of the dead to his inheritance" (verse 5). What Boaz has in view is the so-called levirate marriage (Deut. 25:5-10; Lev. 25:25; 27:9-33), although that usually involved a brother of the widow's husband (see also Gen. 3). What fear or concern motivates the next of kin's reluctance is unclear.

Our narrator then reports in precise terms how Boaz fulfilled all the legal obligations and followed due process to take possession of the property and to marry Ruth. There is reference to the symbolic removal of a sandal to seal the transaction (verses 8-9) and the account of the formal notarizing of the agreement. This was done orally, with the elders affirming that they were witnesses (verses 10-11), but it was as binding as a written contract. The elders go further to pronounce a blessing on the new family (verses 11-12).

The story began with trouble and tragedy, but it ends with the happiest of reports, that of the birth of a child. Not only is the welfare of Naomi and Ruth secure, but also a future for the family that seemed doomed. The child is surrounded by mother, grandmother, and the women of the town, who bless Naomi and name the child (verses 14-17).

It is highly significant that this child is the father of Jesse, the father of King David. Ordinary people, but people who go beyond what the law requires to act with compassion for others, are the ancestors of kings. There is another remarkable fact here. As the narrator points out over and over, Ruth is a Moabitess, a foreign woman of unusual courage and loyalty. This foreigner is the grandmother of Israel's greatest king, who founded a dynasty that lasted in Judah until the Babylonian captivity. Whether or not the story of Ruth is a polemic against narrow nationalism, it certainly strikes a blow for the acceptance of foreigners.

Psalm 127

In the reading from the Book of Ruth for today, several strands in the story come together to produce a satisfactory resolution of the tensions in the plot and yet the resolution invites the reader to think behind the narrative's beginning and beyond the narrative's conclusion. The behind or before (intimated in the genealogy from Perez to Boaz) and the beyond or afterward (intimated in the genealogy from Boaz to David) point back to the story of divine guidance beginning in Genesis and forward to the stories in Samuel. Among the general themes that get woven together in this conclusion are: the final arrival back home at Bethlehem when Ruth the foreigner becomes an integral part of Israel, the birth of an offspring to bear the name of the deceased, and the new child whose future points to a new house/dynasty.

Psalm 127 is concerned with some of the same themes as those in Ruth—the building of a house/dynasty/family, the blessing of offspring, and the divine guidance of life. The psalm may be examined in terms of the five proverbial components it contains.

1. Verse 1*a* declares that unless Yahweh builds the house workers labor in vain. Human effort without divine blessing is unproductive. How house is to be understood in the text remains ambiguous. It could refer to simply a house, to the temple, to a family, to a royal (the Davidic) dynasty, or, used metaphorically, to mean anything requiring plans and execution of these plans. (We speak about building a career and so forth.) In Ruth 4:11 the building of a house means to rear a family (see Gen. 16:2; 30:3; Exod. 1:21; Deut. 25:9; I Sam. 2:35; II Sam. 7:27).

2. A similar perspective is offered in verse 1*b* but with a different set of metaphors. The idea of a watchman watching over the city seems to reflect more of an emphasis on a continuing, ongoing activity than building a house. At least the imagery of constructing a house suggests a process that is completed at some stage, whereas watching over a city is a continuous occupation. The proverb declares that diligence alone is not sufficient, for matters to function properly, there must also be the presence and blessing of the Deity.

The ancient rabbis told a story that illustrated how they understood the correlation between watching and the presence of God: "Three Rabbis went to visit cities in the Land of Israel, and to set up in them teachers of Scripture and instructors of Oral Law. They came to one city in which they found no teacher of Scripture and no instructor of Oral Law, and they said to the people: 'Fetch us the chief watchmen of the city.' The people brought the watchmen of the city to the Rabbis, and the Rabbis said: 'Are these the watchmen of the city? In truth, they are the destroyers of the city.' And when the people asked the Rabbis: 'Who then are the watchmen of the city?' the Rabbis answered: 'The watchmen of the city are the teachers of Scripture and instructors of Oral Law.' "

3. Verse 2 suggests that human effort, excessive toil, rising early and going to bed late, and anxious toil may in themselves not be productive or rewarding. The last line presents problems. Does it mean that God is the one who rewards a person with sleep? That is, that sleep and rest with confidence and security are not the result of our labors but a gift from God? Or does it mean that spouses who are workaholics only give their companions sleep, that is, they are too exhausted for marital sexual relations?

4. Verse 3 declares that children are a blessing and a gift from God. Modern society with its overpopulation and concern for birth control may not share this outlook. In the ancient world, however, and as the stories of barren parents in the Old Testament illustrate, children were considered differently. (The minister should be aware that the emphasis on "sons" reflects the male-oriented character of ancient Israelite life. The term translated "sons" could be read "children" but it is clear from the remainder of the psalm that "sons" is meant.)

5. In verses 4-5 the person who has many children is pronounced blessed. A person with a retinue of sons possessed clout in public places. Social protection, community influence, personal welfare, social security, survival assurance, continuity of the name, inheritance insurance, comradeship in life, all of these were involved in male progeny. In ancient societies, much would have been lost without them.

I Thessalonians 2:9-13, 17-20

Today's epistolary lection continues directly from last week's New Testament lesson. The topic is still Paul's reflections on the nature of his ministry among the Thessalonians when he was first with them.

The first item mentioned in today's text is his practice of working to support himself financially in his apostolic work. "Labor and toil" often refer specifically to work done for the sake of the gospel, what we might call "church work" (I Thess. 1:3; Rom. 16:6, 12; I Cor. 3:13-15; 15:10; Phil. 2:30). To be sure, Paul has in mind his work of ministry in the broadest sense, but especially in view is his "secular" work as a tentmaker (I Cor. 4:12; Acts 18:13). His justification for this practice has several elements: providing for the necessities of himself and others (Acts 20:34) and avoiding being a burden on his churches (II Thess. 3:8). Also related to this was his theological principle of preaching the gospel free of charge (I Cor. 9:18). To support oneself while preaching the gospel conformed to the more general expectation that Christians would not only work at their jobs but be diligent in doing so (II Thess. 3:10-13; Eph. 4:28).

A further item is his exemplary behavior. He reminds them of "how holy and righteous and blameless was our behavior to you believers" (verse 10). The importance of personal examples was well understood in the Greco-Roman world, as seen in the remarks of Julian the Apostate (d. ca. A.D. 363), in reflecting on the Cynics of an earlier era: "Deeds with them came before words, and if they honoured poverty they themselves seem first to have scorned inherited wealth; if they cultivated modesty, they themselves first practised plain living in every respect; if they tried to expel from the lives of other men the element of theatrical display and arrogance, they themselves first set the example by living in the open market places and the temple precincts, and they opposed luxury by their own practice before they did so in words" (*Oration* 7.214, as cited in A. J. Malherbe, *Moral Exhortation, A Greco-Roman Sourcebook* [Philadelphia: Westminster, 1986], p. 39).

To give his remarks more specific point Paul compares his relationship with his church to that of a "father with his children" (verse 11). Though the image shifts from that of wet nurse (2:7-8), it has the same effect of rendering his relationship with his church as intensely personal and intimate. It was common for him to view himself as the father of the churches he established and of Christians whom he converted (I Cor. 4:14-15, 17; II Cor. 6:13 Gal. 4:19). Like a parent, he could be stern in rebuking immature behavior (I Cor. 3:1-4), but also tender in nurturing growth (I Cor. 4:14).

In presenting himself as an exemplary father, Paul conforms to a well-established practice within the Greco-Roman moral tradition. This is illustrated especially well in the remarks of Pseudo-Isocrates (ca. fourth century B.C.): "Nay, if you will but recall your father's principles, you will have from your own house a noble illustration of what I am telling you. For he did not belittle virtue nor pass his life in indolence; on the contrary, he trained his body by toil, and by his spirit he withstood dangers. Nor did he love wealth inordinately . . . neither did he order his existence sordidly. . . . I have produced a sample of the nature of Hipponicus (the father), after whom you should pattern your life as after an example, regarding his conduct as your law, and striving to imitate and emulate your father's virtue; for it were a shame . . . for children not to imitate the noble among their ancestors" (*To Demonicus* 9-11).

Several elements of Paul's fatherly ministering are mentioned: exhorting, encouraging, and charging (verse 11). The first two refer to the positive, more gentle work of guidance and nurture, while the third has a sterner element. The sense is captured especially well by NEB: "appealing to you by encouragement, as well as by solemn injunctions." Both the softer and harder, the positive and negative, dimension of the task has a single purpose: to get them "to live lives worthy of the God who calls you into his kingdom and glory" (verse 12, NEB). To live "upward" in response to the noble calling of God and to conform one's life in an appropriately "high" manner is to adopt a life-style worthy of the kingdom (II Thess. 1:5; 2:14; Eph. 4:1; Phil. 1:27; Col. 1:10; I Pet. 5:10).

At this point, the *Common Lectionary* omits verses 13-16, doubtless because of the severity of the language Paul uses to describe the opposition of the Jews to the gospel. It is commonly read as one of the most anti-Jewish texts in the New Testament, and for this reason it has figured prominently in Jewish-Christian dialogue and in ecumenical efforts in this regard.

After this brief hiatus, today's text turns to more personal concerns—Paul's anxiety at not being able to see the Thessalonians and his justified pride in their steadfastness and fidelity to the gospel (verses 17-20). It is the concern of an anxious parent who is unable to see his children and the recognition that there is no substitute for a "face to face" visit (3:6, 10; Rom. 1:11; II Tim. 1:4). We are also hearing a father boast about his children, who are for him a source of constant joy (3:9). His hope for their acceptance and vindication "before our Lord Jesus at his coming" (verse 19; 3:13; 4:15; 5:23; II Thess. 2:1, 8; I Cor. 15:23; James 5:7-8) also expresses the inmost desire of the Christian parent.

As was the case in last week's epistolary lection, the primary focus here is on the nature of ministry. Yet the concerns expressed here loom larger than this. The worthwhileness of a parental example obviously has vast import for Christian moral teaching. Parents can be charged to be worthy examples and children can be charged to be grateful for parents whose lives are exemplary. The Christian minister might also reflect on the hermeneutical problem presented by the omission of verses 13-16. While this may be justifiable for the purposes of constructing an ecumenically constructive lectionary, the passage nevertheless stands as part of the church's canonical text. The best solution may be to confront and struggle rather than to omit.

Matthew 23:1-12

Matthew 23:1 begins the fifth and last of the major sections of teaching in this Gospel. This section ends at 26:1 and has at its center the apocalyptic speech of chapter 24. Since the Synoptic apocalypses are traditionally read the First Sunday of Advent, the lessons from Matthew during this season after Pentecost will not include chapter 24. This teaching section is a compilation of sayings and, like the other four, not to be regarded as a single discourse. Some of these teachings are paralleled in Mark, more are found in Luke, but clearly are gathered here from a variety of settings. It is not possible to recover the original contexts, but obviously Matthew did not regard that as important. Jesus' teachings have been brought forward to address the Matthean situation.

In 23:1 the crowds are included in the audience for the sayings which follow. Perhaps Matthew is joining this section to the preceding, picturing the multitude that gathered during Jesus' debates with religious leaders. However, it is quite clear, at least beginning at verse 5, that the real audience consists of the disciples, for it is to them the warnings and instructions are addressed. In other words, in Matthew 23:1-12 Jesus is talking to his church, and especially to its leaders. At 24:1, that the disciples are the intended audience for Jesus' discourse becomes even more explicit.

And what is Jesus saying to the church? In general terms Jesus warns against arrogance and self-exaltation among leaders in the faith community. The method of the warning is to point to the scribes and Pharisees as negative examples. That the scribes and Pharisees were skilled in and devoted to the precepts of Moses is not questioned. That they were successors to Moses as teachers of Israel is accepted and affirmed (verses 2-3). This endorsement is in accord with 5:17-18. The warning, however, points elsewhere to two glaring weaknesses among the scribes and Pharisees: the failure to practice their teaching and the love of place and honor. Matthew's rebuke seems general, as though all scribes and Pharisees were guilty. Actually, the rabbis themselves lamented and condemned these evils among their number, just as Christian leaders do within their ranks. That the law was loved and followed by many is amply testified (Ps. 1:2; 119:97).

Our lection is reminiscent of 6:1-18 which addresses the same problems of love of chief seats, special greetings, and titles of honor. The phylacteries and fringes refer to special attire worn especially at prayer time. Phylacteries were leather boxes containing Scripture verses (Deut. 6:6, 8; 11:18), and fringes were tassels on the corners of prayer shawls (Deut. 22:12). The charge here is that they had become quite ornate and decorative. The titles—rabbi, father, and master (verses 8-10)—are to be rejected because all are brothers and sisters before one teacher, father, and master. The closing verses (11, 12) are appropriate in principle but are clearly independent sayings of Jesus found in other contexts in the Gospels. For example, see Matthew 20:25-28 and Luke 22:25-27.

It is quite clear that Matthew is not simply reciting the flaws to be found among synagogue leaders so the Christian leaders can say, "I thank God I am not as they are," thereby revealing that they are. Matthew is addressing the problem that infected Judaism, early Christianity, and the church ever since: the love of place and preference among the servants of God. The restrictions in our text are severe and allow no titles, a practice followed by some groups. In some such groups, pride and love of recognition show up even in humble terms such as "Brother." But the point of the text is clear and is found repeatedly in the teaching of Jesus. Neither the problem nor its solution lies in clothing and terms designating one's place in the community. Until the model of Jesus' ministry is embraced, games such as prizes for the most humble will continue.

Proper 27

Sunday Between November 6 and 12 Inclusive

Amos 5:18-24; Psalm 50:7-15; I Thessalonians 4:13-18;
Matthew 25:1-13

The Gospel, the Epistle, and the Old Testament reading join in speaking of the "Day of the Lord." A day of reckoning, a time of God's bringing history to a close is a theme found throughout the Bible. But will that day be one of joy or sorrow, of darkness or light? The texts before us offer both encouragement and warning, both promise and threat. The readers of these passages will differ in what they hear, a difference due in large measure to their commitments, their circumstances, and their life-styles.

Amos 5:18-24

With the readings for today and next Sunday we prepare to meet the end of the liturgical year with our faces turned toward the future. Two prophetic texts with eschatological themes, from Amos for today and from Zephaniah for next Sunday, begin to set the stage for the conclusion of the season and the year which ends with the festival of Christ the King.

This reading from the Book of Amos, brief as it is, contains two distinct units of prophetic discourse, verses 18-20 and 21-24. Each is a different form of prophetic speech, and each * has its own particular message.

Amos 5:18-20, like many other prophetic addresses, begins with the cry "woe." Typically, what follows this exclamation is a description of the prophet's audience in terms of their sinful actions. Thus Amos 6:4 ff:

> "Woe to those who lie upon beds of ivory,
> and stretch themselves upon their couches."

(See also Isa. 5:8-22.) In this case, however, the prophet accuses those "who desire the day of the Lord." With a series of rhetorical questions and metaphors he then attacks and corrects some unspecified false expectations concerning the day of the Lord.

The day of the Lord, which later becomes an apocalyptic expectation of the end of history, is a persistent and important theme in the message of Amos. Obviously, however, expectation of the day of the Lord was already well-established when this prophet came onto the scene in the middle of the eighth century B.C. While it is not possible to know for certain what Amos' audience expected, it seems most likely that the day of the Lord was associated in their thinking with the ancient tradition of the holy war. As in the holy war, on that day the Lord would arise to defeat his enemies, usually believed to be also the enemies of his people. In the thought of Amos, the day of the Lord is still the day of the Lord's warfare against his enemies. The difference, however, is that his own people Israel have become the enemy!

So Amos 5:18-20 is filled with reversals and irony. The people who look forward to the day will see it, but it will be darkness and not light. Just as one escapes from a lion and is met by a bear, or escapes into his house to be bitten by a snake, so will be the day of the Lord for Israel. The little discourse is thus an announcement of judgment upon the people, not of the end of history, but of their military defeat and exile.

In the second unit, verses 21-24, the prophet quotes the Lord directly. The speech is not an announcement of the future, like most of the individual discourses in the Book of Amos, but a prophetic torah (law, instruction) speech, like the ones found in Isaiah 1:10-17 and Micah 6:6-8. Following the pattern of a priest's response to a question from the laity concerning a particular matter of sacrifice, worship or the distinction between clean and unclean, the prophet hears Yahweh give an answer that is quite contrary to what is expected. The purpose of the speech is thus to instruct people in the actions God expects from them.

The torah speech has two unequal parts, verses 21-23

specifying what Yahweh does not want and verse 24 stating what he wishes. The matters rejected include most of the important aspects of the cult: worship gatherings (verse 21), various forms of sacrifice (verse 22), and the lyrics and music of worship (verse 23). We cannot be certain whether Amos means to reject all forms of established cultic practice, or simply to insist that such things are no substitute for right behavior. Taken in themselves, however, these lines amount to a radical indictment of established religion.

What God expects is the full and regular outpouring of justice and righteousness. These two powerful words frequently are linked in prophetic address, as elsewhere in the Old Testament. To Amos, justice refers to what we would call due process (cf. 2:6-7; 5:10-12), and the fair and equitable distribution of resources. The prophet is particularly concerned about the oppression of the poor by the rich (4:1-3; 5:10-13; 6:4-7), about equity and fairness in human society. But the substance of justice stems from the fact that the God of Israel is just, and will not tolerate unfair actions. Righteousness refers more to the internal characteristics of devotion and piety from which stem just behavior.

When these two units are considered together they point to the fuller message of Amos. Because of the failure of justice and righteousness and the arrogant reliance upon ritual practice, the people of God are doomed to destruction at the hand of a foreign invader. Looking beyond Amos to the belief in the reign of God as expressed in this liturgical season, we are reminded that the day of the Lord is to be defined by justice and righteousness. The kingdom of God is that time and place when God's justice reigns among all.

Psalm 50:7-15

This psalm is in keeping with the eschatological emphasis of the final weeks of the liturgical year. The opening verses of this psalm (verses 1-6) form an extended call to worship. They affirm Yahweh's coming to judge the people. The reference to "the rising of the sun to its setting" (verse 1) may not refer to the geographical extent of judgment (that is, from east to west) but rather to the fact that one day, from sunrise to sunset, would be a special day of calling Israel to accountability and judgment. If so, this would be most likely one of the days of the fall festival.

The remainder of the psalm consists of two divine addresses. The first, in verses 7-15, is addressed apparently to the faithful members of the community. These would be the faithful ones (the *hasidim*) mentioned in verse 5. The second speech, in verses 16-23, addresses the wicked (note verse 16*a*).

Undoubtedly, in the context of worship it would have been left for the individual persons to place themselves in one camp or the other. The terms "faithful ones" and "the wicked" are thus more rhetorical than specific. Verses 5*b* and 16*bc* would suggest that the special day being celebrated was a time of covenant renewal. Verse 5*b* can be translated: "the ones making a covenant with me by sacrifice." The statements in verse 16 about reciting the divine statutes and taking the covenant on the lips could refer to the ceremony of covenant renewal. According to Deuteronomy 31:10-13, all the people were to be assembled every seventh year at the Feast of Booths (the fall festival). At this convocation, the law (the book of Deuteronomy) was to be read.

The lection for today is comprised of only the speech to the faithful ones. Since the NJPSV provides a better translation than the RSV, the lection is given here in its entirety.

> "Pay heed, My people, and I will speak,
> O Israel, and I will arraign you.
> I am God, your God.
> I censure you not for your sacrifices,
>   and your burnt offerings, made to Me daily;
>   I claim no bull from your estate,
>   no he-goats from your pens.
> For Mine is every animal of the forest,
>   the beasts on a thousand mountains.
>   I know every bird of the mountains,
>   the creatures of the field are subject to Me.
> Were I hungry, I would not tell you,
>   for Mine is the world and all it holds.
> Do I eat the flesh of bulls,

or drink the blood of he-goats?
Sacrifice a thank offering to God,
and pay your vows to the Most High.
Call upon Me in time of trouble;
I will rescue you, and you shall honor Me."

Three elements in the speech are noteworthy. (1) Yahweh declares that as ruler and governor of the universe, he is not dependent on the sacrifices of humans for survival. The text, however, does not condemn the offering of sacrifices and should not be seen as condemnation of cultic worship. (2) Worshipers are requested to offer a sacrifice of thanksgiving or to offer thanksgiving to God (verse 14). The term for "thanksgiving" can refer to both the attitude and the sacrifice, so the issue is not completely clear (see the marginal note in the RSV to the verse). Thanksgiving is the attitude requested. Thanksgiving services required conspicuous consumption and sharing since all the sacrifice had to be eaten on the day it was offered (see Lev. 7:11-5). (3) Yahweh appeals to the people to call upon him in time of trouble (an authentication of foxhole religion!) with the promise that he would respond and grant deliverance. The human response for such deliverance was to glorify Yahweh through testimony and thanksgiving sacrifice (verse 15).

I Thessalonians 4:13-18

There was a conspicuous number of Gentile converts among the membership of the Thessalonian church (Acts 17:4; I Thess. 1:9-10). With little or no familiarity with the Jewish apocalyptic tradition, especially as it developed during the Hellenistic period, the so-called intertestamental period (e.g., Isa. 26:19; Dan. 12:2-3; II Macc. 7:9-14), many of them were understandably puzzled about certain features of Christian eschatology. In some traditions of Greek thought, it was possible to conceive of the immortality of the soul. By this was meant that the soul had an eternal existence, but could take up residence temporarily within a human body. This was thought of as a tomb in which the soul was captured. While Greeks could look forward to a time when the soul would be released from the body and return to its eternal state, they did not find the notion of a resurrected, or revivified body, attractive. When Christian preachers spoke of the resurrected body of Christ and the time when the bodies of the dead would be raised, the Gentiles were bound to have questions.

Today's text points us to some of these questions raised by young converts to the faith. From remarks by Paul in this passage, it appears that one of their questions was not so much *whether* there would be a resurrection (cf. I Cor. 15:12) or even *what form of existence* they would experience. Their question was rather what would happen to those who died prior to the coming of Christ.

It is an understandable query. Paul had been with them only a short time during his founding visit, and he doubtless was able to introduce them only to the barest essentials of the early Christian kerygma. Perhaps Timothy had followed through with his instruction (3:1-10). But as we have seen, a central element of the early missionary preaching to Gentiles was the proclamation of the risen Christ who would come at a future date to rescue the saved from the coming wrath of God (1:10). The natural expectation was that this would occur soon, certainly within their lifetime (Rom. 13:12; I Cor. 7:29, 31; 16:22; Heb. 10:37; James 5:8; I Pet. 4:7; Rev. 22:20). Indeed, Paul himself at one point expected that he would be alive at the coming of Christ (4:17), although he apparently finally came to reckon with the possibility that even he might die prior to the Lord's coming (II Cor. 4:16–5:10). Assume, then, that a person has responded to the gospel, becomes a Christian, and fully expects to be rescued from the coming wrath by the returning Son of God. Then assume that this person dies, or falls asleep (verse 13). The natural question is, does that person lose out on the promised deliverance of the coming Messiah?

Paul's response is to reassure those Christians who are troubled about their fellow Christians who have died: "God will bring with him those who have fallen asleep" (verse 14). They are reminded that the destiny of the dead lies with the God who raised Jesus from the dead. God, like Jesus, should be seen as the "Lord both of the dead and of the living" (Rom. 14:9).

Paul goes even further in his answer to their question. He establishes the sequence of events at the end-time. For comparison, one might recall a similar sequence in I Corinthians 15:23: "Each in his own order: Christ the first fruits, then at this coming those who belong to Christ." Here no distinction is made between the dead and the living who belong to Christ at his coming. This, however, is precisely the distinction made in today's text: first the dead in Christ will rise (verse 16), then in a second stage those in Christ who are alive "who are left, shall be caught up together with them in the clouds to meet the Lord in the air" (verse 17). Thus, according to his vision of the end-time, the dead in Christ will be resurrected and will be joined by those who are still alive, so that a single host of believers join Christ in the heavens. Interestingly, he does not address the point here whether those who are alive in Christ will be transformed into another form of existence, although this can be inferred from his discussion in I Corinthians 15:35-50.

What precipitates this is the "coming of the Lord" (verse 15; cf. 2:19; 3:13; 5:23; II Thess. 2:1, 8; I Cor. 15:23 James 5:7-8). His coming is described in terms drawn from Jewish apocalyptic: the Lord descends from heaven, the archangel calls, and the trumpet of God sounds (verse 16; cf. Matt. 24:30-31; Mark 13:26-27; II Thess. 1:7).

The intention of this set of instructions is paraenetic: "Therefore comfort one another with these words" (verse 18; 5:11). This is worth noting since eschatology often functions in Christian preaching to terrify rather than to comfort. It is also worth noting that Paul leaves much unanswered. The focus of his remarks is on those who are "in Christ," and thus he leaves unanswered the question of the fate of those outside of Christ. Neither does he in this context discuss the agenda that he follows in I Corinthians 15, namely the kind of body with which we will be raised. In a word, he responds directly to the questions posed by his hearers, attempts to answer them simply and directly, without complicating their understanding even further. In this instance, less is better.

As we approach this text homiletically, we do well to note

268

the concrete setting in which these eschatological questions arose. The questions of the Thessalonians were quite specific, and they arose because of their expectation of an imminent return of Christ. Naturally our situation is different, and our questions will also be different. Even so, it is a common Christian concern to wonder about "those who have fallen asleep," even more to grieve over them. But Paul calls us not to grieve "as others do who have no hope" (verse 13). Like everyone else, Christians die. This is inescapable. But what distinguishes the Christian understanding of death is our fundamental belief that "Jesus died and rose again" (verse 14) and that the God in whom Jesus placed his own destiny is the God in whom we have placed ours. From this cardinal element of our faith does Christian hope spring. It is this that renders Christian exhortation as reassuring rather than unsettling (verse 18).

Matthew 25:1-13

On these last three Sundays before Advent we will attend to Matthew 25: two parables and the vision of the coming of the Son of man. This chapter not only concludes the fifth major teaching section begun at 23:1 but also marks the end of Jesus' ministry to the public (26:1). From this point on, Jesus will move toward his passion in the presence of close friends and disciples.

Matthew 25:1-13 contains the parable of the ten maidens, found only in the first Gospel but with fragments of similar parables in Luke 12:35-36 and 13:25. Matthew offers very brief commentary on the parable. In verse 1, the word "then" tells the reader that the story concerns the future, and in this case, the future that governs the discussion from 24:36 to 25:46: the certain but uncertain final day and hour. In verse 13, the exhortation to "watch" is commentary on the entire section and not particularly on the parable of the maidens. In this parable, it is not watchfulness that is being enjoined; after all, the wise maidens slept also. The issue is preparedness in the face of uncertainty. The major commentary on this story, as we shall see, is offered by the context.

Gospel parables are basically of two types: those that offer a surprise of grace at the end (a party for a prodigal, a full day's pay for one-hour workers, a tax collector justified, and others) and those that follow the direct course from cause to effect as surely as the harvest comes from what is sown. There are no gifts and parties. Together the two types present justice and grace, either of which becomes distorted without the other. Today's parable moves straight from cause to predictably painful effect: the door is shut and will not be opened.

The preacher will find in the commentaries ample discussion of wedding practices in the writer's time and place, clarifying for modern readers the text's attention on the groom and on the movement of the groom's wedding party. In this brief space, we need to attend to Matthew's emphasis in the story: "the bridegroom was delayed" (verse 5). When one looks at the larger context, the delay theme is seen more clearly as the key to the story. This parable is one of three successive stories bearing this theme: "My master is delayed" (24:48); "As the bridegroom was delayed" (25:5); and "Now after a long time the master of those servants came" (25:19). It may have been that on the lips of Jesus the parable was designed to speak of preparation in view of the Kingdom having arrived at the door, but in the Evangelist's hand, the story is in the futuristic mode. Perhaps Matthew's church faces the problem of how appropriately to live and work as Christians in view of a delayed Parousia. As the parable has it, the delay created the crisis for some of the maidens; the delay was the circumstance about which some proved wise and some foolish; the delay triggered the series of events ending in the final exclusion of those unprepared.

We do not know how widespread and how intense the expectation of the imminent return of Christ really was. However, since many New Testament writers devote attention to the delay (for example, Mark 13:7; II Pet. 3:3-10), we may surmise that such an expectation lay at the heart of the faith of many. But in the face of the problems created by the delay, Matthew refuses to abandon eschatological fulfillment. Whatever the nature and extent of present realizations of the kingdom, the future remains the time of completion and reckoning.

Matthew presents, then, a theology for the delay, for the ongoing life of the church in the world. The maidens who calculated an immediate arrival of the groom were the ones in trouble. But accurate or inaccurate calculating is not at all the issue. The issue has to do with responsible behavior *in the meantime.* After all, it is not the coming of the bridegroom that makes some wise and some foolish; it merely reveals who is.

Proper 28

Sunday Between November 13 and 19 Inclusive

*Zephaniah 1:7, 12-18; Psalm 76; I Thessalonians 5:1-11;
Matthew 25:14-30*

The image of the coming day of the Lord continues with even greater vividness as we draw near the festival of Christ the King. The psalmist parades the power of God before the readers and the prophet warns those who assume God's inactivity that there is wrath to come. Paul instructs the church that the proper response to the Lord's return is not calculating the time and place but in appropriate conduct and relationships. And all these threads are tied together in Jesus' parable of the talents. It may be "after a long time" but the question of how one has handled one's position of trust will eventually be raised.

Zephaniah 1:7, 12-18

This reading continues and expands one of the main themes of last week's Old Testament lesson from Amos, the announcement of the day of the Lord. In fact, Zephaniah must have had the Book of Amos before him as he composed this announcement, for 1:15 picks up the language of Amos 5:18 and 8:8-14 characterizing the day as one of darkness, and 1:13 is a paraphrase of Amos 5:11.

According to the first verse of the book, Zephaniah was active during the reign of King Josiah of Judah, which we date 640–609 B.C. Other seventh-century prophets were Jeremiah, Nahum, and Habakkuk. One of the most important international events during the time of Josiah was the fall of the Assyrian city of Nineveh in 612 B.C. Whether the conflicts that led to the fall of Nineveh or some earlier international crises influenced the message of Zephaniah is not known. The prophet sees disaster on the horizon, but his interpretation is moral and theological: Judah and Jerusalem will be punished for their sins.

Our assigned reading comes from the first major section of the book, 1:2–2:3, a graphic announcement of judgment against Judah and Jerusalem. Except for the occasional messenger formulas (1:2, 3, 7, 10) and the concluding paragraph (2:1-3) in which the prophet calls for the humble among the people to assemble and seek the lord, the speaker throughout is the Lord. The doom announced is so total that it is almost apocalyptic. It alternates between a cosmic destruction of all living things (1:2-3a, 18) and the destruction of the wicked inhabitants of Judah and Jerusalem, or some particular group among the people (1:3b-6, 8-9). In particular the Lord singles out those who have led or participated in idolatrous worship and refuse to inquire of the Lord (1:4-6), the officials and even the sons of the king (1:8). In addition the Lord condemns people for their attitudes as well as for their actions, especially those who say in their hearts, "The Lord will not do good, nor will he do ill" (1:12). Whereas Amos had accused people of religious arrogance, Zephaniah attacks religious cynicism.

As today's reading begins, the prophet is commanding the people to be silent before the Lord God (1:7). In the end he is calling for a solemn assembly, for those who are willing to humble themselves to seek righteousness so that they might "perhaps" escape the wrath of God (2:3). What stands between these prophetic injunctions is the description of the sounds and sights of the day of the Lord as judgment day. The sounds and sights are those of warfare, for the day is the time when the Lord will arise to defeat his enemies, not beyond but among the chosen people. (For further discussion of this point see the comments on last week's Old Testament lesson.)

The sound of the day is "bitter," and even the mighty warrior cries out (verse 14). One hears the war trumpet and the battle cry, not of the defenders but of those who attack the fortified cities (verse 16). The sights are visions of attacking armies, plundering hordes (verse 13), people stumbling about like the blind, and blood spilling on the ground (verse

17). Above all, the imagery of darkness and gloom is used both literally and figuratively (verse 15). The message focuses on the dark side of the intervention of God in history.

As in Amos, this announcement of judgment is directly related to the justice of God. The Lord will bring about the day of wrath because of the sinfulness of the people, especially of their officials, priests, princes, and all those who look cynically on the Lord's willingness to act in history. As far as the reading for today goes, the prophet's purpose is to make the will of the Lord clear and—through the creative power of the word—to set the future into motion. However, in the paragraph that immediately follows (2:1-3) he holds out the bare possibility that some may escape the wrath to come. In the broader context of the book as a whole, the day of the Lord is to be the initial step in the establishment of the kingdom of God, the just reign of the Lord. The punishment is to be purging and cleansing, leaving Jerusalem inhabited by those who are humble, who seek the will of God, and who are just and righteous.

Psalm 76

Like other Zion psalms (Pss. 46, 48, 125), this composition draws on the ancient beliefs about the city of Jerusalem (= Zion). The following beliefs about Zion found expression in the Psalms and were celebrated in worship: (1) God had chosen Zion out of all the cities as his special place; (2) Zion was the dwelling place of God and the sanctuary his abode; (3) Zion was identified with the cosmic divine mountain from which flowed the life-giving streams; (4) God was the protector of Zion, defending her against the threat of chaotic waters and the onslaught of national and historical enemies; and (5) in Zion, God was the great king ruling over his people, the nations, and cosmic order.

Psalm 76 opens with a hymn in praise of Zion (verses 1-3); contains a hymn addressed to God in verses 4-10; and concludes with an appeal to the participating worshipers. The opening hymn proclaims Zion (= Salem; see the name Jerusalem) as the abode and dwelling place of God. The concept of God's dwelling in Zion was based on the presence of the ark of God in the temple. From several narratives in the Old Testament, we know that the ark was closely associated with the presence of God. Where the ark was, there was God. The ark was considered God's throne (Num. 10:35-36; I Sam. 4:4) and was taken into battle so God could aid the Israelite forces. The ark was box-shaped, was carried on poles, and was decorated with cherubim, which were probably composite figures with human faces, bull bodies, and bird wings (Exod. 25:10-22). Two huge cherubim with fifteen-foot wing spans stood over the ark in the Holy of Holies of the Jerusalem temple. When David brought the ark to Jerusalem (II Samuel 6), it was with great fanfare and with all the features of a solemn religious procession. When the temple was completed by Solomon, the ark was placed in the sacred Holy of Holies (I Kings 8:6). The presence of the ark in the temple meant that God was there; the temple was his dwelling place.

Psalm 76:3 refers, as did Psalms 46 and 48, to God's triumph and the destruction of the weapons of war. Many interpreters have sought in this verse (and Ps 76:5-9) a reflection of David's defeat of the Philistines in the environs of Jerusalem (II Sa. 5:17-25). However, what we have in this passage is cultic terminology. In the worship services God was proclaimed as the king over nations and creation and as victorious over all his and Israel's enemies, historical and otherwise.

The second section of this psalm, verses 4-10, is a hymn praising God. God is here described as terrible in his anger, as one who pronounces judgment upon the earth, and as one who stands in judgment to save the oppressed of the earth. The judgment proclaimed is not judgment against God's own people but judgment upon the enemies of Zion.

The psalm concludes with a call to the worshipers to make their vows and to perform them and to offer gifts to God, who cuts off the rulers of the earth (Ps. 76:11-12). The laws regulating the pilgrim festivals required that "none shall appear before [God] empty-handed" (Exod. 23:15). That is, the people must offer to God sacrifices on these occasions. The making of vows—resolutions and promises—at festive celebrations is reflected in the story of Hannah and her husband in I Samuel 1. Hannah was childless and prayed that she would become the mother of a child. As part of her request, she vowed to give the child to God if it were a son (I Samuel 1:11). After the child was born and weaned, Hannah offered him at the sanctuary to fulfill her vow to God. Her husband, Elkanah, was said to have gone up to Shiloh every year to offer sacrifice and to pay his vow (I Sam. 1:21). This yearly festival attended by Elkanah was no doubt the great autumn festival, a time when people made commitments to God, binding vows for the coming year.

I Thessalonians 5:1-11

Like last week's epistolary text, today's New Testament lesson addresses an eschatological question. If it was natural to wonder about the fate of those who died before Christ came, it was only natural to wonder *when* Christ would come. It was common to speculate about the "times and seasons" that would presage the coming of Christ (cf. Matt. 24:36; Acts 1:7).

Paul's opening remark is to reassure his readers of the futility of constructing eschatological timetables (verse 1). Much more important than speculating *when* it would come is to know *how* it would come—suddenly and unexpectedly. The image of a thief coming in the night is frequently used to illustrate the unpredicability of the time of the day of the Lord (Matt. 24:43; II Pet. 3:10; Rev. 3:3; 16:5; cf. Wisd. of Sol. 18:14-15).

Another favorite image used to depict the sudden coming of the Lord is the woman expecting a child (verse 3). It can be used differently. In Isaiah 13:6-8, the day of the Lord is said to be near and those unprepared for it are promised that pain and agony will seize them and that they "will be in anguish like a woman in travail" (cf. also Jer. 6:24; Hos. 13:13). In today's text, however, the point of the image is the suddenness with which a woman can go into labor and a child be born (cf. Mark 13:17 and parallels). At the critical moment, the process is irreversible: "there will be no escape" (verse 3).

Both of these images—the stealthy thief and the pregnant

woman—serve as vivid reminders that we cannot pinpoint precisely when the moment of crisis comes. We are cautioned against reading false signals. When we hear "peace and security" (verse 3; cf. Jer. 6:14), rather than relaxing our guard we should put our systems on alert. The message here is not to try to calculate the hour, but to be alert so that we are prepared at any hour.

After this first set of warnings about the unpredicability of the time of the Lord's coming, Paul urges us to be in a constant state of preparedness. Not that this requires us to be something we are not, or do something we do not normally do. Instead, he instructs us about the true character of Christian existence; "You are all sons of light and sons of the day; we are not of the night or of darkness" (verse 5). Christian conversion can be conceived as a transition from darkness to light (I Pet. 2:9; I John 1:5-7). The dualistic outlook reflected here is also common in Jewish apocalyptic thought. But the point of this reassuring knowledge is that "children of light" need not be frightened by enemies who flourish in darkness, most notably Satan and his denizens.

Since we "belong to the day" (verse 8), we are expected to behave accordingly. The two activities that are excluded are sleeping and drunkenness, both of which presuppose that one is not fully conscious, at least not to the point of being able to make rational, clear-headed decisions. We are urged, then, to "keep awake and be sober" (Rom. 13:11; Eph. 5:14). The proper mood in which to prepare for the day of the Lord is alertness (Mark 13:37; Acts 20:31; I Cor. 16:13; I Pet. 5:8).

Yet another image is introduced with the mention of "the breastplate of faith and love . . . and for a helmet the hope of salvation" (verse 8). Here we are to think of the soldier fully equipped for battle, ready to engage the enemy, on call rather than asleep or drunk in a stupor. Although the metaphor is not developed in as much detail as it is in Ephesians 6:14-17, it is vivid nevertheless as it recalls the image of God as a fully equipped soldier (Isa. 59:16-17; cf. Wisd. of Sol. 5:18). What is striking in the New Testament appropriation of this metaphor is that the Christian is being asked to take on the very attire that God wears!

We should also note the occurrence here of the familiar

triad of virtues: faith, love, and hope (1:3; cf. Rom. 5:1-5; 12:6-12; I Cor. 13:7, 13; Gal. 5:5-6; Eph. 1:15-18; 4:2-4; Col. 1:4-5; I Tim. 6:11; Titus 2:2; Heb. 6:10-12; 10:22-24; I Pet. 1:3-9).

If we are properly equipped with the soldier's armor, we can expect to be protected by God from the coming wrath (verse 9; cf. 1:10; Rom. 5:9). It is not God's intention that any one should be condemned to stand under the divine wrath, especially those who are called through the gospel "to obtain salvation through our Lord Jesus Christ" (verse 9). This is possible because he "died for us" (verse 10; cf. 4:14; Rom. 14:9; I Cor. 15:3-4, 12). As he stressed earlier, regardless of whether we "wake or sleep," that is, whether we die before the Lord comes or whether we are still alive when he comes, "we [will] live with him" (verse 10; cf. 4:17; also Rom. 6:8; Phil. 1:23).

As before, this eschatological discussion concludes with exhortation: "encourage one another and build one another up" (verse 11). Part of the Christian's ongoing responsibility is to engage in mutual encouragement (cf. 4:18; Heb. 3:13) and corporate edification (cf. Rom. 14:19; 15:2; I Cor. 10:23; 14:12, 26; II Cor. 12:19; also Jude 20).

In spite of the span between Paul's time and ours, his words are surprisingly modern, considering the continued apocalyptic speculation that goes on around us. Those who would circle the calendar and predict the date of the Lord's coming are still with us. Their fixation is on "times and seasons." Paul's advice is as sage now as it was then: the important question is not *when* but *how* the Lord will come. The proper response is not frenzy but preparedness that comes from knowing that "we are of the day." It is this, after all, that translates into mutual encouragement and upbuilding, not the feverish fits of the clock watchers.

Matthew 25:14-30

Matthew's parable of the talents and Luke's parable of the pounds (19:12-27) are sufficiently similar to have come from the same story. However, they are sufficiently different to alert the preacher to avoid trying to interweave them. The parable before us is enough for the sermon. The early church historian Eusebius reported on a third version in a work referred to as the Gospel of the Nazarenes, a second-century writing. In that version there were three servants: one multiplied, one stored, and one wasted. Upon his return the master received one with joy, rebuked one, and put one in prison.

This is a story of financial activity. A talent was not the ability to sing or paint but a large sum of money, approximately the amount a laborer would receive for fifteen years of hard work. A capitalist wants his money to be working while he is away and so he entrusts sums of money with servants, expecting a return on his investment. According to the third servant's description of him, the master loves deals without risk and without hard work (verse 24). The preacher will want to beware of making the parable an allegory, having the talents represent one thing, the journey another, the servants another, and the master another. To do so could lead to making the master a representation of Christ, which would, of course, be a misrepresentation. It was not unusual for Jesus to use persons of less than admirable qualities to provide lessons in other parables, the dishonest steward and the unjust judge being two examples. All this assumes the truth of the third servant's portrayal of the master, a description not denied in the master's response.

Having been warned against allegorizing the parable, the reader will, of course, notice that Matthew himself has inserted into the story language that belongs not to a story of financial dealing but to the kingdom. Notice at verses 21 and 23 the reward extended to the first two servants: "enter into the joy of your master." This is not business talk. Likewise, in the conclusion (verse 30) the reference to outer darkness where there is weeping and gnashing of teeth has no meaning in the financial world but is very much a part of Matthew's description of eternal judgment. Matthew uses the expression eight times, most recently occurring in the conclusion of the parable of the marriage feast (22:1-14).

After these many Sundays with Matthew we have become familiar with two characteristics of the first Gospel: the insertion of "spiritual truths" into parables and frequent reminders of the final judgment. And we must acknowledge that at times Matthew's sermonic insertions, no doubt prompted by conditions being addressed, do not seem to flow naturally from the story itself. We saw this in verse 13 as a comment on the parable of the ten maidens and we see it here in verse 29. This is a proverbial saying, sometimes spoken in cynicism, very much like, "Them that has gets" or "The rich get richer and the poor get poorer." Here Matthew probably means to moralize to the effect that gifts unused atrophy while gifts exercised increase. Many sermons on this parable take verse 29 as the central thrust of the story.

However, to do so is to miss the high-risk activity of the first two servants. They doubled the money entrusted to them, hardly a possibility without running the risk of losing the original investment. (Recall Luke's story of a shepherd leaving 99 sheep "in the wilderness" to go in search of one that was lost, 15:3-7.) The major themes of the Christian faith—caring, giving, witnessing, trusting, loving, hoping—cannot be understood or lived without risk. To take verse 29 as the total thrust of the parable is also to miss the problem of the third servant. He was motivated by the opposite of faith; he was afraid (verse 25). While some degrees and occasions of fear are not inappropriate, this is a case of being immobilized at the very center of one's responsibility and purpose. Fear of failure, fear of punishment, fear of loss have not only paralyzed this servant but many servants and many congregations.

Finally, notice again verse 19: "Now after a long time." As discussed in last Sunday's lection, this and the two preceding parables deal with Christian living in view of the delay of the return of Christ. Faithfulness in service is neither determined by nor destroyed by the time of the Parousia.

Proper 29 (Christ the King)

Sunday Between November 20 and 26 Inclusive

Ezekiel 34:11-16, 20-24; Psalm 23; I Corinthians 15:20-28; Matthew 25:31-46

The Season After Pentecost concludes with the festival of Christ the King. In this respect, this Sunday anticipates Epiphany which also celebrates the lordship of Christ. The dramatic vision of Christ coming to reign on his glorious throne (Matt. 25) governs all the texts for today. The sub-theme of Christ as shepherd separating sheep and goats has attracted as companion passages Ezekiel 34 and Psalm 23. Paul joins Matthew 25 in declaring the reign of Christ but only until all things have been brought into subjection to him. Then all is delivered to God who becomes "all in all," the one to whom ultimately the whole creation bows in praise.

Ezekiel 34:11-16, 20-24

This passage from Ezekiel is a highly appropriate reading for the last day of the liturgical year, the focus on Christ as King. On the one hand, the text calls attention to important Old Testament roots of New Testament images and ideas concerning Jesus Christ and the kingdom of God. On the other hand, it has its own particular contributions to make to the Christian proclamation of messianic and eschatological themes.

Ezekiel was a prophet of the period of the Babylonian Exile. He was taken with the first of the deportees when the Babylonians captured Jerusalem in 597 B.C., and reports that he received his call to be a prophet in Babylon in the fifth year of the Judean king Jehoiachin, that is, 593. He emerged as one of the leaders of the exiles in Babylon, although he was

281

frequently in conflict with them concerning the Lord's plans for their future. He clearly stands in the tradition of his prophetic predecessors, such as Hosea, Isaiah, and Jeremiah, but in many ways he is a transitional figure. On the one hand, he shows clear priestly interests, and his thought is related in some ways to the Priestly Document of the Pentateuch. Moreover, he is deeply aware of the legal traditions for which the priests were primarily responsible. On the other hand, both the form and the content of many of his messages move in the direction of apocalyptic literature. Although his visions are not so extended as, e.g., those in Daniel, some of his dramatic images are almost as bizzare as those of later apocalyptic literature. And while he does not look to an end of history, his expectations for transformation tend to go beyond those of earlier prophets.

Ezekiel's discourses include the full range of announcements known to the prophets. There are vision reports, reports of symbolic actions, prophecies of punishment, especially from his earlier period—prophecies against foreign nations and announcements of salvation. The assigned reading for today is part of a larger collection (Ezek. 33–39) consisting mainly of announcements of the return of the exiles and the restoration of the nation with its center in Jerusalem. Most of this material comes from the later period of his activity, after the second fall of Jerusalem and the total destruction of the city in 586 B.C. (cf. Ezek. 33:21-22).

Ezekiel 34, either as a single lengthy discourse or as a collection of several smaller ones, employs the imagry of the shepherd to recapitulate the history of Israel, past, present and future. Throughout, the prophet introduces and quotes the words of Yahweh. The chapter begins (verses 1-6) with an indictment of "the shepherds of Israel," the kings who did not feed the sheep, that is, the people of Israel. Then there is an announcement of judgment against those shepherds, the Lord vowing that he himself will take charge of the sheep (verses 7-11). The chapter concludes with an announcement of the restoration of the people and the promise of a "covenant of peace" (verses 25-31).

Within that framework, the verses assigned for today contain two distinct units, verses 11-16 and 20-24. Both employ the metaphor of the shepherd in proclaiming the Lord's concern for his people, but they use it differently. In the first case the "shepherd" is Yahweh himself (verse 15). Like a shepherd, the Lord will search out the sheep that have been scattered, "bring them out from the peoples, and gather them from the countries, and will bring them into their own land" (verse 13). This clearly is a promise of a return from the Babylonian Exile and restoration in the Promised Land. The Lord further promises to provide the main elements necessary for life: food—and in abundance—and security (verses 14-15). He will take particular care of the lost, the strayed, the crippled, and the weak (verse 16).

There are two distinctive elements in verses 20-24. First, the "one shepherd" is not Yahweh but "my servant David, and he shall feed them" (verse 23). The promise of a future David is not to be taken literally, but is a messianic hope, the expectation of a new and righteous king from the Davidic line. Second, the prophet's expectation of a restored nation includes the element of judgment, as in Matthew 25:31-46. The Lord will judge the sheep, punishing the "fat sheep" who have pushed aside the others, thus making them "lean sheep" (verse 20). He accuses these fat sheep of scattering the flock abroad, that is, of being responsible for the exile of the nation. Remarkably, no specific punishment is noted. Rather, the emphasis falls upon the Lord's provision of proper and just leadership for the nation.

In the concluding line the tension between the Lord as shepherd and David as shepherd would appear to be resolved. Employing the language of covenant, Yahweh affirms: "I, the Lord, will be their God, and my servant David shall be prince among them" (verse 24). The passage is an announcement of salvation, especially for those who have suffered under bad leadership. The kingdom of God envisioned here is not beyond history but within it. God is concerned that his people have food to eat and security with justice (verse 16).

Psalm 23

This widely known and frequently read psalm has been used several times elsewhere in this lectionary series (Fourth

Sunday of Lent, Year A, and the Fourth Sunday of Easter, Years A, B, C). The reader should consult these for details and further exposition of the psalm.

Psalm 23 was selected for today because of the shepherding imagery that it shares with the readings from Ezekiel and Matthew.

Since Psalm 23 has been discussed elsewhere in this series, here remarks will focus on ancient rabbinic interpretation of this text. First of all, the rabbis recognized that shepherding was a difficult task but sensed that in speaking of God as shepherd, the psalm (understood as written by David) was expressive of an ancient wisdom: "These words are to be considered in the light of the verse *I understand more from the ancients* (Ps. 119:100). R. Jose bar Hanina taught: In the whole world you find no occupation more despised than that of the shepherd, who all his days walks about with his staff and his pouch. Yet David presumed to call the Holy One, blessed be He, a shepherd! But David said: I understand more from the ancients, meaning that Jacob called God Shepherd, as it is said *The God who hath been my shepherd all my life long* (Gen. 48:15); so I, too, call God shepherd: The Lord is my shepherd, I shall not want."

Second, the rabbis understood this psalm with reference to God's care for the Hebrews during the wilderness period. The reference to not wanting and such texts as Psalm 78:19 ("Can God spread a table in the wilderness?") helped the interpreters connect the psalm with the wilderness period and the travel from Egypt to Canaan: "R. Judah said in the name of R. Eleazar: 'The road does three things: it makes man's clothes worn, his body lean, and his money scarce. But the Holy One, blessed be He, dealt not thus with Israel. For it was said to Israel,' *Thy raiment waxed not old upon thee* (Deut. 8:4); *the Lord thy God hath been with thee* (Deut. 2:7) in thy health of body; and *thou hast lacked nothing* (ibid.) for thy spending.' "

All the needs of the people were supplied as if they were guests of God: "R. Judah said: 'As when a king is in a city, the city lacks nothing, so *These forty years the Lord thy God hath been with thee, and thou hast lacked nothing* (Deut. 2:7). In the world's use, when a man receives a wayfarer, the first day he kills a calf for him; the second day, a lamb; the third day, a chicken; the fourth day, he serves pulse to him; the fifth day he gives him even less, so that the last day for the wayfarer is not like the first. Now lest one think that it was the same with the wayfaring children of Israel, Scripture states, *These forty years the Lord thy God hath been with thee, thou hast lacked nothing,* and the last day in the wilderness for the children of Israel was like the first.' "

Even the children's clothes grew with them and as a consequence of God's care and never needed repair or cleaning. Even the smell of sweat did not taint their garments. One rabbi declared: "The well of living waters brought up certain plants and certain spices for the children of Israel, and in these they were made to lie down, as is said *He maketh me to lie down in green pastures: He leadeth me beside refreshing waters* (Ps. 23:2), and so the fragrant smell of them was carried from world's end to world's end."

Finally, parts of the psalm were interpreted eschatologically. "To dwell in the house of Yahweh for ever" was understood as life in the world to come or in terms of the rebuilding of the destroyed Jerusalem temple.

I Corinthians 15:20-28

Today's text overlaps the first option for the New Testament lesson (I Cor. 15:19-26) for Easter in Year C. The reader may wish to consult our remarks in that connection in *Lent, Holy Week, Easter, Year C.* There is also slight overlap with the epistolary lection (I Cor. 15:12-20) for the Sixth Sunday After Epiphany (Proper 1) for Year C, which is discussed in *Advent, Christmas, Epiphany, Year C.*

The overall context in which this passage occurs is Paul's discussion of the resurrection in I Corinthians 15. It will be recalled that some of the Corinthian Christians denied, in some sense, the resurrection of the dead (15:12). In what sense they found the notion of resurrection incredible we are not certain, whether they were denying a *future* as opposed to an already realized resurrection (cf. II Tim. 2:18), a *bodily* as opposed to some spiritualized form of resurrection, or the sheer possibility of resurrection itself (cf. Matt. 22:23-28).

In any case, some Christians found it difficult to believe that they would be raised from the dead. Paul's response has several features. He begins by rehearsing the basic Christian kerygma (15:1-11), thereby showing the centrality of the resurrection of Christ within early Christian faith. Apparently the doubters had no difficulty believing that *Christ* had been raised. But would they be raised in the same way? This they were uncertain about.

In response, Paul insists that the two stand or fall together: the resurrection of Christ and the resurrection of all Christians. We cannot accept the former and in principle deny the latter (15:12-19). The thrust of Paul's remarks is to push the doubters to a position of absurdity. They can only account for their existence as a community of the Easter faith because of their belief in the death and resurrection of Christ. Their identity is an expression of their prior faith. To deny the possibility of resurrection in general is to call into question their own existence and identity, to say nothing of Paul's own preaching.

Having pursued this line of argument, Paul then turns his thoughts toward the future to discuss what will happen at the end-time. This is the focus of today's text.

He begins by reiterating a cardinal element of the Christian creed: "But in fact Christ has been raised from the dead" (verse 20; cf. 15:4, 12). This constitutes the heart of the Easter faith and shapes the identity of the Easter community. It is an emphatic declaration, the axiom of Christian belief. It is the "if" clause, the protasis, on which the "then," the apodosis, of Christian faith and praxis depend.

The image used to link Christ's resurrection with our own is "first fruits" (verses 20, 23). It is supplied by the Old Testament (Exod. 23:19; Lev. 23:10; Num. 15:20-21; Deut. 26:1-21) and refers to the practice of setting aside the first part of the harvest as an offering to God. Naturally "first fruits" implied that "other fruits" were to come at the general harvest. The first batch of grain that was harvested was a sure sign that the whole field would eventually be harvested.

A similar relationship, Paul insists, exists between Christ and "those who belong to Christ," literally "those who are of Christ" (verse 23; cf. I Cor. 3:23; Gal. 3:29; 5:24). To speak of

Christ as the "first-born from the dead" (Rom. 8:29; Col. 1:18; Rev. 1:5) implied that Christ was the first one ever to be raised from the dead *in the absolute sense.* As such, he was the first to experience resurrection life. In the image of harvesting, he was the first shock of grain to spring forth from the ground and be harvested (John 12:24). To shift the metaphor, he was the first to awake from the sleep of death (verse 20).

To be "of Christ" means that one participates fully wih Christ and has complete solidarity with Christ (Rom. 6). It is to share in the fate and destiny of Christ as part of the body of Christ (I Cor. 12). In no way, then, can the destiny of Christ be radically separated from the destiny of all Christians. Theirs is a common destiny.

How can we imagine such solidarity between one human and all humans? By remembering the story of Adam (verses 21-22). As Paul interpreted Genesis 1–3, he saw a clear analogy between Adam and Christ (cf. Rom. 5:12-21). Each was a representative figure whose "act" reached far beyond himself. Through the act of the one, the destiny of the many was altered. In the case of Adam, it was altered for the worse; in the case of Christ, it was altered for the better. Through Adam came death; through Christ comes life (verse 22).

But there is a proper sequence, "Each in his own order: Christ the first fruits, then at his own coming those who belong to Christ" (verse 3). By distinguishing separate stages in the process, Paul is perhaps countering some form of realized eschatology which collapsed into a single period the two resurrections of Christ and all Christians. Whether this was the case or not, his remarks have the effect of underscoring the futurity of the Parousia of Christ (cf. I Thess. 2:19; 3:13; 4:16; 5:23; II Thess. 2:1, 8; James 5:7-8).

At this point, an exegetical problem arises which the preacher will do well to notice. In verse 24, the phrase "then comes the end *(telos)*" is taken by some commentators to mean "then come the remainder," in the sense of the rest of humanity. This way of rendering the phrase would suggest yet a third group who participate in God's eschatological work. It would also make possible a more universalistic reading of the passage. The larger question is whether Paul, in these remarks, is focusing specifically on the fate and destiny of Christians only, or whether he is thinking more broadly in terms of the whole of humanity.

With verse 24 we are introduced to the part of the passage that has the clearest resonance with the celebration of Christ the King. Here the imagery of "kingdom" occurs, as we are assured that in the end-time Christ will transfer the kingdom to God. It is remarkable language, if for no other reason, because of the relative infrequency with which Paul speaks of the kingdom of God (15:50; Rom. 14:17; I Cor. 4:20; 6:9-10; Gal. 5:21; I Thess. 2:12; II Thess. 1:5).

Behind these remarks is the Christian conviction that Christ was the Son exalted to God's right hand, thus the fulfillment of Psalm 110:1 (cf. Matt. 22:44 and parallels). From this exalted, kingly position, Christ enjoys an interim reign during which competing forces, here represented as "every rule and every authority and power" are gradually being vanquished (Rom. 8:38; I Cor. 2:6; Eph. 1:21; 2:2; 3:10; 6:12; Rom. 8:38; Col. 1:13, 16; 2:10, 15; I Pet. 3:22; Heb. 2:5; II Pet. 2:10). The last in the line of enemies is death (verse 26; cf. Rev. 20:14; 21:4).

When the work of Christ is finally accomplished, the Son hands over the kingdom to the Father (Dan. 2:44; Eph. 1:20-21). All of this should be seen as being done under the auspices of God, who, after all, is preeminent in power (Eph. 1:22; Heb. 2:8). In no sense, should the power of Christ be understood to supersede the preeminent status of God (verse 27). Thus, when we confess that "all things are put in subjection under [Christ]" (verse 27), God is naturally excepted. Indeed, Christ himself finally yields in ultimate submission to God (verse 28). The epitome of power and authority finally belongs to God before whom Christ yields his authority (I Cor. 3:23).

We can see how our passage for today becomes an important text for celebrating the kingship of Christ. Certainly his role in the eschaton is stressed but also his intermediate role as the Sovereign of the earth. Yet today's passage also imposes some constraints on how we understand Christ as King, for it clearly qualifies his sovereignty with respect to the ultimate sovereignty of God.

Matthew 25:31-46

The festival of Christ the King concludes the post-Pentecost season and immediately precedes Advent. One could hardly imagine a more appropriate text than Matthew 25:31-46. With this teaching Jesus concludes his public instruction, and if the principle of end stress is at work here, then Matthew wants this to be the lingering lesson in his auditors' ears. These verses have no parallel in Mark or Luke; their kinship is with the throne scene in Revelation 20:11-15 and with Son of man passages in the Old Testament (Daniel) and in extracanonical writings such as Enoch.

This text is not a parable but an apocalyptic vision of the last judgment. The purpose of the vision is not speculation about the end or for the fascination of the community. Rather the vision is the vehicle for ethical instruction. The heart of it is the coming ("Parousia," 24:3) of the Son of man. His coming is not to the earth, but to the throne in heavenly glory. The scene is an enthronement, the Son of man being installed as King and Judge (Son of man appears only in verse 31; thereafter the term is "King," verses 34, 40). The "coming" has been dealt with already: it will be sudden as the lightning (24:27); it will be on clouds of glory and with great power (24:30-31); the day and hour are unknown (24:36-42); it will be as a burglar entering at night (24:43); it will be a time of reckoning and woe to the unprepared (24:45-51). Three parables have dealt with the delay of the coming (24:45–25:30). But now comes the full vision, glorious in appearance, cosmic in scope, and yet personal in that every life must appear before the judgment seat.

Terms used to describe the event are drawn from the treasury of Jewish thought. "Right" and "left" (verse 33) were common terms in both Jewish and Gentile culture for the favored and unfavored position. "Inherit the kingdom" (verse 34) comes from Israel's tradition about the Promised Land. "From the foundation of the world" (verse 34) draws upon the view that all which was essential for God's eternal purpose was created before the world was made. In other words, all which pertains to God's will is not contingent upon anything in the created order.

Three elements in the vision draw special attention. First, the basis for the final judgment is one's response to human need (verses 35-36). These needs are not unusual but present themselves in the ordinary coming and going of one's life. Second, both those at the right and at the left are surprised that they have so served or failed to serve Christ (verses 37-39, 44). This touch of being surprised is a beautiful portrait of those saints whose service to others is so much a part of their behavior that they are embarrassed at the recital of their deeds and amazed that service to those in need is service to Christ. And the element of surprise also describes vividly those who, in Matthew's community, were busily religious in attention-getting ways but who bypassed the scenes of human anguish. Recall 7:21-23 and those who are rejected even though they make valid claims to having prophesied, cast out demons, and performed miracles. What could be more religious, Matthew says, than attending to those who need care?

And finally, the vision reminds the reader that service to another is service to Christ. Matthew said this earlier (10:40-42), but here the point is dramatized and elevated to ultimate importance. However, the reader will want to avoid turning this truth into a strategy for assuring one's salvation. This is to say, one must avoid reading this text and then concluding, "From now on, every time I see a person alone or in prison or hungry or thirsty I will not see that person but I will see Christ." Such behavior would render every needy person faceless and nameless by those joyfully "serving Christ" rather than human need. Most likely these, too, would be surprised at the final judgment.

Visitation, May 31

I Samuel 2:1-10; Psalm 113; Romans 12:9-16b;
Luke 1:39-57

This service focuses on Mary as God's servant and not on the advent of the Christ Child. Luke's account of Mary's visit to Elizabeth does, of course, anticipate Advent, and so the preacher will want to keep the camera on Mary who is for Luke the model of humble obedience to God. Mary's song makes much use of the Song of Hannah (I Sam. 2), both of which speak of God's favor upon those who serve with little attention and less praise. This theme naturally attracts Psalm 113 and Romans 12.

I Samuel 2:1-10

This text has found its place as the Old Testament lesson on Visitation primarily because Hannah, the mother of Samuel, has been seen as a type of Mary, the mother of Jesus. In addition, the occasions of the Song of Hannah and the Magnificat are quite similar; both concern the birth of babies who are divine gifts, and both of the babies are dedicated by their mothers to the service of God. Moreover, several themes in Hannah's Song parallel those of the Magnificat, especially those that focus on God's care for the lowly.

Hannah's Song, like Mary's, comes at a critical point in history. In the lengthy history of Israel from the time of Moses to the Babylonian Exile, Samuel is an extremely important figure who spans two distant eras, the end of the period of the judges and the beginning of the monarchy. The baby whose birth Hannah celebrates will be the last and most significant judge, but he will be more, serving both priestly and prophetic functions as well. Finally, he will be the one to

291

preside over Israel's debate about whether or not to have a king, and will designate first Saul and then David as kings.

None of this is told in the account of the birth of the boy Samuel, but it is made clear from the outset that he is a child of destiny. In his birth the devotion of a woman and the graciousness of God work hand-in-hand. Long past the age of childbearing, Hannah goes to the sanctuary at Shiloh, presided over by Eli the priest, to pray for a son, vowing that he would be dedicated to serve the Lord. The Lord heard her prayer and when the child was weaned, she took him to Shiloh to hand him over to service in the sanctuary.

The Song of Hannah is presented as part of the service for the consecration of Samuel. However, its relationship to the context is quite loose. Within the song there are no specific allusions to the persons or the period but, on the other hand, an anachronistic allusion to the king (verse 10). It is likely that the song itself is a later addition to the narrative, supplied as an appropriate expression of Hannah's piety and a typical part of a service of worship.

Hannah's Song is similar in many respects to other Old Testament lyrical poetry that arose and was used in worship. In particular, it is a song of thanksgiving which has, like many such songs, features of hymns of praise. The thanksgiving song typically was part of services of worship not found on a liturgical calendar. When an individual or the nation found itself in trouble, a prayer service was held, in which the central part was a prayer of complaint. When the individual or the nation was delivered from the distress, a service of thanksgiving was called. When Hannah first went to the sanctuary at Shiloh she went to complain about her barrenness and ask the Lord's help. Now, fulfilling the vow made as part of that prayer, she gives thanks.

Songs of thanksgiving and praise spring from the human experience of God as both powerful and caring. Hence they are filled with the mood of joy and confidence. Since that experience takes many forms, the themes of such songs are almost unlimited. They may celebrate the world as God's creation, or particular acts of salvation in history or in one's life. Among the themes of the Song of Hannah are the following: (1) joy and rejoicing because of the Lord's help (verse 1); (2) the incomparability of the Lord, as a sure support (verse 2); (3) the Lord chooses the weak over the powerful (verse 4); (4) the Lord cares for the needy, whether they are hungry or barren (verses 5, 8*a*); (5) the Lord's power extends to all things, over life and death and to the foundations of the earth (verses 6, 8*b*); and (6) the Lord protects the faithful against the wicked, defeating his adversaries, and his reign will extend to the ends of the earth (verses 9-10).

Psalm 113

Three general considerations about this psalm should be noted initially: (1) it, along with Psalms 114–118, was employed in both temple services (at the time of the slaughter of the lambs) and home celebrations (as part of the meal ritual) during the Passover festival; thus the imagery of the psalm came to be associated with the events of the Exodus which was commemorated in the Passover ritual; (2) the psalm has many similarities to the Song of Hannah in I Samuel 2:1-10 with which it may be profitably compared; the similarity of both of these to Mary's Magnificat in Luke 1:46-55 has led to their connection with Visitation; and (3) the psalm shares in a common biblical motif, which might be called the "reversal of fate" or the "from rags to riches" sentiment.

The genre and structure of the psalm are clear. It is a hymn utilized to express and instill faith and particular beliefs by and in the congregation. The initial verses (1-4) are a summons to praise God, temporally in all times and forever (verse 2), and geographically in all places and everywhere (verse 3). Verses 5-9 provide the motivations, the reasons why God should be praised. These are presented in the form of a question (verses 5-6) and an answer (verses 7-9).

The psalm develops a dialectic in the divine and thus speaks about God in contrasting ways. In the question (verses 5-6), God is highly exalted who, sitting above looks far down upon earth and even far down upon the heavens. If such a transcendent God must squint to see the earth, then surely the course of events and the status of individual persons must be beyond divine purview. The answer given to, "Who is like Yahweh?" comes, however, as unexpected in its content. Yahweh is the one who reverses the fate of the unfortunate, who transforms the status of those whom society judges as failures. Yahweh is not an unconcerned transcendent Deity but the caretaker of the dispossessed and the unpossessing.

Verses 7-8 concern the reversal of status of the male. The poor and the needy would have been those condemned by fate and fortune to marginal participation in the life of the community. These would have been forced to live in poverty at the peripheries of society. Perhaps they had gotten in that condition by misfortune, poor harvests, illness, or debt. The dust and the ash heap refer to the city garbage dump where the dispossessed and unpossessing as well as the sick and leprous (see Lam. 4:5; Job 2:8; Lev. 13:45-46) made their domicile, grubbed for survival, begged for a handout, got food and clothing from family and friends if they had any. Such places of last resort are similar to modern old folks' homes and public shelters as well as dump hovels where the world's refugees congregate. A male living under such conditions in ancient times would have been without social standing and without self-respect and confidence. So much for verse 7, the "before" in the psalmic commercial.

The "after" we find in verse 8. The ones suffering deprivation and ostracism are made to sit with the nobles/princes, that is, with the rich and the powerful. To "sit with" implies acceptance by others and self-assurance by the new participant. (Remember the difference between standing integration and sitting integration in the South. "Sit-ins" marked a new state in the civil rights movement because to "sit with" is to share.) For the ideal of one who sits with the nobles, see Job 29:1-25.

The transformation of the unfortunate female is noted in verse 9. The mother was not really "at home" in the extended family of her husband, that is, she had no real security or sense of fully belonging and participating, until she and her children created their own space and place in the family. The wife, always brought into the husband's family, was an outsider to her in-laws until children transformed her into an insider and made her "at home." It must have been lonely in such a situation for the barren wife, so much so, that barrenness could be understood as a disgrace if not a curse from God (see Gen. 16:2; 20:18; I Sam. 1:5; Luke 1:25). Many of the matriarchs of Israel, however, were barren (Sarah, Rachel, Hannah) for a long time before they produced a child viewed as the result of divine intervention.

Romans 12:9-16*b*

Most of this passage (verses 9-13) has already been treated earlier in this volume in connection with the epistolary lection (Rom. 12:1-13) for Proper 17. Since the same text serves as the New Testament lesson for Visitation in all three years, the reader may also wish to consult our remarks on this passage in *After Pentecost* for Years B and C.

Verses 14-16*b* contain several injunctions that echo sentiments found in Matthew's collection of Jesus' teachings otherwise known as the Sermon on the Mount.

"Bless those who persecute you: never curse them, bless them" (verse 14, JB). In the Matthean tradition, the command to pray for our presecutors is linked with love for our enemies, which reverses the normal pattern of loving our friends and hating our enemies (Matt. 5:44). Perhaps the most visible and memorable instance of this is the Lukan portrait of the crucified Christ who asks the Father to forgive those who crucified him for acting in ignorance (Luke 23:34). The portrait of Stephen in Acts is clearly modeled on the earlier depiction of Jesus (Acts 7:60), Luke's way of indicating that the church is to emulate the example of Jesus in this respect. It is a form of reverse response that is enacted in the apostolic ministry of Paul (I Cor. 4:12). In I Peter 3:9-12, blessing as the appropriate response to reviling is justified by appealing to Psalm 34:12-16, which says to eschew speech that is evil and full of guile.

"Rejoice with those who rejoice and be sad with those in sorrow" (verse 15, JB). In the second Beatitude, those who mourn are promised solace (Matt. 5:4). The Jewish Wisdom tradition also made it obligatory to minister to those in mourning: "Do not fail those who weep" (Sir. 7:34). What is envisioned here in this double-pronged injunction is a level of genuine community where "not just the exceptional situation but everyday life with its alternation of laughter and tears summons us away from the Stoic ideal of *ataraxia* not merely to participation but beyond that to demonstrated brotherhood with all" (Käsemann following Conzelmann). Not that a sense of community was absent among the Stoics, for Marcus Aurelius insisted that one should be a "rational and civic creature" who fulfills social obligations: "That which is not in the interests of the hive cannot be in the interest of the bee" (*To Himself* 6.54).

"Live in harmony with one another" (verse 16*a*). This is the call to be of the same mind (cf. Rom. 15:5; II Cor. 13:11; Phil. 2:2; 4:2). "This does not mean that [we] must think the same thoughts, which is only seldom realized and not even desirable. It is rather a matter or orientation to the single goal of the community united in grace, which . . . enables us to be of one spirit in spite of tensions, and which comes to expression in unanimity" (Käsemann).

"Do not be haughty, but associate with the lowly; never be conceited" (verse 16*b*). The flavor of the first injunction is expressed especially well by JB: "Never be condescending but make real friends with the poor." Arrogance and self-assertion are inappropriate forms of Christian behavior, not only because they reverse the true nature of the work of Christ (Phil. 2:5-11; cf. Mark 10:45), but because they reflect an egocentrism that becomes debilitating to any genuine form of community (I Cor. 4:6-7; 11:22). We should also note that more is being called for here than mere change of attitude toward the lowly. We are enjoined to "associate with the lowly," which can only suggest community and solidarity at its most basic level (Mark 2:15-17; Luke 4:18-19).

Several features of today's epistolary text make it especially fitting for the celebration of Visitation. In the Gospel lesson Elizabeth is so taken with the visit of Mary that she exclaims, "And why is this granted me, that the mother of my Lord should come to me?" (Luke 1:43). Clearly Elizabeth is being visited by one who has been uniquely blessed. Mary recognizes that it is in her own "low estate" that she has been visited by God (Luke 1:48). Consequently, she can in no way be conceited and condescending toward her cousin Elizabeth. In the Lukan narrative, the visit of Mary to Elizabeth is an unselfish gesture, an occasion for two expectant women to rejoice together. Eventually both would lose their sons to violent deaths, and although the Gospel does not record it, we can well imagine their weeping together.

Luke 1:39-57

The service of Visitation recalls Mary's visit to her kinswoman Elizabeth in the hill country of Judah. This celebration not only provides the occasion for the church to anticipate Christmas yet six months away, but also the opportunity to hear Luke sing and expound on that beautiful moment. Before the births of either John or Jesus the reader of Luke is made privy, through their mothers, to the profound Christian themes yet to be lived out and proclaimed.

Elizabeth and Mary are not nameless and faceless women who are no more than the wombs that carry great sons. They are persons with names, addresses, beliefs, hopes, and joy in service. Such is Luke's treatment of women in the Gospel story. Mary will reappear in trust and devotion (Acts 1:14), as will other women who join in the mission (Luke 8:1-3), and to them is entrusted the one sustained hallelujah of the Christian faith: He is risen (Luke 24:1-12).

Mary's visit to Elizabeth provides the occasion for the two women to celebrate the angel's word to Mary, which was also the angel's word to Abraham and Sarah: "For with God nothing will be impossible" (1:37; Gen. 18:14). As Paul was to express it, God gives life to the dead and calls into existence things that do not exist (Rom. 4:17). It does not matter whether it is a case of an old and barren couple or a virgin without a husband. The Visitation is, therefore, a double celebration of the power of God to give life.

The Visitation is also a study in contrasts. Elizabeth is old, wife of a priest who was part of an ancient order of things in

Israel. Having a child in her old age is a reminder of the past: Abraham and Sarah, Manoah and his wife, Elkanah and Hannah, from whom came Isaac and Samson and Samuel. The promises of God survived and continued through the unlikely births to the old and barren. But Mary was young, a life new, virgin, and all promise. She and her child do not remind one of the past; in fact, in them begins a new history. Mary's child is continuous with the past, to be sure, the fulfillment of a promise, but in him God is doing a new thing. So radically new is this act of God that the only appropriate means was a woman young, and a virgin.

The Visitation is also a beautiful reflection, through the women, of the futures of their unborn sons. As Elizabeth is humbled by the visit of "the mother of my Lord" (verse 43) so John was witness and servant to Jesus. As John leaped in Elizabeth's womb when Mary entered the house (verses 41, 44), so John's joy was that of a groomsman when the bridegroom arrived (John 3:29-30). As Elizabeth blessed Mary not only for her child but also because Mary believed the word of God (verses 42-45), so John would come calling for faith in Jesus as the means of life in the kingdom. There is never any question for Luke that Jesus and not John is the Messiah, but neither is there any question that both Elizabeth and Mary are servants of God's purpose, both their sons are gifts of God, and both sons have appointed ministries in God's plan for the ingathering of the nations.

The Visitation is also a preview of reversals yet to come. The ordinary structures of history, the usual cause and effect sequences of events, could not sustain or contain what God would be doing. The empty will be full and the full, empty; the poor will be rich and the rich, poor; the powerless will reign and the powerful will be dethroned. In a close approximation of the Song of Hannah (I Sam. 2:1-10), Mary sings of the eschatological reversal of stations and fortunes in the realm where and when God's love and justice rule supreme.

Holy Cross, September 14

Numbers 21:4b-9; Psalm 98:1-5 or Psalm 78:1-2, 34-38;
1 Corinthians 1:18-24; John 3:13-17

The "lifting up" of Jesus is a frequent reference in the Fourth Gospel to Jesus' death on the cross and to his exaltation to God's presence. In John 3 the expression is joined to the analogy of the brazen serpent story in Numbers 21. In the Epistle, Paul speaks of the preaching of the cross as God's weakness and foolishness which is stronger and wiser than all human accomplishments. In a similar vein, both readings from the Psalms praise the triumph, not of God's power, but of God's forgiving goodness.

Numbers 21:4b-9

Like many other Old Testament readings for special days, this one has been connected with the particular occasion on the basis of typological exegesis. The association of this passage from Numbers with the cross of Jesus comes from New Testament times. "And as Moses lifted up the serpent in the wilderness, so must the Son of man be lifted up" (John 3:14). It continues to be instructive to reflect on the ways the story of the serpent in the wilderness is like the cross.

It seems as if Moses had nothing but trouble from the people of Israel in the wilderness. On other occasions in the readings for this season we have encountered those people complaining against Moses and the Lord, even objecting to the burdens of their election, the fact that they were set free from slavery in Egypt (see the commentary on the Old Testament lessons for Proper 15 in this volume).

Although this story of complaint begins like most of the others, its results are quite different from the previous ones. There is the general observation that the people "became

299

impatient on the way" (verse 4). The reader familiar with the story of Israel's travels from Egypt will already find this remarkable: They had been impatient and dissatisfied almost from the first day! Then follows the grumbling that is a summary of all the things they have complained about from the beginning. They grumble against God and Moses about being in the wilderness, about the lack of food and water, and—inconsistently—about the food they do have. This doubtless is an objection to the manna, never especially appealing, but certainly boring after the traditional forty years in the desert.

Usually what has happened at this point in the story is Moses' intercession with the Lord, who graciously meets the needs of the people, either for food, water, or security. But we hear without explanation that the Lord sent "fiery serpents among the people, and they bit the people, so that many people of Israel died" (verse 6). Now the people do two things. They confess their sin of rebellion against the Lord and the leadership of Moses, and they ask Moses to intercede wtih the Lord to remove the serpents (verse 7).

When Moses prays for the people, the Lord responds but he does not "take away the serpents." Instead he instructs Moses to make a fiery serpent and set it on a pole so that those who are bitten may look at it and live (verse 8). Moses did as instructed, setting up a bronze serpent, and it functioned as promised (verse 9).

The religious background of the traditions in this passage are complex. The belief is widespread that the image of a dangerous animal can function as protection against it, and the image of the snake in particular is associated with healing rituals in various religions. But does not the very fashioning of such an image violate the second commandment (Exod. 20:4) and thus threaten to violate the first commandment (Exod. 20-3)? Perhaps that is why the text mentions cautiously that the people were only to "look at" the bronze serpent. It is not an idol but a gift of the Lord. There must have been such an image in the temple in Jerusalem, for II Kings 18:4 reports that when Hezekiah purified the worship he destroyed "the bronze serpent that Moses had made." Even healing symbols can become objects of idolatry.

SPECIAL DAYS

Theologically, the most important factor here is the pattern of sin, punishment, and God's means of grace. Once the people sin, experience the punishment, confess their sin and pray for relief, the Lord responds. On the one hand, it appears that God was eager to respond almost before they asked. On the other hand, the prayer is not granted in the form it was presented. Sin has—and will continue to have—its effects. The dangers remain, and the people continue to suffer from the potentially death-dealing snakes. However, now there is healing from the Lord, although the scars of the snake bites—the effects of sin—doubtless will remain.

Psalm 98:1-5

The exaltation of the cross is a sign of triumph and victory, of restoration and healing. That Psalm 98 should be chosen for reading on this day is quite appropriate since the psalm celebrates a triumphant Deity.

This text is one of the enthronement psalms (93–99) which were used in the fall festival as part of the ritual reenthronement of Yahweh. The festival celebrated, as the psalm proclaims, the triumph and reign of Yahweh as king. In the first five verses of the psalm emphasis falls on the victorious triumph of God (verses 1-3), which is paralleled in the triumph of Christ on the cross, and on the call to praise (verses 4-5), which is paralleled in the cross as the exaltation of Christ.

The term "victory" is repeated three times in the opening three verses. The victory of God is declared to be (1) the consequence of his power symbolized by his right hand and holy arm, (2) his vindication among the nations or the establishment of his status and reputation among the peoples of the world, and (3) the manifestation of his love and fidelity to Israel. God himself, the nations of the world, and all his chosen people are thus seen as involved in the divine victory.

The response to the victory of God is human praise. Verses 4-5 call upon the world to respond in song and sound with voice and instrument.

Psalm 78:1-2, 34-38

Part of this text as well as its general content was discussed under Proper 15 on pages 143-45. Verses 34-38 emphasize that although God had reason to destroy the Hebrews in the Wilderness he did not. One such example of his care and long-suffering is reported in the narrative of Numbers 21:4*b*-9.

The two sections selected for this lection are part of the introduction (verses 1-2) and a portion of the psalmist's interpretation and preaching on the wilderness theme (verses 34-38). The opening verses present the historical synopsis and interpretation that follow as a teaching or a parable, that is, not as a pure recital of history but as an interpretative reading of the past intended to speak to the present.

Verses 34-38 are a portion of the homily on Israel's behavior in the wilderness. Although cared for, preserved, and fed in the desert, the Hebrews are described as having constantly sinned. The people are depicted as demurring and demanding, unappreciative and uncooperative. Over and over again, God has to act to reprimand them. Verses 34-38 proclaim two things about the people: (1) they were not repentant until they were punished; they did not turn toward God until God had turned against them; their repentance was the product of divine coercion and (2) their devotion was superficial and temporary. Their mouths and their tongues were committed to religious expression, not their hearts. Flattery and lies not fidelity and loyalty were their hallmarks.

In spite of the people's behavior and their transient faith, they depicted God as their refuge and redeemer (verse 35). Long-suffering and forbearing, God forgave and did not destroy; he withheld his anger and did not give vent to his wrath (verse 38).

I Corinthians 1:18-24

It is a tribute to this celebrated Pauline passage that we hear it read every liturgical year. It is featured prominently each year when I Corinthians 1:18-31 serves as the New Testament lesson for Tuesday in Holy Week. In Year A, the same text is heard on the Fourth Sunday After Epiphany. In Year B, a portion of this text (verses 22-25) is heard on the Third Sunday of Lent. And for the celebration of Holy Cross each year, verses 18-24 serve as the New Testament lesson. How it is heard and read will obviously differ at each of these times, as each liturgical setting creates its own nuance and causes us to attune our ears accordingly. The preacher may wish to consult our remarks on the passage in each of these settings since its full implication can hardly be grasped with any one reading or set of interpretive remarks.

We should first read it—and understand it—in its own context, within Paul's first letter to the church at Corinth. It occupies a prominent position toward the beginning of the letter, immediately following his appeal for unity (I Cor. 1:10-17). Its placement here is crucial, for it introduces a theological perspective that serves as an important corrective. Within the Corinthian church there was an emerging theological position, if not a position at least an outlook, that placed a high premium on wisdom and knowledge. Paul had already begun to see the debilitating effects this viewpoint was having on the church, creating pockets of loyalty and rivalry, stratifying the community into levels—levels of knowledge and ignorance, levels of gifts, levels of concern or lack of concern for one another, levels of strength and weakness. Some scholars have characterized the viewpoint as "gnostic," and perhaps it was in the sense of an amorphous outlook but not in the sense of a developed theological system as was the case in the second century.

In the face of the situation as he perceived it, Paul casts anchor at the very outset. The point at which he pitches the battle for the hearts of the Corinthians is "the preaching of the cross" (verse 18). With these words we are close to the heart of Paul's gospel. In his original missionary preaching among the Corinthians, he had made an intentional choice to focus primarily, if not exclusively, on "Christ and him crucified" (I Cor. 2:2). If asked to define his own psychological center of gravity, Paul would answer: the cross. Somehow the cross had become for him more than a narrative event, more than a story dramatically unfolded in the Passion story

(Mark 15:16-47; Matthew 27:27-44; Luke 23:26-56, John 19:1-42). Doubtless when he preached about the cross, he rehearsed this story, if not in whole at least in part. The "preaching of the cross" was preaching whose content, as well as motivation, was the story of the crucified Christ. In this sense, it was a past event, for he could speak of those who had "crucified the Lord of glory" (I Cor. 2:8).

But just as surely as the cross was for Paul a past event, it was more than this. It was narrative, but it was also symbol. Somehow the word "cross" captured the essence of God's dealings with humanity. Somehow it became for Paul a riddle, an inescapaple enigma. His word for it is "stumbling block," or "scandal" (*skandalon*, Gal. 5:11). We know some of the reasons why. The notion of a crucified Messiah created a severe hermeneutical problem. Deuteronomy 21:22-23 stated that "a hanged man is accursed by God," and given the undeniable nature of Jesus' death by crucifixion, he was implicated by this passage. We know how incredible Peter found the notion of a suffering Messiah (Matt. 16:21-23).

There was also the sheer incredibility of the message of the cross. Jews found it offensive, and Greeks found it irrational. Or, in the words of today's text, "a stumbling block to Jews and folly to Gentiles" (verse 23). Judged in the arena of public opinion, "the word of the cross" did not fare that well. It came as a minority opinion, voted down by the majority.

Yet as Paul understood the cross, it revealed something unique and fundamental about God. The sheer fact that humans found it difficult to accept, if not an inconceivable way for God to act, was itself revelatory, for in this way the cross illustrates God's capacity to confound us. Our tendency is to rationalize the work of God so that it conforms to our own expectations. We make it fit, or else we implicate God; but this is the height of human arrogance, Paul insists, this inclination to call God's hand. God can do without consultants! (verses 19-20).

Rather than repelling Paul, the cross attracted him. Not because of the beauty or power of the Passion story. It was neither beautiful nor powerful. If anything, it was a story of human savagery, of misguided human motives, of human conspiracy, and human ignorance. If anything, it was an unfolding drama of powerlessness, of events turning in on themselves, of the inability of divine intervention. Yet it was precisely in and through an event, or series of events, where human weakness reigned, where divine power was conspicuously absent rather than dramatically present, that Paul saw God most visibily revealed. The cross was a vacuum where neither "signs" nor "wisdom" were present to save the day. It was its own sign, its own peculiar symbol, its own form of wisdom, its own revelatory word. And if we look closely, we see God at work in a way that "makes sense" of the world as we know and experience it.

The cross as event, symbol, and enigma thus becomes the clue to who God really is. It reveals a God who is made known in weakness rather than strength, in suffering rather than robust health, in powerlessness rather than in shows of force, in moments of darkness rather than in shafts of dazzling sunlight. It is the God who is experienced in the underside of life, in the shadows not in the sun.

So construed, the cross becomes for Paul a point of psychological redefinition. "Far, be it from me to glory except in the cross of our Lord Jesus Christ, by which the world has been crucified to me, and I to the world" (Gal. 6:14). His angle of vision on the world was radically altered by the cross. From this vantage point, the world's values were reversed (Phil. 3:5-7). Indeed, the "world" became crucified in the sense that it ceased to lay hold on him in the way it once did. It died. It ceased to exist. It no longer had the finality it once had. After the cross, "the form of this world [began to pass] away" (I Cor. 7:31; II Cor. 4:16–5:5).

The reverse was also true. Just as the "world" died, so had "Paul" died. The "I" which figured so prominently in his self-understanding died. Through the cross, and his co-participation with Christ in the crucifixion, the form of his personal existence radically shifted from an "egocentric" to a "Christocentric" form of existence (Gal. 2:19-20).

Paul was the first to admit that such an understanding of the cross was reserved for "those who are called" (verse 24). It was, after all, a matter of being summoned by God. In this sense, the cross beckons, and its beckon must be heard over the objections of scandal and irrationality.

John 3:13-17

As a magnet, the subject of the cross has been held over the text for the day, drawing to itself those verses pertaining directly to that event. Fairness to the subject and to the text demands, however, that verses 13-17 be set back into the context in order to extract them again.

John 3:1-21 is usually regarded as a conversation between Jesus and Nicodemus. However, where the Evangelist ends the conversation and where his own comments begin is not clear. One had but to look at different red-letter editions to see this uncertainty illustrated: Do Jesus' words end at verse 15, at 16, or at 21? the question is, however, a moot one, because the text reveals clearly that John is doing more than reporting a conversation. Such a shift begins at verse 7 with a change from the singular to the plural "you." The message from Jesus, says the writer, is to all and not to Nicodemus alone. The plural continues in verses 11 and 12. In addition, at verse 11 the "conversation" becomes more openly a debate between the church and the synagogue over the subject of life in the kingdom. Note the "we" versus "you" (plural). Furthermore, at verse 13 the passage becomes even more obviously a post-Easter Christian message by the statement in the past tense, "No one has ascended into heaven but he who descended from heaven, the Son of man." The earthly sojourn of the Savior is viewed as a completed event. It would be unfair, therefore, to treat this text within the confines of a private conversation at the beginning of Jesus' ministry, and it would be grossly unfair to be critical of Nicodemus for not understanding it. The Evangelist, by means of Nicodemus, is addressing the reader.

And what is the Evangelist saying to the reader? Let us confine courselves to the bearing of the text on our subject, the cross of Christ. Since the cross is not mentioned in verses 13-17, how is it to be discerned here? To be sure, in traditional church art, music, and theology, John 3:16 is associated with Golgotha. It is as though it were to be translated, "For God so loved the world that he gave his only Son *on the cross*." That the cross is a part of the Johannine understanding of salvation is beyond question. Jesus lays down his life for the sheep (10:11); he lays down his life for his friends (15:13); he dies as the Passover lamb providing the freedom of a new exodus for the people of God (19:31-37). But the cross in this Gosepl is the means of glorifying the Son (12:23-28); that is, of returning the Son to the presence of God. Hence the double meaning of being "lifted up" (verse 14; 8:28; 12:34)—up on the cross and up into glory. This being lifted up is as surely an act of God's grace and love as was the provision for salvation in the camp of Israel when they suffered God's judgment and punishment for their unbelief and disobedience (verse 14; Num. 21). Jesus' being lifted up was an act of love from God toward the world, and to be understood as this Evangelist presents it, that act needs to be seen in the full movement of the descending and the ascending of the Son of man (verse 13).

In summary fashion, John's message may be stated this way: the Son came into the world to reveal God (1:18), whom to know is life eternal (17:3). That revelation is not only in signs and discourses but also in the cross.

The God revealed in the Son is a God who loves, who loves the whole world, and who desires none to perish but that all have life eternal. God does not simply wish this; God sends the only Son to offer this life as a gift.

However, the cross refers not only to Jesus' death but to his being lifted up to God. This also is a part of the salvation event in that the glorified Christ sends the Holy Spirit to his church (7:39). "Nevertheless I tell you the truth: it is to your advantage that I go away, for if I do not go away, the Counselor will not come to you; but if I go, I will send him to you" (16:7).

All Saints, November 1, or on First Sunday in November

Revelation 7:9-17; Psalm 34:1-10; I John 3:1-3; Matthew 5:1-12

All the readings for today announce the blessed estate of the saints of God. Both the Gospel and the psalm describe the nature of this happiness and those to whom it is given. The Epistle quietly and modestly extends the thought: if we are children of God now, consider how it will be with us when Christ appears and we share in his likeness. The Apocalypse, replacing the Old Testament lection, envisions that future glory of the saints who have endured, purified by having been bathed in the suffering of Christ.

Revelation 7:9-17

Even though this text is normally associated with All Saints Day, it serves as the New Testament lesson for the Fourth Sunday of Easter in Year C. In that setting, it occurs as part of the semicontinuous reading of the book of Revelation from the Second through the Sixth Sunday of Easter. In order to place the passage in its wider literary context, the reader may wish to consult our remarks in *Lent, Holy Week, Easter, Year C*.

As the first lesson for All Saints Day, this is a most impressive reading. One of several visions of the heavenly court in the book of Revelation, it recalls the earlier vision of God sitting enthroned, surrounded by the twenty-four elders, the four animals, and the angelic host (4:1–5:14). The focus of their attention is the Lamb who had been slain but vindicated by God as the one with "power and wealth and wisdom and might and honor and glory and blessing" (5:12).

In the heavenly scene depicted in today's lesson the audience around God's throne is further extended to include a vast host of people, an innumerable multitude "from every nation, from all tribes and peoples and tongues" (verse 9).

We should imagine a truly universal audience that includes people from every part of the globe. When first introduced, they are all "clothed in white robes, with palm branches in their hands" (verse 9). As we envision this sea of white stretching out through the heavens, we recall an earlier scene when the Lamb opened the fifth seal and saw underneath the altar "the souls of those who had been slain for the word of God and for the witness they had borne" (6:9). They are easily recognized as the slain martyrs who cry out to God for vindication, "O Sovereign Lord, holy and true, how long before thou wilt judge and avenge our blood on those who dwell upon the earth?" (6:10). Although their cry for vindication is not immediately answered, they are given white robes, the attire of those who have been sanctified through their martyrdom. It is the proper attire of the heavens, as the elders around the throne are similarly described (4:4).

In addition to white robes they are described as holding palm branches in their hands (verse 9). This may serve to underscore the celebrative atmosphere, given the use of palm branches in festal celebrations (Lev. 23:40, 43). This was certainly part of the symbolism associated with the triumphal entry of Jesus which was accompanied by the spreading of palm branches (John 12:13; cf. Matt. 21:1-9 and parallels).

All the angels surround the throne and ascribe blessings of glory and honor to God (verse 12); but as yet the multitude of people is unidentified. To this point, we know that it is an innumerable multitude, international in scope. The mention of their white garments causes us to reflect on the earlier vision of the martyrs in chapter 6, but no direct link is made with that earlier vision.

As we ask ourselves who they are, one of the elders puts the question for us, "Who are these, clothed in white robes, and whence have they come?" (verse 13). In almost the same breath he tells us their identity: "These are they who have come out of the great tribulation; they have washed their robes and made them white in the blood of the Lamb" (verse 14). In apocalyptic thought, "the great tribulation" signified the time of unprecedentedly fierce persecution that would precede the end-time (cf. Dan. 12:1; Matt. 24:21; cf. Joel 2:2).

These, then, are not merely those who have undergone suffering on behalf of the kingdom, but intense suffering and violent death.

By now, the identity of this innumerable host is known to us: they are the martyred saints, those who have died on behalf of the faith. The vindication that they sought in the vision in chapter 6 is now achieved (verses 15-17). It is described in terms of almost unimaginable bliss: worshiping God in the temple night and day; free of hunger, thirst, and scorching heat; sheltered by the Lamb, their shepherd, who guides "them to springs of living water" (verse 17); without tears.

As the vision unfolds, it is easy to understand why this text is chosen as the first lesson for All Saints Day. It is a heavenly vision focused on those who have died for the faith and whose cause is finally vindicated in the heavenly court. Such a clear focus on the martyred saints takes us close to the original significance of All Saints Day as a day celebrating unnamed martyrs who died in persecution. Yet we should recall that the word "saints" (hagioi) in the New Testament is used in a much broader sense. It may in fact have been the most common designation of the early Christians (cf. Rom. 1:7; 8:27; 12:13; I Cor. 1:2; 14:33). In certain traditions the celebration of this wider circle of faithful Christians occurs on the following day, All Souls' Day.

Whether this day is observed in the narrow or the broad sense, it serves as a day of remembrance and celebration. Technically, today's text focuses more narrowly on the martyred saints, but the book of Revelation eventually extends the heavenly host to include all the redeemed (21:1–22:5). Given the usage of "saints" within the New Testament as a whole, we are justified in making it a more inclusive celebration, a time to remember all those who have preceded us in the life of faith—and all those who will succeed us.

Psalm 34:1-10

Psalm 34 is an individual thanksgiving psalm intended for use by persons who have moved through trouble and distress and now enjoy security on the "redeemed" side of the turmoil. Like most thanksgiving psalms, this composition has a strong autobiographical or testimonial quality about it. Such psalms were used to look back on the trouble from which one had been freed.

The use of this psalm on All Saints Day shifts the focus from a this-worldly to an other-worldly orientation. That is, the original usage of the psalm was concerned with offering thanks for redemption from some "ordinary" predicament in this life. It was not concerned with giving thanks for having passed through life in its entirety and having gone to one's final state or having died in the faith.

Verses 1-10 (for a discussion of verses 11-22 see Proper 13, Year B) contain an opening affirmation of thanks (verses 1-2), an invitation to others to join in the thanksgiving (verse 3), an autobiographical statement (verses 4-7), and an appeal to the human audience to learn from the worshiper's experience and to share in the sentiments expressed (verses 8-10).

Several points can be noted about this psalm: (1) even though cast in general terms and stylized language, the autobiographical section shows that rehearsing one's story was considered a valuable and therapeutic experience; this is a basic element in modern therapy just as it has been in testimonal meetings throughout church history; (2) persons can learn from the experiences of others; the mutual sharing of burdens and triumphs is thus encouraged; (3) the psalm assumes that life, even for the good and the faithful, is filled with its own troubles and distresses; (4) the psalm testifies to the encouragement that faith gives to life; (5) and the optimism of the psalm, especially in verses 7-10, may seem a bit idealistic but such sentiments help set the pace and orientation of people who share them and thus contribute to particular attitudes with which they face life and its problems and triumphs.

I John 3:1-3

This epistolary lection is also included within the longer reading (I John 3:1-7) that serves as the New Testament lesson for the Third Sunday of Easter in Year B. The reader may wish to consult our remarks in *Lent, Holy Week, Easter, Year B.*

There is some merit in reading today's text closely with what immediately precedes (2:28-29). Even though JB and RSV make a decisive break between 2:28 and 3:1, NEB takes 2:28–3:3 as a single paragraph (cf. also NIV). What favors this editorial decision of NEB is the occurrence of "children" in 2:28 and the use of the image of divine begetting in 2:29: "every one who does right is born of him." An eschatological thread also runs through the entire section (cf. 2:28 and 3:2).

In any case, the main theme of today's text as defined by the *Common Lectionary* is the status we enjoy as God's children. The notion of divine paternity, which is introduced in 2:28, is rendered specific with the mention of "Father" (verse 1). To understand God through this image is a pervasive Johannine theme (1:2-3; John 1:14, 18; 5:17; 10:30; cf. Matt. 11:27). It is axiomatic that the Father loves the Son, and by extension every child (John 3:35; 5:20; 10:17; 15:9; 16:27). The opening note of today's text is the incredible lavishness of the Father's love: "Think of the love that the Father has lavished on us" (verse 1, JB). A similar note is struck by Paul who insists on our inseparability from God's love in Christ (Rom. 8:38-39; cf. 8:14-17; Gal. 3:26; also Eph. 1:5).

Several angles of this rather incredible status are explored. On the one hand, it is present reality—"and such we are" (verse 1)—"here, and now, dear friends, we are God's children" (verse 2, NEB). Yet the full realization of this gift is still a future hope—"what we shall be has not yet been disclosed" (verse 2, NEB). The tension between "already" and "not yet" is vividly present within our text. And this conforms to our own experience. As children, we have some vague notion of our relationship to our parents, but it becomes more concrete as we grow older, even more so when we become parents. Yet as undefined and elementary as our understanding is, it is no less real and meaningful. In a similar fashion, today's text projects our filial relationship into the future, and as the future unfolds, our awareness of the true significance of being God's children compounds geometrically.

We are struck by how our text hammers home this present reality. We are told in the most emphatic terms that we are children. At one level, it should appear obvious to us, yet at another level we have to be reminded of our true identity, primarily because it is called into question by "the godless world" (vrse 1, NEB). This sharp distinction between the children of the world and the children of God is typical of Johannine dualism (4:4-6; John 8:23; 15:19; 17:16). It seems to reflect a sectarian outlook that not only defines the church against the world but also understands Christ as an alien figure, a "stranger from heaven," who is misunderstood and finally rejected by the world (John 1:10-11). Here we see how ecclesiology is reinforced by Christology: the church's own fate is an extension of the fate of Christ. It goes unrecognized because he was unrecognized. In Johannine theology, the world was oblivious to the way in which the Father was at work in the world through the Son (John 7:28; 8:55; 14:7; 15:21; 16:3; 17:25; also Acts 13:27; I Cor. 2:8). The world's ignorance of the divine mystery was its failure to see the unfolding revelation of God before its very eyes (John 9).

The danger of having our identity constantly called into question by the world is that it may not only skew our present understanding but undermine our future hope. We are thus assured that being God's children opens us to a future when even fuller recognition occurs: "What we shall be has not yet been disclosed, but we know that when it is disclosed we shall be like him, because we shall see him as he is" (verse 2, NEB). The future disclosure is the coming of Christ, before whom God's children will be able to stand "confident and unashamed" (2:28 NEB). It is presented here as a moment of transparent vision, when our view of Christ is completely unobstructed.

But more is promised than a clear view of Christ: "we shall be like him" (verse 2). With full revelation comes transformation, what Paul refers to as an exchange of "our lowly body" for "his glorious body" (Phil. 3:21; cf. Rom. 8:29; II Cor. 3:18; Col. 3:4).

The effect of this vision of the future is moral purification: "everyone who has this hope before him purifies himself, as Christ is pure" (verse 3, NEB). Moral purity is commonly understood as a prerequisite for seeing God (Matt. 5:8; Heb. 12:14; also II Cor. 7:1).

This second lesson serves as a useful complement to the first lesson, where the heavenly hope is sketched in such vivid terms. In a sense, the first lesson is maximalist, the second lesson minimalist. In one instance, we see the saints exalted, vindicated, clothed in white, equipped with palm branches, gathered around an elaborately configured throne. They join the twenty-four elders, the four living creatures, the angelic host in giving praise and honor to God and the Lamb. Little is left to the imagination. In the other instance, the promise is: "we shall be like him . . . we shall see him as he is." Here much is left to the imagination. Much is left unsaid. Yet we are no less reassured of the hope that awaits us.

On All Saints Day, the preacher may wish to contrast these very different ways of conceiving the future hope, perhaps consider the relative merits of the more graphic depiction over against the less graphic depiction. Or, another possibility is to explore the tension within our text between present reality and future hope, what we know to be our present identity, the way it can be called into question, and the kind of expectation it shapes within us. How other saints have lived in this tension, and how their lives have been empowered by their vision of the future, may provide valuable clues.

Matthew 5:1-12

All Saints is an occasion for remembering with gratitude those whose lives bear witness to the blessing of God. It will be with them in mind that the Beatitudes are said and heard.

The Sermon on the Mount is the first of five major sections of Jesus' teachings recorded in Matthew. All five sections conclude with the same formula (7:28; 11:1; 13:53; 19:1; 26:1), giving the impression of careful structuring. Most likely Matthew has the memory of Moses in mind as he portrays Jesus bringing God's instruction from the mountain. However, given the wide range of subject matter in these three chapters, plus the fact that portions of this material are found in parallels scattered through Mark and Luke, one is persuaded that the "sermon" is a compilation of teachings from Jesus, the original audiences and occasions now being lost to us. Such a view does not rob any of the sayings of their authority or meaning, but it does free the interpreter from having to discover or construct a single audience for all the material. Matthew's audience, of course, is the church. Were a title to be given to this collection of sayings, it could well be "Life Under the Reign of God."

Matthew has these teachings of Jesus addressed to an audience that is described as a crowd (4:23-25; 5:1; 7:28) and yet as a group of his disciples (5:1). Does this mean that he taught the crowds or that he taught those from the crowd who were his disciples? Luke's parallel offers little help, speaking of a great crowd of his disciples and a multitude of people (6:17), concluding with the words, "in the hearing of the people" (7:1). This question is important. Is the Sermon on the Mount for the church or for society as a whole? It seems safe to say that Jesus is not offering a way of reordering society regardless of one's faith in or relationship to Jesus. Rather these teachings are for those who are the community gathered around Jesus. However, the presence of the crowd keeps the invitation open. Speaking to his followers in the presence of the public keeps all of them honest about who they are and where their commitments lie. The church is a community but not a ghetto; meetings are aware of and open to the world.

The Sermon on the Mount begins with blessings or Beatitudes. Instruction is prefaced with blessing just as the Ten Commandments were prefaced with a recital of God's favor toward Israel (Exod. 20:1 2). In other words, God's imperative is couched in and surrounded by grace. Obedience is thus to be understood as response to, and not an effort to gain, God's favor. The Beatitude says, "Blessed are those who"; that is, it gives its blessing, it is not a formula for happiness such as, "If you want to be happy this is what you do." Neither is a Beatitude an exhortation. The preacher will want to avoid giving the impression that Jesus said, "We ought to be poor in spirt" or "Let us be meek." He pronounces his blessing and the language is performative, conferring the favor in the very saying of it.

The preacher cannot in one sermon give detailed word studies and exegetical analyses of all the Beatitudes. And on All Saints there will be no desire to do so. There will be occasions for that. In this sermon, several accents might be helpful. First, brief attention to what a blessing is (Ps. 84:5-6, 12; 128:1; Ecclus. 25:7-10) and the powerful dynamic of saying and receiving the blessing can give life to the passage. Second, notice that these Beatitudes completely reverse the values of most societies, including our own. No doubt many in Jesus' audience were upset, preferring to take the kingdom in their own hands, and by force if necessary. These blessings elaborate on the description in Isaiah 61:1-3 of those to be visited with God's favor. The meek, the poor in spirit, the peacemakers, those who mourn; these need to be seen and heard as persons, not merely defined and described. And finally, the preacher would do well to distinguish between Jesus extending his blessing to victims and Jesus calling people to be victims. The former he does; the latter he does not do. Even victims do not have to have a victim mentality. Blessed victims take initiative to claim a life appropriate to the blessing. Those who give the coat, turn the cheek, love the enemy, and go the second mile are no longer victims. They are kingdom people.

Thanksgiving Day

Deuteronomy 8:7-18; Psalm 65; II Corinthians 9:6-15; Luke 17:11-19

A first reading of these texts will fix in mind one sentence: God is a God of abundance. The Deuteronomist, the psalmist, and Paul all sing of God's overflowing gifts. But dangers to the human spirit lurk, and prosperity casts its own kind of shadow. One can soon forget the source of all things (Deuteronomy); one can fail to express gratitude to God for creating and sustaining life (Luke); and one can refuse to match God's generosity with a cheerful generosity toward those in need (II Cor.). Although Thanksgiving is not a traditional festival of the church, these texts help build an altar on what is otherwise a national holiday.

Deuteronomy 8:7-18

The book of Deuteronomy is full of excellent texts for Thanksgiving Day. This is because the book, presented as the last words of Moses in the plains of Moab just before the entrance of the people of Israel into the Promised Land, anticipates the life of those people in a rich land given to them by their God. The book actually was written in the centuries after the time of Moses, by preachers and writers who had experienced the land as a gift. They knew, and wanted to remind others, that their wealth was not the fruit of their own strength, but had been given to them.

Today's reading includes most of a sermon (Deut. 8:7-20) on the attitude of the people of God toward the gift of a rich land and the behavior that results from that attitude. It is preceded by another sermon on a similar theme (Deut. 8:1-6). Like virtually all the book of Deuteronomy, it is in the form of second person address, looking toward the future. The speaker appeals to the audience in order to promote the right attitude and actions, using the logic of rhetoric. There are also implied and expressed (verse 19) threats and promises: It is dangerous to ignore these injunctions, but to follow them leads to the abundant life.

One of the most important elements of thanksgiving is to count one's blessings. This the preacher invites his hearers to do in verses 7-10, giving a catalog of the good things in and of the land. The style of that description is almost poetic. The land is well-watered (verse 7), a factor that certainly could not be taken for granted in the terrain in and around Canaan. It is agriculturally rich, producing all kinds of good things to eat (verse 8), and in fact the people will lack for nothing in it (verse 9a). Its resources even include the metals, iron and copper, that were most important in the Old Testament period.

In order to be thankful one must cultivate a good memory. Thus the preacher warns his hearers not to forget (verse 11). In this context, as elsewhere in Deuteronomy, "forget" refers to two different matters. On the one hand, it refers to the commandments of the Lord, which must not be forgotten, that is, ignored (verses 1-6, 15-16). On the other hand, it refers to God and what he has done and continues to do for Israel: Do not forget the Lord your God, and therefore assume that you have brought yourself into the land and provided all the good things in it (verses 11a, 12-14, 17-18). Memory is an essential element in the theology of the book of Deuteronomy. It is an active remembrance, the recital of the mighty acts of God that then shapes behavior. One who remembers what the Lord has done will obey the stipulations of the covenant, and thus live the abundant life in the land (verse 18).

With its two major sections, then, this sermon urges that one be thankful for the natural resources of the land (verses 7-10) and for the acts of God in the past (verses 11-18). Behind the sermon is the preacher's concern that the wealth of the land can be dangerous. A people who are rich certainly will be tempted to be self-sufficient. Those who have plenty of food, "goodly houses," herds and flocks, and even gold and silver (verses 12-13) may become arrogant (verse 14) and even say in their heart, "My power and the might of my hand have gotten me this wealth" (verse 17). Such persons have short memories. The way to avoid that corrupting attitude and its attendant behavior is to remember. Remember that the Lord brought you in and gave you the land, and even gave you "the power to get wealth" (verse 18). Finally, in the allusion to the "covenant which he swore to your fathers" there is an allusion to the promise of the land and descendants to the patriarchs, reminding the hearers that they stand at the end of a long line of other persons who have made their good life possible.

Psalm 65

Very few psalms of community thanksgiving are found in the Psalter (see Pss. 67; 92; 107). A hymn may have served as the community's response to specific acts of divine providence, and thus no great need existed for writing special thanksgiving psalms. Psalm 65 is probably one of the exceptional psalms of communal thanksgiving.

All of the psalm is direct address to the Deity, although some scholars see a radical change of tone between verses 1-4 and 5 following. Some even argue for three psalms (1-4, 5-8, 9-13). The composition appears, however, to be a unity and the elements of sin, creation, and divine blessing of the crops/harvests are not so unrelated.

Verses 1-4 focus on the human admission and divine forgiveness of sin. Difficulties in translating verses 1-2 make the exact meaning uncertain. For example, in the Hebrew, the opening line says, "To thee praise is silent" or "is waiting." Note the KJV which reads, "Praise waiteth for thee." Verses 2b and 3a can be translated, "Unto thee all flesh shall bring the requirements of iniquity." At any rate certain factors seem clear.

1. The occasion for the celebration and the praise of God is the fulfillment of vows. There may have been vows made to be carried out if certain conditions were met by God, such as

his providing a good crop year or forgiving sins, probably the latter. Moderns look judgmentally on vows or deals with God or at least we publicly express ourselves that way. Ancient Israel was unashamed of such arrangements.

2. A public, communal acknowledgment of sin is made. A basic feature of Israelite religion was a routine day of national repentance (Yom Kippur). Others days of repentance were held when deemed necessary. The minister who preaches on this psalm should imaginatively think about what such days of national repentance might do in contemporary cultrue where admitting wrong and guilt is itself considered to be a national sin.

3. Worship in the temple is viewed as an exhilarating source of joy and blessedness. The goodness of the temple (verse 4c) probably refers to the sacrificial feasts eaten in the temple in conjunction with thanksgiving. (The covered dish dinner has a long genalogy and a most sumptuous ancestry!)

In verses 5-8, the psalm shifts to focus on the divine creation of cosmos and the establisment of order in the world. Chaos is represented by the seas, the waves, the people (and the roaring and tumult). Over against these, God establishes, stills, and pacifies so that the regularity of the mornings and evenings follow each other in successive shouts for joy.

The material in the psalm most appropriate for the theme of thanksgiving as an agricultural festival are verses 9-13. The entire cycle of the harvest year is reflected in these verses. There is reference, first of all, to the autumn rains (called the early rains) which water the ground and make plowing and sowing possible. In Palestine, the summer, from about mid-May until late September or early October, is completely rainless. During this period, the land dries up and vegetation dies. The early fall rains, from "the river of God" in the heavenly world, softens the land and seeding follows. The winter rains make possible the growth of grain. Then in the late spring harvest occurs. The harvest in verses 11-13 speak of the bounty of the spring season; God's wagon drips fatness upon the land. Pastures, hills, meadows, and valleys give forth their crops and new-born animals, all considered the blessings of God.

II Corinthians 9:6-15

The context in which today's epistolary lection occurs is Pauls' discussion of the contribution for the Jerusalem poor, which occurs in II Corinthians 8–9. At an early stage in his ministry, Paul had agreed not to forget the poor in Jerusalem (Gal. 2:10). During the period of his Aegean mission, collecting money for this relief fund became an important priority for him (I Cor. 16:1-3). Besides the way it would provide relief for the impoverished in Palestine, it would also serve as an expression of solidarity between the newly founded Gentile churches in the Aegean and the largely Jewish church in Palestine (Rom. 15:25-27).

At a critical stage, the Corinthians seem to have dragged their feet. We do not know the reasons, but we do know that their reluctance did prompt the longest discussion of this topic we have in Paul's writings. Some scholars have plausibly suggested that this two-chapter section of Second Corinthians actually consists of a series of shorter notes sent to the church at different times, later compiled into a separate letter, and finally redacted into what we know as "Second Corinthians."

In these remarks, Paul appeals to the Corinthians to complete their part of the relief fund, reminding them that the churches of Macedonia, their northern neighbors, had already given generously (II Cor. 8:1-7). He makes a number of appeals: the example of Christ (II Cor. 8:8-9), the need for equal distribution of resources (II Cor. 8:13-14), his own reputation as one who had testified of their generosity (II Cor. 8:24-9:5). Today's text continues these appeals.

We do know that his appeal was finally successful. The Corinthians finally came through and Paul was able to complete the project. As he concludes the Letter to the Romans, he is en route to Jerusalem with the gift, even though he is apprehensive about how it will be received (Rom. 15:15-32, esp. verses 30-31).

The first appeal in today's text is *the principle of return:* sow sparingly and you will reap sparingly; sow bountifully and you will reap bountifully (verse 6). It was common in moral exhortation to cite examples from nature to reinforce one's case (Gal. 6:7-8; cf. I Cor. 15:35-41). The Jewish wisdom tradition offered similar advice: "One man gives freely, yet grows all the richer;/another withholds what he should give, and only suffers want" (Prov. 11:24).

A second observation is the *need for voluntary rather than forced generosity* (verse 7). Paul makes a similar distinction in his Letter to Philemon in calling for kindness that is "a matter not of compulsion . . . but of [his own] free will" (Philem. 14. NEB). It would be kindness in either case, and doubtless it would have salutary effects, regardless of the motivation, but Paul is more interested in the motivation that gives rise to the act than the consequences that result from the act. What especially pleases him about the generosity of the Macedonian churches is that they gave of their "own free will" (II Cor. 8:3). When Israel was commanded to provide for the poor, they were enjoined to give freely, not begrudgingly (Deut. 15:10). The Old Testament attested God's love for cheerful givers (verse 7).

Third, our text mentions the *generosity of God* (verses 8-10). We are reminded of God's capacity to provide for our needs, to do so abundantly, so that we can be equipped for good works (verse 8; cf. Eph. 2:10; Col. 1:10; II Thess. 2:17; II Tim. 3:17; Titus 2:14). Again, Scripture supplies the warrant for this claim: God provides rain and snow to water the earth, making it productive to give "seed to the sower and bread to the eater" (Isa. 55:10).

This is an important point, for it suggests a close correlation between faith and generosity. We may withhold our goods and money as an act of self-protection and self preservation, but to do so implies that our preservation is in our own hands. To let go of our possessions, by contrast, becomes an expression of faith because it symbolizes the commitment of ourselves and our future to someone other than ourselves—God. To cling to our possessions symbolizes our doubt in God's ability to provide.

Fourth, *generosity produces thanksgiving* (verses 11-13). Any act of charity obviously benefits the one in need. In this case, the Corinthians' contribution would "supply the wants of the saints" (verse 12). Benefit also accrues to the free-hearted giver: God's abundance is opened up even more. But, in addition, God will be honored: acts of generosity "produce thanksgiving to God" (verse 11); they "overflow in many thanksgivings to God" (verse 12). In mind here are prayers of thanksgiving that occur on the lips of the recipients, those who benefit from the generosity of others. Paul goes ahead to add that the Corinthians' generosity would "glorify God" because it would be an expression of "obedience in acknowledging the gospel of Christ" (verse 13).

It matters to Paul that acts of generosity result in more prayers being offered to God, not because God needs our prayers and acknowledgments but because it expresses the right kind of faith—faith in God as Creator (Rom. 1:18-25). For Paul, the sure mark of being pagan is the inability, or refusal, to give thanks. Those incapable of thanksgiving are those who have exchanged the creature for the Creator, and in doing so have forfeited "the truth about God" (Rom. 1:25). By contrast, the capacity to give thanks becomes the earmark of true faith, for it recognizes who is creature and who is Creator.

Not surprisingly, his remarks end with a thanksgiving: "Thanks be to God for his inexpressible gift!" (cf. Rom. 6:17; 7:25; I Cor. 15:57; II Cor. 2:4; 8:16).

This is an important text to read and hear at Thanksgiving if, for no other reason, because it properly anchors thanksgiving in theological reflection. There is much here about God's generosity and God's ability to provide for us in abundance. There is also the call for generosity of heart. Our text says no to the zipped pocket. It calls nature as a witness against the sparing sower. Above all, it sees thanksgiving as an expression of faith in God the Creator.

Luke 17:11-19

"On the way to Jerusalem." With this phrase (verse 11 Luke reminds the reader that the story which follows occurs in the travel narrative begun at 9:51. Otherwise, the preacher need not struggle to join the story of the healing of the lepers with what precedes it. Verse 11 is a clear transition. This account is found only in Luke, with vague similarities to Mark's account of Jesus healing a leper (1:40-45).

One is impressed with the realistic details of the account. Lepers tended to live in groups (II Kings 7:3) and they avoided contact with non-lepers (verse 12; Lev. 13:45-46; Num. 5:2), but they kept close enough to populated areas to receive charity. Jesus' command that they show themselves to the priest (verse 1) was according to the Law of Moses (Lev. 14:2-32). However, one is also struck by elements in the story that raise questions. For example, the location between Galilee and Samaria (verse 11) is a bit confusing in view of the fact that Jesus is on his way to Jerusalem and had much earlier entered Samaria (9:52). Very likely Luke uses the Galilee-Samaria border as a literary avenue for introducing a story involving Jews and a Samaritan (verse 16). Another uncertain element is the command to go and present themselves to the priest. Did that apply to the Samaritan? Also, why reproach the nine for not returning when they had been commanded to go (verses 17-18)? In fact, their healing occurred in their going; their obedience was apparently the expression of faith essential for their healing (verse 14). One can understand why some commentators believe Luke has idealized an event in order to join faith, obedience, and gratitude.

However, it seems more natural to understand this passage as a two-part story: verses 11-14 and 15-19. The first part is a healing story: a case of evident need; a cry to Jesus for help; Jesus treats them as already healed, sending them to the priest, and their healing occurs in their response of faith. (In Mark 1:40-45, the leper is sent to the priest *after* the healing.) The second part (verses 15-19) is a story of the salvation of a foreigner. it is the foreigner who praises God and gives thanks to Jesus. It is the foreigner to whom Jesus says, "Your faith has made you well" (verse 19). The verb translated "made you well" is a form of the verb "to save." There is more given to the Samaritan than the cleansing that they all received. This additional blessing is termed "salvation."

The story makes two points vital to Luke: the faith of foreigners (7:9; 10:25-27; Acts 10–11) and Israel's blindness to what is available in Jesus (Acts 28:26-27). It is important to note that Jesus did not reject the nine Jewish lepers; they were blessed with healing. Neither did Jesus set aside Jewish law; he sent them to the priest for the post-cleansing rituals. But the Gentile responds in ways beyond that of the Jews. Probably by the time Luke was written such stories noting the differences between Jewish and Gentile responses to Jesus were told in abundance. Very likely this story was inspired by the one to which Jesus had referred earlier (4:27), the healing of a leper, a foreigner, who was converted to Israel's faith (II Kings 5:1-14).

We cannot suppose that Luke told this story simply to paint a favorable picture of a Gentile and an unfavorable one of the Jews. Some condition is being addressed in Luke's church. Possibly some Christians were seeking benefits from Jesus' ministry but not salvation. Perhaps some were taking their blessings for granted, without gratitude. If so, again it was, and is, the outsider who reminds the church what faith is, what praise is, and what thanksgiving is.

Scripture Reading Index